Hospitality Management

HOSPITALITY MANAGEMENT

Mahesh Chandra Singh

CENTRUM PRESS
NEW DELHI-110002 (INDIA)

CENTRUM PRESS
H.O.: 4360/4, Ansari Road, Daryaganj,
New Delhi-110002 (India)
Tel: 23278000, 23261597, 23255577, 23286875
B.O.: No. 1015, Ist Main Road, BSK IIIrd Stage,
IIIrd Phase, IIIrd Block, Bengaluru-560085 (INDIA)
Tel: 080-41723429
Email: centrumpress@gmail.com
Visit us at: www.centrumpress.com

Hospitality Management

First Edition, 2013

ISBN 978-93-81293-96-6

PRINTED IN INDIA

Printed at Balaji Offset, Delhi.

Contents

Preface

Hospitality management is both a field of work and a field of study. In the work sense, it refers to management of hotels, restaurants, travel agencies, and other institutions in the hospitality industry. As a field of study, it refers to the study of the hospitality industry and its management needs. People who are interested in careers in hospitality management may opt to pursue it as a field of study so that they can start their careers on solid footing.

The hospitality industry is vast and very diverse. Any time people travel, stay in a hotel, eat out, go to the movies, and engage in similar activities, they are patronizing establishments in the hospitality industry. The management of such establishments is very challenging, as managers need to be flexible enough to anticipate and meet a wide variety of needs. They must also handle tasks such as training employees, handling staff, setting standards, and so forth.

Some people develop careers in hospitality management by working from the ground up. They get experience in various low level positions before gradually being promoted into supervisory positions, and eventually attain managerial status. For people who plan to work with a single organization for life, this method can be a great way to advance, as it familiarizes them with all of the nuances of the organizations they work for and gives them a better idea of the amount of work involved at all levels to run a facility like a busy resort.

People who attend hospitality management training can opt for certification programs, associate's degrees, or bachelor's degrees in hospitality management. Training is designed to prepare people to take on managerial positions immediately, familiarizing people with everything from payment processing systems to what to do when a natural disaster strikes a hotel. People with training can often enter the job market right away and command excellent salaries, especially if they graduate from well known schools.

This kind of work is not for everyone. People who work in hospitality management need excellent customer service skills, but they also need to the ability to be hard, since managers need to be tough, but fair, with employees. It is also important to be able to identify and anticipate needs, ranging from organizing orders of food for a restaurant to preparing for the arrival of an important guest. People who can think quickly on their feet, who like working with the public, and who enjoy solving puzzles may enjoy employment in this field.

It is an approachable and readable text for students at all levels, from undergraduates to professionals retraining.

—Author

1

Introduction

Meetings are a crucial part of an organization's overall strategy, and planning them requires special skills and tools. This article describes how to get the job done and where to turn for help.

Introduction

So you've been handed the responsibility of organizing an off-premises meeting. Welcome to a task that isn't as easy as it seems. Before long, you'll be making decisions and following up on all manner of details. You may find yourself searching madly for reference materials or interviewing professionals to help you organize. Don't worry, there's no shortage of either.

Measuring Value

The best meetings support an organization's business objectives and help convey its overall message to those attending. The best meeting planners actively participate in honing the content to ensure that the meeting furthers the goals of the organization and is consistent with its mission. To measure the meeting's effectiveness, they are prepared to demonstrate its return on investment (ROI) to management.

Through ROI, organizations justify the dollars spent on meetings by measuring desired criteria, i.e., the knowledge gained by attendees or the increase in sales directly attributable to their participation. Determining ROI is accomplished through a variety of means, such as feedback from management, post-meeting evaluations, and surveys.

Questions to Ask

When handed the task of planning a meeting, first ask yourself whether there are alternatives to having a meeting at all. Is there a less costly way to communicate with this group, say, with videoconferencing or computer conferencing?

Chances are your organization will decide there is no substitute for a face-to-face gathering, so two other questions are in order:

* What is the objective of this meeting?
* Who will attend?

The answers to these questions will form the basis of all logistical decisions to come, such as where the meeting is to be held, the size of the budget, what type of hotel or other facility you will use, the content of the agenda, what type of recreation will be called for, and even how the chairs in the meeting room will be set up.

The importance of these early steps cannot be overemphasized, in particular the question: "Why are we having this meeting?"

An incentive meeting held as a reward for salespeople, for example, will likely be held in an upscale resort hotel with recreation as part of the program. On the other hand, a short, hastily called brainstorming meeting is best staged at a business hotel, perhaps one located near an airport so that attendees can get in and out quickly. Obviously, fancy meals and recreation will not be necessary. And a meeting called to teach salespeople a new skill will best fit in a conference center that specializes in training and team-building programs. There, some form of recreation may provide a welcome break.

Site Selection

Only after you are sure of the nature of the meeting and what type of hotel or facility you will use, can you go about selecting a venue. For openers:

- Contact the convention and visitors bureau in the destination you are considering. The bureau will send you literature that describes local hotels.

- Consult a hotel directory, such as SourceBook, a special issue of Successful Meetings magazine, Gavel, a special issue of Meetings & Conventions magazine, or the Official Meetings & Facilities Guide, a web-based facility guide. (For details, see Publications.)
- Contact the sales offices of major hotel chains for directories of their properties.

After compiling a list of possible venues, send the sales department of each a request for proposal (RFP) outlining the requirements of your meeting. (If you're contacting several hotels in a destination, the convention and visitors bureau may serve as a middleman). The RFP should include such information as the preferred dates for your meeting, the number and type of sleeping rooms you require, the range of acceptable room rates, food and beverage requirements, a tentative agenda, and the amount and type of meeting space needed. This information will help the hotel decide whether it is able to host the meeting according to your specifications.

Based on the hotels' responses to your RFP, narrow down the field and arrange to inspect the hotel or hotels you're considering. Things to consider during a site inspection: overall appearance of the hotel and its guest rooms, lobby, and meeting space; proximity to the airport and availability of shuttle services; attitude of the service staff; whether meeting rooms have obstructions, such as pillars or overhangs, that interfere with audiovisual presentations; accessibility for people with disabilities.

If you cannot inspect the site in person, a detailed questionnaire will suffice. Also, many hotels have Web sites that include layouts of their meeting space.

Negotiating a Contract

By now, you should be ready to accept a letter of agreement from one property. This outlines the space reserved for your group. You can begin to negotiate with the salesperson from the property on the terms of the contract that will eventually be signed. If you've held a similar meeting before, you may strengthen your bargaining position by mentioning how much was spent on basic items. Nearly everything is negotiable: the sleeping room rate; the meeting room rental, which may be waived if the group generates sufficient guest-room and food and beverage revenue; upgrades to suite accommodations; meeting room equipment; and the complimentary room ratio (typically, hotels "comp" one room for every 50 booked).

Negotiating with a conference center is simpler, because such properties offer a complete meeting package (CMP). This provides a per-person cost for everything from sleeping rooms and meals to conference space and audiovisual needs.

Regardless of the venue, make sure you have a written contract that outlines the guest room commitment, room rate, complimentary accommodations, reservation and deposit procedures, method of payment, meeting space, banquet space, and cancellation policy.

Before the contract is signed, however, you might want to include special provisions that could be difficult to add later on. For instance, you could insert a clause stipulating that certain organizations, such as a competing company, may not meet in the hotel at the same time. Or you could provide for financial relief in the event that the hotel is double-booked and can't honour its commitments.

Keep in mind that you have the option of outsourcing your meeting to meeting specialists who will undertake all logistics (or only those elements you wish to outsource) from site selection to on-site management of the meeting. This company need not be based in the city where you hold the meeting.

Details

After the contract is signed, your meeting file will be turned over to the property's convention services manager. Think of this person as your in-house meeting planner, the person who, from now until your meeting ends, will coordinate all your needs and serve as a liaison between you and other departments within the property. Leading up to the meeting, you will be confronted with countless details (meeting publications often publish diagrams showing what must be done and when). Among the critical details:

- *Transportation*: Will flights be booked by your organization's in-house travel department or an outside agency? Airlines have special departments that handle groups. They offer discounted fares and cargo rates, complimentary tickets (depending on the number of seats booked), and special ticketing and billing. How will attendees get from the airport to the meeting property? Taxi? Hotel shuttle? If you're expecting high-level executives or other VIPs, you'll have to arrange limousine transfers.
- *Check-in*: To expedite check-in, the property will need to be briefed on the arrival pattern of attendees.
- *Agenda*: As the meeting nears, a schedule of meeting-related activities and food-and-beverage functions should be drafted and shared with the convention services manager.
- *Meeting-room Setup Depends on the Nature of the Sessions*: Use an auditorium-style setup when a speaker is addressing the group. Arrange tables in a U for sessions where attendees will be interacting.
- *Audiovisual*: Well before the meeting, talk to the convention services manager about your requirements and how the equipment should be set up. Bear in mind that some rooms have structural elements that are not conducive to audiovisual presentations.
- *Food and Beverage*: Menus should be discussed and confirmed with the convention services manager and with the catering department.
- *Recreation and Special Events*: The convention services manager can assist in setting up recreational programs on the property, such as a golf tournament. Off-site events, such as dinners and outings, are best arranged through a destination management company (DMC), a type of tour operator that focuses on groups. Production companies can assist you with organizing themed banquets, Broadway-style shows, or multimedia presentations. Ask the local convention and visitors bureau for a list of such companies.

Interactive Meeting

Interactive technology provides ways to improve understanding and learning at your meeting, then measure the progress. It gives planners a more precise and immediate system for evaluating the results of a meeting.

A key interactive element is the audience response system, which enables a presenter to ask questions and have the answers displayed instantly on a large screen in front of the audience. (Questions and answers can also be printed out and distributed after the meeting.) Attendees are each given a wireless keypad with which they answer questions. They can pick Yes or No or punch in a number that corresponds to a multiple-choice answer. Answers are tabulated by an on-site computer, then displayed on the screen in various formats, such as bar graphs or pie charts.

Besides getting people involved in the learning process, the system makes it possible to obtain immediate feedback. That makes it especially useful for business meetings, media testing, and focus groups. Often, the audience is divided into teams that compete for the best score.

Audience response systems can be used at virtually any meeting facility, whether in-house, off-site, or at several remote sites linked by videoconferencing. Setup time is nominal. A 500-pad meeting can be set up in an hour and a half. The price varies, depending on the size and duration of the meeting and the amount of customization required.

On Site/Aftermath

Ideally, the meeting planner should arrive at least a day before the attendees. At that time, the meeting planner, the convention services manager, and the appropriate department heads can discuss last-minute needs. Some form of post-meeting evaluation is necessary to determine the meeting's ROI. Example: a questionnaire distributed to attendees plus follow-up interviews with attendees and managers.

Employee Recognition and Motivation

The foundation of recognition and motivation is that people need and want Acceptance, Approval and Appreciation. Almost all positive motivation is based on these needs. People want to know that what they do makes a difference. Just recognizing the staff is the most important step one can take. You may want to count the number of "we's that are said instead of "I's in order to assess the extent to which your staff feels part of the team and part of the business' future. One saying is, "Powerlessness corrupts, absolute powerlessness corrupts absolutely."

These nine actions will help immensely to give your staff what they need: Communicate, Communicate, Communicate, Recognize, Recognize, Recognize, Thank, Thank, and Thank!

From various sources, Vicki developed a list of ideas for ongoing weekly or monthly programs to keep employees connected to the hotel or restaurant emotionally, to create excitement and to make your business unique relative to your nearby competitors for employees. Remember, the competition for staff may be from other industries such as retail, manufacturing, etc. Pick a few and try them for a while; but, you must give them a chance, one time will not do it. The staff will see right through you.

- Gift certificate for the most challenging question posed to the President
- Money or chocolates or lottery ticket to a spouse with a note thanking for his/her support during overtime
- Thumbs-up certificates redeemable for merchandise
- Soda, fruit, snacks to housekeeping staff all the time
- When anyone makes a negative comment, put $0.25 or $0.50 into a pot and use the money for a Fun Committee
- Bring Polaroid camera to work occasionally and take candids of staff and post pictures on a bulletin board for all to enjoy
- Selection of employee of the month/quarter/year by peers not just management
- When he/she is employee of the month, give him/her a special name tag highlighting that status
- Points given out at any time for anything, good attendance, helping out a guest, etc., and are redeemable for prizes

- When you reach a certain level in revenues, give all staff a reward, being sure to give them the goal in advance
- Spontaneous calls from corporate to line staff saying how they are appreciated
- Allow line workers to participate in all personnel function decisions, hiring, training, evaluating, firing, schedules
- Fine those who arrive late to a meeting and distribute the money to those who were there on time
- Create a symbol of the team, maybe just property logo but put it on T-shirts, mugs, caps
- Certificate of achievement, lunch, and mug for perfect attendance, gift certificate to the one with longest perfect attendance
- Allow those with perfect attendance record to enter a lottery to get a $100 or $200 gift certificate
- Quarterly teleconference with all employees and support staff, especially CEO
- Family orientation for new employees with slide show or video program with refreshments
- Several line staff call new hire to welcome him/her to the team the day before he/she starts
- Toll-free hot line to President where they can leave any question, suggestion, etc. and will get a response
- Hold a regular meeting to tell staff what is going on and how they are doing
- Always hang charts, graphs, etc. to depict regularly how the property is doing
- Full page ad in newspaper once a year thanking employees and name all individually
- Public praising of an individual at a department or hotel meeting
- Make sure all rewards, praise, bonuses, etc. are in public

- Have the General Manager spend at least an hour with every new employee
- Golden Broom Award to all (excluding housekeeping staff) who are seen picking up trash-after two, they can redeem them for a gift
- Pick a trophy that is passed from rewardee to rewardee so it is much desired, it does not matter what it is and actually the odder the better so it is fun
- Pre-printed "you done good" or "a pat on the back" or "bravo" note cards to have management inscribe whenever appropriate spontaneously
- Praise immediately and tell them specifically what they did right and how it helps the company
- Always find ways to get staff's input into the operation-just simple suggestion box works great
- Work hard at finding a way to implement each suggestion and give a clear explanation why it cannot be used if that is the case
- Acknowledge all suggestions, even if not implemented, express appreciation perhaps also a small reward If you implement an idea, give a reward, and widely publicize it
- Pins for uniforms that say "The guest comes first" or "I will do my best" or "We're glad you're here" or something similar
- Periodically hold contests like a TV game show where employees answer questions about the property hotel, perhaps in teams
- Use an 800# service which employees call periodically to be given randomly selected test questions and win a prize if they get them all correct
- Give a small gift on the date of their anniversary
- Hold an annual banquet for those with more than a certain number of years of service
- Give every employee printed business cards

- At Ritz Carlton, all employees throughout the hotel are authorized to spend up to $2,000 each incident to resolve a guest's complaint, but few spend anywhere near that amount
- Ask employees regularly what else we can do for them to enable them to do a good job
- Tell employees regularly what else they can do for management to enable you to do a good job
- Hold weekly meetings with small groups of employees to discuss anything, serve food
- Hold a weekly 20 minute meeting with one employee to discuss anything
- Make it personal, people naturally commit themselves to other people, not to organizations
- Hold monthly employee meetings at which the financial performance of the previous month and other goals are discussed in specific
- Distribute daily reports of revenue performance last night and month-to-date
- Send employees and family to a competitive property and have them write a report
- Send employees and family to your property and have them write a report
- Imprint the hotel's four key business goals on T-shirts
- Include career development discussion in all performance reviews
- Send line staff to schools to do recruiting and interviewing
- Tell staff that if they achieve x,y,z, etc., you will call their mothers and tell them how great their child is and actually do it
- Always make sure their work environment is positive, attractive, and reflective of your goals and values
- Ideas for back-of-the-house areas: plants, framed art (let them choose), clean unworn carpets, adequate ventilation,

natural light, meeting space, adequate work-space, well-functioning equipment, attractive break facilities

- Form a recreation committee to plan monthly activities
- Regular employee newsletter
- Ask for input on cost-cutting programs during times of low demand
- Implement management reviews where line staff assess management's performance

These are only a few of the infinite number of ideas to keep good staff members and motivate them to work hard toward common goals.

Whatever you choose to do, keep doing it consistently and make sure that you are sincere. Good luck on making your hotel or restaurant a unique and rewarding place to work.

2

General Hospitality: Links and Business

Hotel

A hotel is an establishment that provides paid lodging on a short-term basis. The provision of basic accommodation, in times past, consisting only of a room with a bed, a cupboard, a small table and a washstand has largely been replaced by rooms with modern facilities, including en-suite bathrooms and air conditioning or climate control. Additional common features found in hotel rooms are a telephone, an alarm clock, a television, and Internet connectivity; snack foods and drinks may be supplied in a mini-bar, and facilities for making hot drinks. Larger hotels may provide a number of additional guest facilities such as a restaurant, a swimming pool or childcare, and have conference and social function services.

Hotels rooms are usually numbered to allow guests identify their room. Some hotels offer meals as part of a room and board arrangement. In the United Kingdom, a hotel is required by law to serve food and drinks to all guests within certain stated hours; to avoid this requirement it is not uncommon to come across *private hotels* which are not subject to this requirement. In Japan, capsule hotels provide a minimized amount of room space and shared facilities. In the United Kingdom, Australia, Canada and Ireland (and rarely in some parts of the United States), the word may also refer to a pub or bar and might not offer accommodation. In India and Bangladesh, the word may also refer to a restaurant.

Etymology

The word *hotel* is derived from the French *hotel* (coming from *hote* meaning *host*), which referred to a French version of a townhouse or any other building seeing frequent visitors, rather than a place offering accommodation. In contemporary French usage, *hotel* now has the same meaning as the English term, and *hotel particulier* is used for the old meaning. The French spelling, with the circumflex, was also used in English, but is now rare. The circumflex replaces the 's' found in the earlier *hostel* spelling, which over time took on a new, but closely related meaning. Grammatically, hotels usually take the definite article-hence "The Astoria Hotel" or simply "The Astoria".

Classification

The cost and quality of hotels are usually indicative of the range and type of services available. Due to the enormous increase in tourism worldwide during the last decades of the 20th century, standards, especially those of smaller establishments, have improved considerably. For the sake of greater comparability, rating systems have been introduced, with the one to five stars classification being most common and with higher star ratings indicating more luxury.

Hotels are independently assessed in traditional systems and these rely heavily on the facilities provided. Some consider this disadvantageous to smaller hotels whose quality of accommodation could fall into one class but the lack of an item such as an elevator would prevent it from reaching a higher categorization.

In some countries, there is an official body with standard criteria for classifying hotels, but in many others there is none. There have been attempts at unifying the classification system so that it becomes an internationally recognized and reliable standard but large differences exist in the quality of the accommodation and the food within one category of hotel, sometimes even in the same country. The American Automobile Association (AAA) and their affiliated bodies use diamonds instead of stars to express hotel and restaurant ratings levels.

Hotels are also classified by service type ranging for all-inclusive full-service resorts that cater to vacationers to small limited service hotels that cater to transient business travellers. The main categories of hotels are as follows;

- Full Service Upscale :
    - o *Examples include Conrad Hotels, Ritz Carlton, Four Seasons Hotels, and JW Marriott*
- Full Service :
    - o *Examples include Hilton, Marriott, Doubletree, and Hyatt*
- Select Service :
    - o *Examples include Courtyard by Marriott and Hilton Garden Inn*
- Limited Service :
    - o *Examples include Hampton Inn, Fairfield Inn, Days Inn, and La Quinta Inn*
- Extended Stay :
    - o *Examples include Homewood Suites by Hilton, Residence Inn by Marriott, and Extended Stay Hotels*
- Timeshare :
    - o *Examples include Marriott Vacation Club, Westgate Resorts, and Disney Vacation Club*
- Destination Club.

Historic Hotels

Some hotels have gained their renown through tradition, by hosting significant events or persons, such as Schloss Cecilienhof in Potsdam, Germany, which derives its fame from the Potsdam Conference of the World War II allies Winston Churchill, Harry Truman and Joseph Stalin in 1945. The Taj Mahal Palace & Tower in Mumbai is one of India's most famous and historic hotels because of its association with the Indian independence movement.

Some establishments have given name to a particular meal or beverage, as is the case with the Waldorf Astoria in New York City, United States where the Waldorf Salad was first created or the Hotel Sacher in Vienna, Austria, home of the Sachertorte. Others have achieved fame by association with dishes or cocktails created on their premises, such as the Hotel de Paris where the crepe Suzette was invented or the Raffles Hotel in Singapore, where the Singapore Sling cocktail was devised.

A number of hotels have entered the public consciousness through popular culture, such as the Ritz Hotel in London, United Kingdom, through its association with Irving Berlin's song, 'Puttin' on the Ritz'. The Algonquin Hotel in New York City is famed as the meeting place of the literary group, the Algonquin Round Table, and Hotel Chelsea, also in New York City, has been the subject of a number of songs and the scene of the stabbing of Nancy Spungen (allegedly by her boyfriend Sid Vicious). The Waldorf Astoria and Statler hotels in New York City are also immortalized in the names of Muppets Statler and Waldorf. The luxurious Grand Hotel Europe in Saint Petersburg, Russia achieved fame with its inclusion in the James Bond film GoldenEye.

Unusual Hotels

Many hotels can be considered destinations in themselves, by dint of unusual features of the lodging or its immediate environment:

Treehouse Hotels

Some hotels are built with living trees as structural elements, for example the Costa Rica Tree House in the Gandoca-Manzanillo Wildlife Refuge, Costa Rica; the Treetops Hotel in Aberdare National Park, Kenya; the Ariau Towers near Manaus, Brazil, on the Rio Negro in the Amazon; and Bayram's Tree Houses in Olympos, Turkey.

Bunker Hotels

The Null Stern Hotel in Teufen, Appenzellerland, Switzerland and the Concrete Mushrooms in Albania are former nuclear bunkers transformed into hotels.

Cave Hotels

Desert Cave Hotel in Coober Pedy, South Australia and the Cuevas Pedro Antonio de Alarcon (named after the author) in Guadix, Spain, as well as several hotels in Cappadocia, Turkey, are notable for being built into natural cave formations, some with rooms underground.

Capsule Hotels

Capsule hotels are a type of economical hotel that are found in Japan, where people sleep in stacks of rectangular containers.

Ice and Snow Hotels

The Ice Hotel in Jukkasjarvi, Sweden, and the Hotel de Glace in Duschenay, Canada, melt every spring and are rebuilt each winter; the Mammut Snow Hotel in Finland is located within the walls of the Kemi snow castle; and the Lainio Snow Hotel is part of a snow village near Yllas, Finland.

Garden Hotels

Garden hotels, famous for their gardens before they became hotels, include Gravetye Manor, the home of garden designer William Robinson, and Cliveden, designed by Charles Barry with a rose garden by Geoffrey Jellicoe.

Underwater Hotels

Some hotels have accommodation underwater, such as Utter Inn in Lake Malaren, Sweden. Hydropolis, project cancelled 2004 in Dubai, would have had suites on the bottom of the Persian Gulf, and Jules Undersea Lodge in Key Largo, Florida requires scuba diving to access its rooms.

Other Unusual Hotels

- The Library Hotel in New York City, is unique in that each of its ten floors is assigned one category from the Dewey Decimal System.
- The Burj al-Arab hotel in Dubai, United Arab Emirates, built on an artificial island, is structured in the shape of a boat's sail.
- The Jailhotel Löwengraben in Lucerne, Switzerland is a converted prison now used as a hotel.
- The Luxor, a hotel and casino on the Las Vegas Strip in Paradise, Nevada, United States due to its pyramidal structure.
- The Liberty Hotel in Boston, used to be the Charles Street Jail.

- Built in Scotland and completed in 1936, The former ocean liner RMS *Queen Mary* in Long Beach, California, United States uses its first-class staterooms as a hotel, after retiring in 1967 from Transatlantic service.

Resort Hotels

Some hotels are built specifically to create a captive trade, example at casinos and holiday resorts. Though of course hotels have always been built in popular desinations, the defining characteristic of a resort hotel is that it exists purely to serve another attraction, the two having the same owners. In Las Vegas there is a tradition of one-upmanship with luxurious and extravagant hotels in a concentrated area known as the Las Vegas Strip. This trend now has extended to other resorts worldwide, but the concentration in Las Vegas is still the world's highest: nineteen of the world's twenty-five largest hotels by room count are on the Strip, with a total of over 67,000 rooms.

In Europe Centre Parcs might be considered a chain of resort hotels, since the sites are largely man-made (though set in natural surroundings such as country parks) with captive trade, whereas holiday camps such as Butlins and Pontin's are probably not considered as resort hotels, since they are set at traditional holiday destinations which existed before the camps.

Railway Hotels

Frequently, expanding railway companies built grand hotels at their termini, such as the Midland Hotel, Manchester next to the former Manchester Central Station and in London the ones above St Pancras railway station and Charing Cross railway station also in London is the Chiltern Court Hotel above Baker Street tube station and Canada's grand railway hotels. They are or were mostly, but not exclusively, used by those travelling by rail.

Motels

A motel (Motor Hotel) is a hotel which is for a short stay, usually for a night, for motorists on long journeys. It has direct access from the room to the vehicle (for example a central parking lot around which the buildings are set), and is built conveniently close to major roads and intersections.

World Record Setting Hotels

Largest

In 2006, Guinness World Records listed the First World Hotel in Genting Highlands, Malaysia as the world's largest hotel with a total of 6,118 rooms.

Oldest

According to the Guinness Book of World Records, the oldest hotel still in operation is the Hoshi Ryokan, in the Awazu Onsen area of Komatsu, Japan which opened in 718.

Tallest

Burj Al Arab in United Arab Emirates is the tallest building used exclusively as a hotel. However, the Rose Tower, also in Dubai, which has already topped Burj Al Arab's height at 333 m (1,093 ft.), will take away this title upon its opening.

Hotel Rooms as an Investment

Some hotels sell individual rooms to investors. The buyer is allowed to stay in the room without charge or at a reduced rate for a given number of days each year. The investor is paid a share of the takings for the room. Rooms can be sold on a leasehold basis, sometimes on a 999 year lease. Room owners are free to sell at any time.

Living in Hotels

A number of public figures have notably chosen to take up semi-permanent or permanent residence in hotels.

- Actor Richard Harris lived at the Savoy Hotel while in London. Hotel archivist Susan Scott recounts an anecdote that when he was being taken out of the building on a stretcher shortly before his death he raised his hand and told the diners "it was the food".

Fictitious Hotels

Hotels have been used as the settings for television programmes such as the British situation comedies Fawlty Towers and I'm Alan Partridge, the British soap opera Crossroads, and in films such as the Bates Motel in Hitchcock's 1960 film

Psycho.In an increasingly competitive employment arena, African Americans must prepare for and secure strong, definite jobs which lead them to long-term realistic career options and opportunities.

One of the fastest growing sectors of the economy of our time is the hospitality industry. The hospitality industry alone is a multi-billion dollar and growing enterprise. It is exciting, never boring and offers unlimited opportunities. The hospitality industry is diverse enough for people to work in different areas of interest and still be employed within the hospitality industry. Think about this: It makes sense to prepare for a job in which you have numerous opportunities for advancement, because it is an economic advantage for you in the long run.

The hospitality industry pays those well who have prepared well.

Hospitality management involves the planning, organizing, directing and controlling of human and material resources within the lodging, restaurant, travel and tourism, institutional management, recreational management and meeting and convention planning industries. All of these separate yet related segments of the hospitality industry are interrelated to deliver kind and generous services to guests.

The hospitality industry is one of the oldest businesses in history. People have always gone out to eat sometimes and travelled for work or leisure purposes. However, the face of the hospitality industry has changed drastically. Brenda Scott, president and CEO of the Mobile, Ala., Convention and Visitors Corporation, agrees and says; demographically the world is changing. By the year 2000, 45-50 percent of the workforce and consumers will be non-white. Not only has the industry expanded to include areas such as tourism and meeting and convention planning, but also the face of the workforce in substantial positions has expanded to include all races and colors. The explosion of growth in the hospitality industry demands highly qualified people trained in hospitality management to fill rapidly opening positions.

Although African Americans have had a wealth of experience in hospitality, it has not always been positive. In the past African

Americans have usually performed in low-level managerial positions in hospitality operations holding positions from the lowest realm in service to now having the realistic opportunity of becoming general managers.

The present hospitality industry is extraordinarily healthy and viable and as a result offers excellent opportunities for African Americans in each of the segments; restaurant management, lodging management, recreational management, travel and tourism, meeting and convention planning and institutional management. Scott announces good news: the opportunities are there. The globalization of the hospitality industry creates the availability of jobs in virtually every city in the world. Ed Moore, Jr., regional recruiter for Applebee's International says the restaurant industry is a wonderful field to be in, especially in the 90s. He further states, oftentimes young adults think of flipping burgers when they think of the business. That is not all there is to it. There are positions in middle management as well as the corporate office. We are talking about jobs that range from $26,000 to $100,000 plus. In the growing field of hospitality, it is projected that by the year 2000 an additional two million people will fill new jobs in the industry. According to the U.S. Department of Labour, in the next decade nine out of ten new jobs created will be in the service industry. Through the year 2000, positions for hotel managers are expected to grow faster than the average for all occupations, as reported in the Occupational Outlook Handbook, a publication of the U.S. Department of Labour. It is estimated by Kelley Notes that by the turn of the century the lodging industry will create over 500,000 additional entry-level positions. Kelley Notes also estimates in less than a decade, travel and tourism will become the nation's number one employer with one of every five Americans working in some segment of the hospitality industry.

African Americans do well to actively prepare themselves and aggressively seek employment in the hospitality industry. They should especially investigate opportunities in meeting and convention planning, and travel and tourism. These two areas are hot spots of the industry and presently offer outstanding opportunities for prepared students.

To help African Americans prepare for a successful hospitality career, completing a college degree in hospitality management and/or related area is a great beginning. Phillip Cunningham, general manager of the Tuskegee University Kellogg Conference Centre, believes that success for African Americans in the hospitality industry means being flexible in business and in personal life, understanding the true meaning of customer and employee service, and knowing the job that you are asking others to perform. In addition says Cunningham, with the onslaught of public held hotel companies, today's industry professional must understand how to make a profit. Having great customer skills no longer promotes you to the top. A degree in hospitality management with a strong emphasis in business administration strengthens your preparation for the industry. In additional to classroom preparation, junior and senior students especially should seek hands-on opportunities such as internships, shadowing experiences and mentoring relationships. Internships are very beneficial to students in that they provide immediate access to the real work world and also are the time for students to make mistakes as they learn. These experiences also provide the graduate with a strong level of preparedness for entry-level positions.

Moore contends that students must be prepared and learn as much as possible while still in school. He feels that their education should give them a good solid background before they seek employment in the industry. For those who have properly prepared themselves, entry-level positions may include but are not limited to manager trainee internships, unit manager, food and beverage director, operations manager, sales and marketing, human resources, front office supervisor, executive housekeeper, director of housekeeping, controller, conference manager, rooms divisions manager, travel consultant, meeting planner, events planner, and the assistant manager position in all segments of the industry, etc. In planning and preparing for a successful career in hospitality, take advantage of in-house management training programs and seek mentors which will increase the potential of a steady and timely progression in hospitality. Students obtaining degrees in hospitality are prepared to seek employment in hotels, restaurants, travel and tourism destinations, convention and visitors bureaus, health care facilities, airlines, recreational facilities, and management/contract services, etc.

Successful African Americans in hospitality recognize their role and the importance of mentoring incoming students interested in hospitality management. According to Phillip Cunningham, historically African Americans have not achieved the same level of success in the industry, due to the lack of corporate mentors. It is extremely important to identify people who can help you achieve your goals. Often this means the mentor takes on additional responsibilities without being paid, works more than 50 hours a week, and moves from city to city. Scott agrees that mentoring as well as helping to place students is a responsibility that all successful role models in the industry should take on. She further charges herself as well as fellow colleagues to, assist students' progression in the industry by making opportunities available and by developing outreach programs to disseminate information to students and professionals.

Although competition is tough, well-prepared students can expect steady opportunities for advancement. However, explains Scott, students can compete by participating in internships and working any and every job available in the industry. She also says, if students are to progress upward to managerial level positions, they need practical experience and must have a positive attitude. Overall she feels the most important thing a student can do to be successful is, plan and prepare, have a willingness to work, and be passionate about your career.

The industry is very demanding but rewarding and appreciates those who have paid their dues so to speak. Hospitality companies are looking for confident, well-adjusted individuals with good communication and interviewing skills. In his role as a regional recruiter, Ed Moore, Jr. states, verbal skills are of concern and that students should learn how to articulate well. However, he continues, one of the glaring areas of concern that I have noticed is students are not ready for the interview. This is something that you will need to practice with an experienced person or professional.

Recognizing a shortage of African Americans in key positions in the industry, African-American college graduates are zealously sought and offered substantial positions. To help the industry achieve its goals, many historically Black colleges and universities serve as clearing houses for qualified African-American graduates in hospitality management. This affords colleges and universities the opportunity to maintain ongoing relationships with industry personnel as well as receive constant feedback on the expectations of industry regarding entering employees.

Interested in a career in hospitality management? Where do you go from here? First, complete your college degree in hospitality management and/or related major. Work whenever and wherever possible in any segment of the hospitality industry, be flexible, find a dedicated and concerned mentor in the segment of the industry which interests you most, and talk to successful African Americans in the industry, organizations, and who are in positions of leadership in the field of hospitality management.

The following organizations listed focus primarily on the needs and concerns of African Americans and other people of colour in the industry, as well as serve as a clearinghouse for information and opportunities for students, faculty and the industry.

Preparation inside and outside of the classroom is vital to a progressive and successful career path in the hospitality industry. The opportunities are great, advancement is realistic, and success is attainable.

A Brief History

The history of hotels is intimately connected to that of civilisations. Or rather, it is a part of that history. Facilities offering guests hospitality have been in evidence since early biblical times. The Greeks developed thermal baths in villages designed for rest and recuperation. Later, the Romans built mansions to provide accommodation for travellers on government business. The Romans were the first to develop thermal baths in England, Switzerland and the Middle East. Later still, caravanserais appeared, providing a resting place for caravans along Middle Eastern routes. In the Middle Ages, monasteries and abbeys were the first establishments to offer refuge to travellers on a regular basis. Religious orders built inns, hospices and hospitals to cater for those on the move.

From antiquity to the Middle Ages-The history of hotels is intimately connected to that of civilisations. Or rather, it is a part of that history. Facilities offering guests hospitality have been in evidence since early biblical times. The Greeks developed thermal baths in villages designed for rest and recuperation. Later, the Romans built mansions to provide accommodation for travellers on government business. The Romans were the first to develop thermal baths in England, Switzerland and the Middle East. Later still, caravanserais appeared, providing a resting place for caravans along Middle Eastern routes. In the Middle Ages, monasteries and abbeys were the first establishments to offer refuge to travellers on a regular basis. Religious orders built inns, hospices and hospitals to cater for those on the move.

Inns multiplied, but they did not yet offer meals. Staging posts were established for governmental transports and as rest stops. They provided shelter and allowed horses to be changed more easily. Numerous refuges then sprang up for pilgrims and crusaders on their way to the Holy Land.

Travelling then became progressively more hazardous. At the same time, inns gradually appeared in most of Europe. Some of them have remained famous, for example, l' Auberge des Trois Rois in Basle, which dates from the Middle Ages.

Around 1200, staging posts for travellers and stations for couriers were set up in China and Mongolia.

In Europe, or more precisely in Belgium, l' Auberge Cour Saint Georges opened in Gant, while the Angel Inn was built at Grantham in Lincolnshire, England. The start of the hotel industry-In France, at the beginning of the fifteenth century, the law required that hotels keep a register. English law also introduced rules for inns at that time. At the same time, around 1500 thermal spas were developed at Carlsbad and Marienbad.

During this epoch, more than 600 inns were registered in England. Their architecture often consisted of a paved interior court with access through an arched porch. The bedrooms were situated on the two sides of the courtyard, the kitchen and the public rooms at the front, and the stables and storehouses at the back. The first guide books for travellers were published in France during this period.

An embryonic hotel industry began to develop in Europe. Distinctive signs were hung outside establishments renowned for their refined cuisine. At the end of the 1600s, the first stage coaches following a regular timetable started operating in England. Half a century later, clubs similar to English gentlemen's clubs and masonic lodges began to appear in America.

In Paris in the time of Louis XIV, the Place Vendome offered the first example of a multiple-use architectural complex, where the classical facades accommodated boutiques, offices, apartments and also hotels.

In the nineteenth century, hotels take over the town-The industrial revolution, which started in the 1760s, facilitated the construction of hotels everywhere, in mainland Europe, in England and in America.

In New York first of all, and then in Copenhagen, hotels were established in city centres.

At the beginning of the 1800s, the Royal Hotel was built in London. Holiday resorts began to flourish along the French and Italian rivieras. In Japan, Ryokan guest houses sprang up. In India, the government-run Dak bungalows provided reliable accommodation for travellers. The Tremont House in Boston was the first deluxe hotel in a city centre. It offered inside toilets, locks on the doors and an "a la carte" menu.

The Holt Hotel in New York City was the first to provide its guests with a lift for their luggage.

In 1822, in Venice, a certain Giuseppe Dal Niel transformed an old palace into a hotel and gave it his name, "Le Danieli". As trains began to replace horse-drawn transport, highway inns for stage coaches started to decline.

During this period, the Shepheards Hotel in Cairo was founded, the result of a complete transformation of an ancient city-centre harem.

L'Hôtel des Bergues was built in the spring of 1834 on the shore of the Lake of Geneva. One of its founders, Guillaume Henri Dufour, became a famous Swiss general. In 1840, Hotel des Trois Couronnes was established in Vevey in Switzerland and the Baur au Lac in Zurich, fully refurbished since 1995.

In New York, the New York Hotel was the first to be equipped with private bathrooms.

The "Bayerischer Hof" was built in Munich in 1841, followed in 1852 by the "Vier Jahreszeiten". These two famous establishments were completely renovated after the Second World War.

Le Grand Hotel Paris-The inauguration of the Grand Hotel in Paris took place on 5 May 1862 in the presence of the Empress Eugenie. The orchestra, directed by Jacques Offenbach, played the Traviata. This building was designed by the architect Alfred Armand, in order to "show the élite of travellers from all over the world the progress made under the Second Empire by the sciences, arts and industry".

The exterior facades with their high arched doors and their Louis XIV windows were in the style required for the surroundings of the Opera. The greatest names in painting and decoration participated in the completion of this hotel, the grandest in Europe in its dimensions, luxury and installations. The first hydraulic lift was installed in this hotel. "Lighting was supplied by 4000 gas jets; heating by 18 stoves and 354 hot air vents.

In 1890, the entire hotel was equipped with electric lighting.

Due to the installation of steam central heating in 1901, baskets of wood were no longer sold on the floors. Some years later the hotel was renovated. Further renovation took place in 1970 and 1985. In 1982, it became a member of the Intercontinental chain.

Since 1992 the hotel has been equipped with a central Building Management System.

In June 2003, Le Grand Hotel Paris has reopened its doors following an eighteen-month multi-million dollar renovation.

The Fifth Avenue Hotel in New York City was the first in

that period to provide lifts for its guests. 1869 saw the inauguration, near Cairo, of the Mena House, an oasis of calm and luxury, at the foot of the famous pyramids of Cheops, Chephren and Mikerinos.

In 1870, the Palmer House Hotel in Chicago was the grandest of all hotels. Its structure, the first of its kind, was fire-resistant.

In 1873, the Palais de Würtemberg in Vienna was transformed into a superb luxury residence for the notables of the epoch, hotel Imperial. Kings and queens became regular visitors to what is without doubt the finest example of the refined architecture of the Ringstrasse in Vienna. It is said that Richard Wagner directed the first productions of "Tannhäuser" and "Lohengrin" there. Two years later in 1875, the Grand Hotel Europe opened its doors in St Petersburg. This prestigious place where Tchaikoswky spent his honeymoon and where Shostakovich played a sonata for Prokofiev in his suite.

In 1880, the Sagamore Hotel on Lake George in the state of New York was the very first to provide electricity in all its rooms.

The first school for hoteliers was founded in Lausanne, Switzerland in 1890 by J. Tschumi, Director of the Beau Rivage in Lausanne, and A.R. Armleder, the "father" of the Richemond in Geneve.

In Monte Carlo, hotel Hermitage opened its doors in 1896, offering its guests the refined and luxurious atmosphere enjoyed by the rich at the close of the nineteenth century. Shortly afterwards, the Victoria Hotel in Kansas City offered bathrooms with every room. The Netherland Hotel in New York City then became the first to provide all its guests with their own telephone.

In Athens in 1874, Stathis Lampsas, a chef by profession, realised his dream by building hotel Grande Bretagne. Athens was suffering at that time from a shortage of water. It is said that the personnel bought water from carriers in the street to bring to the 80 bedrooms and... the two bathrooms Of course, the establishment has undergone several renovations since that time.

In 1894, the Grand Hotel became the first Italian hotel to boast an electricity supply.

The Swiss hotelier Caspar Badrutt opened the famous Palace de Saint Moritz in 1896. In 1898, Cesar Ritz, from the Valais in Switzerland, who became, to quote the famous phrase of King Edward VII, the "king of hoteliers and hotelier to kings", opened the hotel which bears his famous name in the Place Vendôme in Paris.

The twentieth century: the age of prosperity-The early years of the twentieth century were rich in new hotels which rapidly became prestigious.

Edouard Niiermans, the "architect of palaces", transformed the Villa "Eugenie", the summer residence of the Emperor Napoleon III and his wife Eugénie de Montijo, in 1900. In 1905, he built hotel du Palais in Biarritz. In 1913 his "Negresco" was opened in Nice, in the presence of seven kings!

In Madrid, King Alphonse XIII was anxious that the capital should have a luxurious and prestigious hotel, and as a result the Ritz was inaugurated in 1910. Seville paid its own homage to the king by opening a splendid establishment, constructed by the architect Jose Espiau, the Alphonso XIII. Not to be outdone, Barcelona inaugurated its own Ritz in 1919. This was equipped with an unheard of luxury at that time, bathrooms with hot as well as cold water!

We could also cite, among many other hotels built in the same period, the Ritz and Savoy in London, the Beau Rivage Palace in Lausanne, le Négresco in Nice, the Plaza in New York, the Metropole in Brussels, the Plaza-Athene and hotel de Crillon in Paris, the Taj Mahal in Bombay and so on. The latter was renovated in 1972 by the Inter-Continental chain.

The prosperous nineteen-twenties saw a veritable boom in the hotel industry. Numerous hotels were established in this decade. In 1923, the architects Marchisio and Prost constructed a hotel in some wonderful gardens in the heart of Marrakech in Morocco, and for decades it was considered the most beautiful hotel in the world: La Mamounia. Winston Churchill helped to forge its reputation by becoming a frequent guest.

Hotels were built not only in cities, but also in the mountains. The first ski resorts in Switzerland (Saint-Moritz, Gstaad,

Montana, etc.) welcomed tourists (often English ones) to some very comfortable establishments.

The worldwide depression which followed in 1929 did not prevent the construction of the famous Waldorf Astoria in New York. This was the greatest hotel edifice of those troubled times.

After the war, the fifties saw the second boom in the hotel industry. The Club Mediterranée (G. Trigano) created the now famous, but then revolutionary concept of the club village. These years were also notable for the construction of the first casino hotels. This was also the time when the airline companies began to develop their own hotels.

In the sixties, new tourist resorts flourished around the Mediterranean. From Spain to Greece and from the Balearics to Yugoslavia, numerous city and beach hotels opened their doors to summer guests hungry for relaxation and a good dose of sunshine. Portugal and the Scandinavian countries soon followed their lead.

Hotels for Business People

1970 saw the beginning of the construction of hotels for business people. This movement was supported by several factors. First of all, there was the will of the airline companies to extend their efforts in the domain of hotels.

Then there was the sudden prosperity, due to black gold, of Middle Eastern countries which attracted business people from the entire world. This engendered an important business travel trend-not limited to this region alone-which initiated the development of hotels primarily designed for business people in Middle-Eastern cities like Dubai, Abu Dhabi, Riyadh and Jeddah, to mention only the most important.

Hotel chains, attentive to their customers' wishes, started to offer an increasingly varied range of services. Their rooms became more spacious and the cuisine more refined.

Gradually, too, various first class hotels (among them former palaces and city centre hotels) which had fallen into disrepair began systematic renovation programmes.

The end of the seventies, when China opened its doors to foreign tourists, also saw the first congresses of international hotel experts. The third hotel industry boom-The third boom in the hotel industry began in 1980, marked by more inventive marketing and the development of hotels increasingly adapted to a particular type of clientele.

This trend prompted the construction of hotels near airports, hotels for conferences, health hotels, ski holiday hotels, holiday villages and marina hotels. The first Property Management Systems (Fidelio, Hogatex, etc.) appear in the hospitality market.

In Istanbul in 1984, work began on the renovation and transformation into a hotel of the prestigious sultans' residence, the Ciragan Palace in Istanbul. The resulting hotel is no less prestigious than the Ciragan Palace was. Managed by the Kempinski chain, it opened its 322 rooms to guests in 1991.

The first administrative hotel management systems, offering hotels greater independence from human resources, then appeared on the market. The hotel industry was becoming more and more competitive. Business travellers and retired people became important target customers.

In the eighties, too, the Far East began to prepare itself to welcome both business people and the tourists who were beginning to discover the countries of the rising sun, such as China, South Korea, Thailand and Japan. The international chains (American for the most part) prepared expansion plans for Europe, the Middle and Far East which were mainly aimed at congress participants and business people.

The nineties: technology starts to make an impact-The early nineties were characterised by a recession in the hotel business, without doubt caused by reductions in multinationals' travel budgets and the growing crisis in the Gulf.

The Gulf War helped to create great insecurity for both individuals and business. 1991 is considered to be the black year of the hotel tradè. It forced hoteliers to become more creative in finding ways of attracting guests (special programmes, offers for "frequent travellers", high performance reservation systems) and thus emerge from the crisis with the minimum damage.

For the first time, the environment and energy conservation played an important role in the marketing activities of numerous chains (thanks in part to the green movement) and even helped to win the loyalty of numerous clients while safeguarding assets at the same time. Reservation systems became more efficient and offered the hotelier a new dimension in the creation of customer loyalty, the database. The records of each guest's individual history have helped create individualised marketing programmes and have enabled hotels to satisfy a guest's personal needs from the moment of his arrival.

Hotel Adlon Berlin is a legend reborn. From its opening in 1907, until it was destroyed in 1945, it was a symbol of Berlin, a lavish host for royalty, heads of government, stage and screen stars, and the greats of literature and science. Now, it has been rebuilt (1997) on its original site, the corner of Unter den Linden and Pariser Platz, facing the Brandenburg Gate. Outside, it is a virtual replica of the original; inside it is testimony to what smart hotel operators (in this case the Kempinski group) can accomplish with an investment of $260 million. The hotel's 337 rooms and suites are the ultimate in luxury. Interiors, designed by England's Ezra Attia and Sweden's Lars Malmquist, dazzle with marble, sandstone, stained glass, gold leaf, stuccowork, cherry wood panelling, and damask draperies. This hotel is today equipped with the most advanced technology with regards to the Room Management System communicating with the Property Management System.

Since 1992, the most important international chains have been vying with each other in ever greater imaginative feats related to the vital process of renovating their establishments worldwide. Technology has started to take its rightful place in hotel administration (simplification of check-in and check-out procedures, global reservation systems, marketing management etc.). In 1995, the first Hotel Room Management System is launched at the European level. It is linked to the most popular Property Management Systems to make the front desk more efficient and near to the guests.

At International Technology Forums, speakers unanimously, underlined the impact of technology on hotel rooms.

Hotel chains have been searching for alliances and some of them. For example: Holyday Inn, Intercontinental, and Crown Plaza have merged to form Six continents hotels Chain; Marriot absorbed Renaissance and Ramada International; Sol Melia opened a new line of Boutique hotels, Accor signed several joint ventures in the East and the Far East, etc.) Forte acquired Meridian to reinforce its global position. Starwoods (Sheraton) absorbed the Italian chain and Westin. The main expansion zones for the hotel industry in 1994 remained Asia (particularly China and India), the Middle East (above all, the United Arab Emirates and Egypt) and Latin America.

In Europe, hotel enterprises in the eastern countries (Russia, Croatia, Slovakia, etc.) decided to renovate dilapidated palaces built at the turn of the century. All the European capitals started to invest in preparations for the major event of this fin de siecle period, that is, the celebration of our entry into the third millennium.

The 3 star hotel Millennium enjoying top level of On-line Room Management System is situated at the best site in Opatija at the Mediterranean coast. Opatija in Croatia corresponds, in terms of reputation, to the level of St. Moritz in Switzerland.

Capitals throughout the world were busy developing the necessary infrastructure to welcome the millions of tourists for the celebration of this event.

Major hotel chains are drawing up development plans in almost all parts of Europe. These plans primarily involve the renovation of numerous prestigious hotels in both western and eastern European countries. Gradually, the great capitals of Europe have been endowed with hotels boasting three, four and five stars, offering quality services, innovative architecture, style, charm, and interior design (city Boutique hotels). Specialised hotels offer wellness programs including health and beauty centres, personalised services and treatments, anti-stress, revitalising, regenerating programs, etc.

Extravaganza-In 1995 construction began in Dubai of one of the most ambitious and prestigious tourist complexes in the region, the Jumeirah Beach Hotels (Jumeirah Beach hotel, Burj Al Arab, etc.). These comprise several establishments capable of satisfying the needs of average tourists, business people and those who can afford real luxury. The talk now is of six-and seven-star hotels, a surprising designation which is nevertheless perfectly justified by the luxury of the bedrooms and the facilities they offer, the impeccable service, the high degree of modern technology, as well as the beauty of the surroundings and the high-quality environment.

In 2004, another Emirate, Abu Dhabi, will welcome the delegates of the Gulf Council Countries. in the new Conference Palace Hotel (CPH). This superior construction has been specified "to offer the most outstanding services with a challenging 9 star definition"... We will, of course, report on it on a later stage.

On-line in seconds, work surf, communicate-everywhere-Today in 2003, travellers, mostly businessmen, carry their personal PC to make presentations, communicate with their office, via e-mails, etc. One possibility offered to them today consists in the use of so-called Pad offering, in particular,

- Cable-free and universal access to Internet or intranet, wherever you happen to be
- Brilliant colour touch screen
- Ready to go in seconds (instant on)
- Freedom in the selection of transmission standards by interchangeable PC cards
- Unlimited flexibility by open platform Windows CE 3.0
- Comprehensive office software package
- Virtual keyboard and handwriting recognition

For sure, new technologies are continuously offering innovative and more comfortable ways to the traveller.

The 160 rooms 5 star Palafitte Hotel in Monruz Neuchatel(CH) offers the visitors of the Swiss Expo 2002 a vision of so called in-room available technologies.

Hotel Management

Seeing to every aspect of operations and functions of the hotel is hotel management. This is spearheaded by the General Manager of the hotel with his able and efficient team of departmental heads. The General Manager is responsible to direct, guide and motivate staff in the day to day operations and will oversee the general operations and diligently monitor all operating costs of the hotel. The Hotel Management is dedicated to improve the performance through cost-effective operations. Team work is an important element in hotel management, as one department cannot function without the support and help of the other departments of the hotel. They constantly plan out new ways and methods to improve the standards and guest experiences. The hotels periodically plan out special promotions and events to allure more guests to the hotel. Hotel management is a strenuous task. From the outset it may be an exciting, people oriented career, but with the hotel industry growing with each passing day, and hotels competing with each other, the demands made by guests, their thinking and value for money expectation increases. Thus, the management has to be prepared to meet this ever increasing demand to sustain and maintain a steady income. "One Room vacant per day is revenue lost forever". As such the managers are on their toes, round the clock to see that the guest is satisfied. Their prime objective is to build a reputation by exceeding the expectations of the guest and the proprietor of the hotel, whereby not only guest satisfaction is achieved but also succeeding in obtaining investment returns to the owner.

Each departmental head is expected to guide their respective staff, for the smooth functioning of the hotel. Co-ordination and cooperation with each other is an important element. Where guest satisfaction and experiences are the key factors, each department sees to the need of the guest with utmost care. No two days will be the same in a hotel.

As such the management has to come up with ideas to see that the guest is happy and content. Some hotels have theme nights, whereby, the guests are given a different kind of experience and food. The management, who works round the clock, are dedicated and committed to ensure that new ideas and methods are brought forward. On a daily basis, the management meets to discuss how best the hotel should function, and to rectify and find solutions to any issue that they have come up with, seeing to guest needs, staff issues, day to day operations of the hotel, costing and budgeting and special events.

To achieve this comprehensive task, motivation and recognition is required. Hospitality is one industry where employees are recognized for their contribution and service. The management records and maintains the achievements of the staff, and they are duly rewarded as individuals and teams. Motivating and keeping the morale of the staff high is very important. As such the management works in a very friendly and cordial manner with the staff, and gives a hand whenever the need arises. There is open dialog all the time between the management and the staff, whereby the staff is able to approach their respective managers without any hesitation. Management continually encourages the staff to work as a team, and hospitality is one industry where 'team work' plays an important role in the functioning of an organization.

Though being a 24-7 job, and the hard work done behind the scene rarely noticed, the success of the Hotel speaks volumes and is all due to the dedicated and committed and effective management.

Hotel Industry in India

Hotel Industry in India has witnessed tremendous boom in recent years. Hotel Industry is inextricably linked to the tourism industry and the growth in the Indian tourism industry has fuelled the growth of Indian hotel industry. The thriving economy and increased business opportunities in India have acted as a boon for Indian hotel industry. The arrival of low cost airlines and the associated price wars have given domestic tourists a host of options. The 'Incredible India' destination campaign and the recently launched 'Atithi Devo Bhavah' (ADB) campaign have also helped in the growth of domestic and international tourism and consequently the hotel industry.

In recent years government has taken several steps to boost travel & tourism which have benefited hotel industry in India. These include the abolishment of the inland air travel tax of 15%; reduction in excise duty on aviation turbine fuel to 8%; and removal of a number of restrictions on outbound chartered flights, including those relating to frequency and size of aircraft. The government's recent decision to treat convention centres as part of core infrastructure, allowing the government to provide critical funding for the large capital investment that may be required has also fuelled the demand for hotel rooms.

The opening up of the aviation industry in India has exciting opportunities for hotel industry as it relies on airlines to transport

80% of international arrivals. The government's decision to substantially upgrade 28 regional airports in smaller towns and privatization & expansion of Delhi and Mumbai airport will improve the business prospects of hotel industry in India. Substantial investments in tourism infrastructure are essential for Indian hotel industry to achieve its potential.

The upgrading of national highways connecting various parts of India has opened new avenues for the development of budget hotels in India. Taking advantage of this opportunity Tata group and another hotel chain called 'Homotel' have entered this business segment. According to a report, Hotel Industry in India currently has supply of 110,000 rooms and there is a shortage of 150,000 rooms fueling hotel room rates across India. According to estimates demand is going to exceed supply by at least 100% over the next 2 years.

Five-star hotels in metro cities allot same room, more than once a day to different guests, receiving almost 24-hour rates from both guests against 6-8 hours usage. With demand-supply disparity, hotel rates in India are likely to rise by 25% annually and occupancy by 80%, over the next two years. This will affect the competitiveness of India as a cost-effective tourist destination. To overcome, this shortage Indian hotel industry is adding about 60,000 quality rooms, currently in different stages of planning and development, which should be ready by 2012. Hotel Industry in India is also set to get a fillip with Delhi hosting 2010 Commonwealth Games. Government has approved 300 hotel projects, nearly half of which are in the luxury range. The future scenario of Indian hotel industry looks extremely rosy. It is expected that the budget and mid-market hotel segment will witness huge growth and expansion while the luxury segment will continue to perform extremely well over the next few years.

Hotel Management Tips for General Managers

Your education and experience provided you with a structured picture of what the business end of your hotel requires, and you continue to enrich yourself through additional training, seminars and workshops. Employee needs are much more basic, and while your first idea may be to give your employees raises and benefits to make them happy, employees expect only respect, honesty, recognition, job enrichment, and feedback to feel fulfilled. Employee morale is emotion based. Here are some management tips to help you as general manager.

Hotel Management Tips for General Managers 1

Get out of your office. Employees need to feel connected to their managers, and it is difficult to create this connection and trust with someone who is always behind closed doors. It is important to be visible!

Hotel Management Tips for General Managers 2

What are you good at? Focusing on your strengths will make your job fulfilling and give you the recognition you deserve. Putting a primary focus on your weakness will only take the pleasure out of your job. No one looks forward to doing things they aren't great at.

Hotel Management Tips for General Managers 3

Don't wait. Don't put off important discussions, meetings, or the elimination of employees. The longer you wait, the more difficult it becomes to face the challenges that you've been putting off.

Hotel Management Tips for General Managers 4

The right qualities make the right hires. Do not hire employees who do not suit the job you are hiring for. It becomes a waste of your time and theirs and can jeopardize the morale of others.

Hotel Management Tips for General Managers 5

Problems are opportunities! Every obstacle you face can lead to amazing breakthroughs, so never see issues as a problem. Looking for the opportunity to learn and grow from it.

Hotel Management Tips for General Managers 6

When employees feel challenged to produce, you will get the best results. Create fun competition to encourage your employees to excel better than where your numbers currently are.

Hotel Management Tips for General Managers 7

Quality service is what customers expect, so caring for your employees will ensure that your customers are well taken care of. Happy employees provide quality in their work.

Hotel Management Tips for General Managers 8

Don't gloat about your success. As a General Manager, it is important to know that your success comes directly from the success of your employees and the way they handle the customers. Praise your employees when you're doing exceptionally well and it will show that you appreciate working with them.

Hotel Management Tips for General Managers 9

Mistakes shouldn't just be cleaned up. The proper management of your hotel should include eliminating as many mistakes as possible to ensure that your hotel is running to the best of its ability.

Hotel Management Tips for General Managers 10

Listening and communication is key! As General Manager, it is important to listen and communicate effectively with employees, associates and customers in order to foresee any challenges and find solutions.

Hotel Management Tips for General Managers 11

How are you caring for your employees? Listen to your employees needs, give them feedback on what they can do to improve their production, and provide them with training to help them grow.

Hotel Management Tips for General Managers 12

Attention to the details creates success. As General Manager, it is important to pay attention to the details that go into the daily maintenance of the hotel environment. When you pay attention to details, you can catch any obstacles as they occur.

Hotel Management Tips for General Managers 13

"Reprimand in private, praise in public." Employees want respect most of all, and calling out your employees mistakes in front of their co-workers belittles them and takes down their respect.

3

Marketing of Hospitality Sector

Introduction

Tourism is one of many activities in a community or region that requires planning and coordination. This bulletin provides a simple structure and basic guidelines for comprehensive tourism planning at a community or regional level. Planning is the process of identifying objectives and defining and evaluating methods of achieving them. By comprehensive planning we mean planning which considers all of the tourism resources, organizations, markets, and programs within a region. Comprehensive planning also considers economic, environmental, social, and institutional aspects of tourism development.

Two Sides of Tourism Planning

Tourism planning has evolved from two related but distinct sets of planning philosophies and methods. On the one hand, tourism is one of many activities in an area that must be considered as part of physical, environmental, social, and economic planning. Therefore, it is common to find tourism addressed, at least partially, in a regional land use, transportation, recreation, economic development, or comprehensive plan.

The degree to which tourism is addressed in such plans depends upon the relative importance of tourism to the community or region and how sensitive the planning authority is to tourism activities. Tourism may also be viewed as a business in which a community or region chooses to engage. Individual tourism businesses conduct a variety of planning activities including feasibility, marketing, product development, promotion, forecasting, and strategic planning. If tourism is a significant component of an area's economy or development plans, regional or community-wide marketing plans are needed to coordinate the development and marketing activities of different tourism interests in the community. A comprehensive approach integrates a strategic marketing plan with more traditional public planning activities. This ensures a balance between serving the needs and wants of the tourists versus the needs and wants of local residents. A formal tourism plan provides a vehicle for the various interests within a community to coordinate their activities and work toward common goals. It also is a means of coordinating tourism with other community activities.

Steps in the Planning Process

Like any planning, tourism planning is goal-oriented, striving to achieve certain objectives by matching available resources and programs with the needs and wants of people. Comprehensive planning requires a systematic approach, usually involving a series of steps. The process is best viewed as an iterative and nagging one, with each step subject to modification and refinement at any stage of the planning process. There are six steps in the planning process:

1. Define goals and objectives.
2. Identify the tourism system.
   (a) Resources.
   (b) Organizations.
   (c) Markets.
3. Generate alternatives.
4. Evaluate alternatives.
5. Select and implement.
6. Monitor and evaluate.

Step One: Defining Goals and objectives. Obtaining clear statements of goals and objectives is difficult, but important. Ideally, tourism development goals should flow from more general community goals and objectives. It is important to understand how a tourism plan serves these broader purposes. Is the community seeking a broader tax base, increased employment opportunities, expanded recreation facilities, better educational programs, a higher quality of life? How can tourism contribute to these objectives?

If tourism is identified as a means of serving broader community goals, it makes sense to develop plans with more specific tourism development objectives. These are generally defined through a continuing process in which various groups and organizations in a community work together toward common goals. A local planning authority, chamber of commerce, visitors bureau, or similar group should assume a leadership role to develop an initial plan and obtain broad involvement of tourism interests in the community. Public support for the planning process and plan is also important. Having a good understanding of tourism and the tourism system in your community is the first step toward defining goals and objectives for tourism development. The types of goals that are appropriate and the precision with which you are able to define them will depend upon how long your community has been involved in tourism and tourism planning. In the early stages of tourism development, goals may involve establishing organizational structures and collecting information to better identify the tourism system in the community. Later, more precise objectives can be formulated and more specific development and marketing strategies evaluated.

Step Two: Identifying Your Tourism System When planning for any type of activity, it is important to first define its scope and characteristics. Be clear about exactly what your plan encompasses. A good initial question is, "What do you mean by tourism?" Tourism is defined in many ways. Generally, tourism involves people travelling outside of their community for pleasure. Definitions differ on the specifics of how far people must travel, whether or not they must stay overnight, for how long, and what exactly is included under travelling for "pleasure". Do you want your tourism plan to include day visitors, conventioneers, business travellers, people visiting friends and relatives, people passing through, or seasonal residents? Which community resources and organizations serve tourists or could serve tourists? Generally, tourists share community resources with local residents and businesses. Many organizations serve both tourists and locals. This complicates tourism planning and argues for a clear idea of what your tourism plan entails. You can begin to clarify the tourism system by breaking it down into three subsystems:

(1) tourism resources,

(2) tourism organizations, and

(3) tourism markets.

An initial task in developing a tourism plan is to identify, inventory, and classify the objects within each of these subsystems.

Tourism Resources are any (1) natural, (2) cultural, (3) human, or (4) capital resources that either are used or can be used to attract or serve tourists. A tourism resource inventory identifies and classifies the resources available that provide opportunities for tourism development. Conduct an objective and realistic assessment of the quality and quantity of resources you have to work with.

Tourism Organizations combine resources in various proportions to provide products and services for the tourist. It is important to recognize the diverse array of public and private organizations involved with tourism.

The most difficult part of tourism planning is to get these groups to work toward common goals.

You should develop a list of these organizations within your own community and obtain their input and cooperation in your tourism planning efforts. Setting up appropriate communication systems and institutional arrangements is a key part of community tourism planning.

Natural Resources

* Climate-seasons.
* Water resources-lakes, streams, waterfalls.
* Flora-forests, flowers, shrubs, wild edibles.
* Fauna-fish & wildlife.

* Geological resources-topography, soils, sand dunes, beaches, caves, rocks & minerals, fossils.
* Scenery-combinations of all of the above.

Cultural Resources

* Historic buildings, sites.
* Monuments, shrines.
* Cuisine.
* Ethnic cultures.
* Industry, government, religion, etc.
* Anthropological resources.
* Local celebrities.

Human Resources

* Hospitality skills.
* Management skills.
* Seasonal labour force.
* Performing artists-music, drama, art, storytellers.
* Craftsman and artisans.
* Other labour skills from chefs to lawyers to researchers.
* Local populations.

Capital

* Availability of capital, financing.
* Infrastructure-transportation roads, airports, railroads, harbours & marinas, trails & walkways.
* Infrastructure: utilities water, power, waste treatment, communications.

Tourism Management Organizations and Services

Off-Site: Coordination, planning, technical assistance, research, regulation:

* Federal & state departments of commerce, transportation, & natural resources.
* Federal, state, regional, & local tourism associations.

* Educational organizations & consultants, e.g., Travel & Tourism Research Association; U.S. Travel Data Centre; Travel Reference Centre, Univ. of Colorado, Boulder; Travel, Tourism, & Recreation Resource Centre, Michigan State University.
* Travel information & reservation services On-Site: development, promotion and management, of tourism resources:
    - Federal agencies, NB. departments of commerce, transportation, & land management agencies.
    - State agencies, NB. departments of commerce, transportation, & land/facility management agencies.
    - Local government organizations, e.g., visitor information, chamber of commerce, convention & visitor's bureaus, parks.
* Businesses: Accommodations: Hotels, motels, Lodges, resorts, bed & breakfast cabins & cottages, Condominiums, second homes, Campgrounds-Food & Beverage: Restaurants, Grocery, Bars, nightclubs.

Fast Food, Catering Services

- Transportation: Air, rail, bus; Local transportation: taxi, limo, Auto, bicycle, boat rental; Local tour services.
- Information: Travel agencies, Information and reservation services, Automobile clubs.
- Recreation Facilities & Services: Winter sports: ski, skating, snow mobile areas; Golf courses, miniature golf; Swimming pools, water slides, beaches; tennis, handball, racquetball courts, bowling alleys; Athletic clubs, health spas; Marinas, boat rentals and charters; hunting & fishing guides; Horseback enterprises; Sporting goods sales & rentals.
- Entertainment: Nightclubs, amusement parks, spectator sport facilities; Gambling facilities: casinos, horse racing, bingo; video arcades; art galleries and studios, craft shops, studios, demonstrations; performing arts: theatre, dance, music, film; historic & prehistoric sites; museums:

art, history, science, technology; arboreta, zoos, nature centres.

- Special festivals and events-Support services: Auto repair, gasoline service stations; boat & recreation vehicle dealers and service; retail shops: sporting goods, specialties, souvenirs, clothing; health services: hospitals, clinics, pharmacies; laundry and dry cleaning; beauty & barber shops; baby-sitting services; pet care; communications: newspaper, telephone; banking and financial services.

Tourism Markets: Tourists make-up the third, and perhaps most important subsystem. Successful tourism programs require a strong market orientation.

The needs and wants of the tourists you choose to attract and serve must be the focus of much of your marketing and development activity.

Therefore, it is important to clearly understand which tourism market segments you wish to attract and serve. Tourists fall into a very diverse set of categories with quite distinct needs and wants. You should identify the different types of tourists, or market segments that you presently serve or would like to serve.

This may involve one or more tourism market surveys. A visitor survey identifies the size and nature of the existing market and asks the following questions:

* What are the primary market segments you presently attract?
* Where do they come from?
* What local businesses and facilities do they use?
* What attracted them to the community?
* How did they find out about your community?
* How satisfied are they with your offerings?

A market survey (usually a telephone survey) also can be conducted among households in regions from which you wish to attract tourists. This type of study helps identify potential markets, and means of attracting tourists to your area.

Tourism Market Segments

In a general tourism plan, some clear target tourism market segments should be identified. You might begin by defining the market area from which you will draw most of your visitors. The size of your market area depends upon the uniqueness and quality of your "product", transportation systems, tastes and preferences of surrounding populations, and your competition.

Identifying the market area will help target information and promotion and define transportation routes and modes, competition, and characteristics of your market. Next, divide your travel market into the following trip length categories:

* day trips from a 50 mile radius,
* day trips from 50 to 200 miles away,
* pass-through travellers,
* overnight trips of 1 or 2 nights (most likely weekends), and
* extended overnight vacation trips.

After you have an idea of your market area and kinds of trips you will be serving, begin defining more specific market segments like vehicle campers, downhill skiers, sightseers, family vacationers, single weekenders, and the like. These segments can be more clearly tied to particular resources, businesses, and facilities in your community.

What kinds of products and services are likely to attract each of these groups? Tourist needs as well as their impact on the local community are quite different for day tourists versus overnight tourists. Areas catering primarily to weekend traffic will experience large fluctuations in use. In deciding the relative importance of these different segments, communities need to assess both their ability to provide required services (do you have enough rooms?), as well as the demand for different types of trips relative to the supply and your competition.

The Environment: A tourism plan is significantly affected by many factors in the broader environment. Indeed, one of the complexities of tourism planning is the number of variables that are outside of the control of an individual tourism business or community. These include such things as tourism offerings and prices at competing destinations, federal and state policy and legislation, currency exchange rates, the state of the economy, and weather. These factors are discussed more fully in Extension bulletin E-1959 as part of the market environment analysis.

Local populations also must be considered in tourism planning. As they compete with tourists for resources, they can be significantly affected by tourism activity, and they are an important source of support in getting tourism plans implemented.

A survey of local residents can be conducted to assess community attitudes toward tourism development, identify impacts of tourism on the community, and obtain local input into tourism plans.

Public hearings, workshops, and advisory boards are other ways to obtain public involvement in tourism planning.

Local support and cooperation is important to the success of tourism programs and should not be overlooked.

Tourism Market Segments

I. Geographic market areas.

II. Trip categories.

Day Trips:

* short-within 50 miles.
* long-up to 200 miles.

Pass through traffic:

* day visitors.
* overnight stays.

Overnight Trips:

* weekend.
* vacation.

III. Activity or trip purpose Outdoor Recreation:

* Water-based Activity:
  - Boating: sail, power, cruise, row, canoe, water ski.
  - Swimming: pool, beach, sunbathing, scuba.
  - Fishing: charter, sport, from pier, boat, shore, ice.

* Land-based Activity:
  - Camping: back packing, primitive, developed.
  - Hiking: climbing, beachcombing, spelunking.
  - Hunting.
  - Skiing: downhill, cross country.
  - Snowmobiling.
  - Bicycling.
  - Horseback riding.
  - Picnicking.
* Air-based Activity:
  - Aeroplane rides, hang gliding, ballooning, parachuting.
* General:
  - Nature study.
  - Photography or landscape painting.
  - Viewing natural scenery.

Sightseeing & Entertainment:

* Visiting particular sites or areas:
  - historic or prehistoric.
  - cultural.
  - amusements.
  - scenic.
* Attending particular events, shows, or demonstrations:
  - ethnic festivals.
  - sporting events.
  - performances.
  - agricultural fair or festival.
  - boat show.
  - shopping.

Other Primary Purpose for Trip:

* Visiting Friends & Relatives.
* Convention & Business/Pleasure.

Step Three: Generating Alternatives. Generating alternative development and marketing options to meet your goals requires some creative thinking and brainstorming. The errors made at this stage are usually thinking too narrowly or screening out alternatives prematurely. It is wise to solicit a wide range of options from a diverse group of people. If tourism expertise is lacking in your community, seek help and advice outside the community. Tourism planning involves a wide range of interrelated development and marketing decisions. The following development questions will get you started:

* How much importance should be assigned to tourism within a community or region?
* Which general community goals is tourism development designed to serve?
* Which organization(s) will provide the leadership and coordination necessary for community tourism planning?

What are the relative roles of public and private sectors? Tourism marketing decision questions include:

* *Segments:* Which market segments should be pursued; geographic markets, trip types, activity or demographic subgroups?
* *Product:* What kinds of tourism products and services should be provided? Who should provide what?
* *Place:* Where should tourism facilities be located?
* Promotion: What kinds of promotion should be used, by whom, in which media, how much, when? What community tourism theme or image should be established?
* *Price:* What prices should be charged for which products and services. Who should capture the revenue?

Step Four: Evaluating Alternatives. Tourism development and marketing options are evaluated by assessing the degree to which each option will be able to meet the stated goals and objectives. There are usually two parts to a systematic evaluation of tourism development and marketing alternatives: (1) Feasibility analysis, and (2) Impact assessment.

These two tasks are interrelated, but think of them as trying to answer two basic questions: (1) Can it be done?, and (2) What are the consequences? A decision to take a specific action must be based both on feasibility and desirability.

Feasibility Analysis: First, screen alternatives and eliminate those that are not feasible due to economic, environmental, political, legal, or other factors. Evaluate the remaining set of alternatives in more detail, paying particular attention to the market potential and financial plan. Make a realistic assessment of your community's ability to attract and serve a market segment or segments. This requires a clear understanding of the tourism market in your area and how this market is changing. Also carefully identify your competition and evaluate your advantages and disadvantages compared to the competition.

Plan toward the future because it takes time to implement decisions and for your actions to take effect. Therefore, look at the likely market and competition for several years to come. Review forecasts for the travel market in your area, if available. Careful tracking of tourism trends in your own community can help identify changes in the market that you will have to adapt to.

Impact Assessment: When evaluating alternative development and marketing strategies it is important to understand the impacts, both positive and negative, of proposed actions. A classification of economic, environmental, and social impacts associated with tourism development. The types of impacts and their importance vary across different communities and proposed actions. Generally, the size, extent, and nature of tourism impacts depend upon:

* volume of tourist activity relative to local activity.
* length and nature of tourist contacts with the community.
* degree of concentration/dispersal of tourist activity in the area.
* similarities or differences between local populations and tourists.
* stability/sensitivity of local economy, environment, and social structure.
* how well tourism is planned, controlled, and managed.

Look at both the benefits and costs of any proposed actions. While tourism development can increase income, revenues, and employment, it also involves costs. Evaluate benefits and costs of tourism development from the perspectives of local government, businesses, and residents.

Impacts of Tourism

Economic Impacts:

* Sales, revenue, and income.
* Employment.
* Fiscal impact-taxes, infrastructure costs.
* Prices.
* Economic base & structure.

Environmental Impacts:

* Lands.
* Waters.
* Air.
* Infrastructure.
* Flora & fauna.

Social Impacts:

* Population structure & distribution.
* Values & attitudes.
* Education.
* Occupations.
* Safety & security.
* Congestion & crowding.
* Community spirit & cohesion.
* Quality of life.

Impacts on Local Government Local government provides most of the infrastructure and many of the services essential to tourism development, including highways, public parks, law enforcement, water and sewer, garbage collection and disposal. Evaluate tourism decisions with a clear understanding of the capacity of the local infrastructure and services relative to anticipated needs, and take into account both the needs of local populations and tourists.

A fiscal impact analysis evaluates the impact of tourism on the community's tax base and local government costs. It entails predicting the additional infrastructure and service requirements of tourism development, estimating their costs, deciding who will pay for/provide them, and how. Will tourism generate increased local government revenue through fees and charges, local sales or use taxes, increased property values or property tax rates, or larger local shares of federal and state tax revenues?

Impacts on Business and Industry Businesses that are directly serving tourists benefit from sales to tourists. Through secondary impacts, tourism activity also benefits a wide range of businesses in a community. For example, a local textile industry may sell to a linen supply firm that serves hotels and motels catering primarily to tourists. A local forest products industry sells to a lumberyard where local woodcarvers or furniture makers buy their supplies. They in turn sell to tourists through various retail outlets. All of these businesses benefit from tourism. If most products and services for tourists are bought outside of the local area, much of the tourist spending "leaks" out of the local economy. The more a community is "self-sufficient" in serving tourists, the larger the local impact.

Impacts on Residents

Local residents may experience a broad range of both positive and negative impacts from tourism development.

Tourism development may provide increased employment and income for the community. Although tourism jobs are primarily in the service sectors and are often seasonal, part time, and low-paying, these characteristics, are neither universal nor always undesirable. Residents may value opportunities for part time and seasonal work. In particular, employment opportunities and work experiences for students or retirees may be desired. Residents may also benefit from local services that otherwise would not be available. Tourism development may mean a wider variety of retailers and restaurants, or a better community library. It may also mean more traffic, higher prices, and increases in property values and local taxes. The general quality of the environment and life in the community may go up or down due to tourism development. This depends on the nature of tourism development, the preferences and desires of local residents, and how well tourism is planned and managed.

Steps Five and Six

Implementation, and Monitoring and Evaluation. We will not attempt a complete discussion of decisionmaking, plan implementation, and monitoring, but these are critical steps in the success of a tourism plan. A set of specific actions should be prescribed with clearly defined responsibilities and timetables. Monitor progress in implementing the plan and evaluate the success of the plan in meeting its goals and objectives on a regular basis. Plans generally need to be adjusted over time due to changing goals, changing market conditions, and unanticipated impacts. It is a good idea to build monitoring and evaluation systems into your planning efforts.

Concluding Remarks

Successful tourism planning and development means serving both tourists and local residents. The bulletins in this series stress the importance of a market orientation for attracting and serving tourists. This market orientation must be balanced with a clear view of how tourism serves the broader community interest and an understanding of the positive and negative impacts of tourism development. Remember, tourism should serve the community first and the tourist second. Tourism development must be compatible with other activities in the area and be supported by the local population. Therefore, the tourism plan should be closely coordinated with other local and regional planning efforts, if not an integral part of them.

4

Growth of Global Hospitality Sector

Globalization Process

Tourism is one of the world economy's growth sectors. Despite crisis-induced slumps the long term growth trend appears to be stable. Tourism is a beneficiary of the irreversible process of globalization and indeed is an accelerating factor for this process. The trend to a division of labour on a worldwide basis has been particularly favourable to tourism, resulting in increased productivity and prosperity in a great many countries. We owe these welcome developments to the introduction of a market economy and democracy in many of the emerging and transitional economies, a process that has been encouraged by the OECD. Tourism is today one of the most internationalised sectors of the world economy. The world tourism market has been extended a lot, adding considerably to the potential for further growth and at the same time bringing about greater competition between tourism countries.

This raises the question whether or not tourism will be able to survive and prosper in such a competitive world economy in countries where the structure in this sector is based mainly on small-to-medium-sized enterprises (SMEs), and if so how.

It is for this reason that the overriding objective of the conference in Gwangju, Korea, is to devise new concepts that can help to make tourism countries in which small businesses dominate more competitive. These efforts require a good analytical understanding of tourism market structures.

Demand-driven Phenomenon: Importance of Visitors' Spending

Tourism is a creation of the modern industrial economy and the leisure society to which it has given rise. It is a sector that can only be defined in terms of demand. The key unit of measurement is the visitor. Whether travelling for business or pleasure the visitor spends money and creates demand for tourism products and services. In each case the decision to travel precedes the act or acts of consumption. There is no tourism industry as such. The supply side structures of tourism are volatile. They only make their appearance once the potential visitor has made the decision to travel and become an actual visitor, consuming a variety of goods and services. Visitors from the home country as well as from abroad pay money for individual goods and services, for reasons and motives that vary considerably. These products and services are produced by many different sectors of the economy and by companies both small and large. In this context it makes a great difference whether or not the goods and services consumed are selected by the individual tourists themselves, or on the contrary are put together by professional tour operators.

Macroeconomic Approach: Typical Tourism Related Industries

Thanks to a concept initiated and developed in the 1980s by the OECD Tourism Committee, the so-called Tourism Satellite Account (TSA), it is possible today to track the spending of visitors and see which specific sectors of the national economy benefit from this spending and to what extent. This makes it possible to measure the extent to which tourism contributes to value added and employment in a given country or region. This complex and time-consuming approach has also made it possible at the macro-level, with the help of a theoretical-statistical construct, to achieve a better understanding of the heterogeneity of production in tourism. Industries which obtain the lion's share of their earnings from the spending of visitors can now be identified as "characteristic branches of tourism, or collectively as the "tourism industry". In addition to identifying these specific tourism-dependent sectors of the economy we can now determine the extent to which the spending of tourists also benefits other industries which are connected or non specific to tourism. The core sectors of the tourism industry are the passenger transport segments, the hotel and catering segments and the leisure, culture and sports segments. It is clear, however, that economic sectors that do not have any formal relationship with tourism, such as the retail trade, the construction industry, or the banking and insurance sector, also benefit a lot from the spending of visitors.

Microeconomic Approach: Tourism Systems and Service Chains

Visitors of course do not see tourism as a statistical construct. For them the journey to and from, and the time spent in the destination, all add up to a single experience. Given this holistic perception of the potential customer we need to adopt a system-oriented view of tourism market structures. The increased value of tourism as an experience has forced suppliers to develop packaged services, and to do everything they can to create a more magical atmosphere, in short to orchestrate and dramatise the whole tourism experience. It is increasingly worthwhile therefore to view the production of tourism goods and services in the context of service chains or networks, made up of a variety of companies and sectors. It follows therefore that tourism product systems must be of a complex nature.

Dual Industrial Structure: The Rise of a New International Travel Industry

The field of tourism has developed a dual economic structure over the years. Whereas in the target countries or destinations SMEs continue to offer such tourism services as accommodation, catering and leisure time activities, an international travel and tourism industry has gradually emerged in the source countries as part of the globalization process.

This new tourism industry is based on many innovations. In civil aviation charter flights were invented as a way of dealing with seasonal peaks in demand. Hotel chains that sprouted from family firms, including the Hilton and Marriott empires, grew out of a desire to satisfy the needs of business travellers, initially those travelling from the USA. The rent-a-car sector, which is today a giant industry, allows visitors to have the same mobility abroad as they do at home. Credit cards have made international money transfers much easier while at the same time reducing the risks involved in foreign exchange operations.

The international travel and tourism industry consists mainly of big companies that organise tours to various destinations on an industrial basis. They offer standardised products, and develop global strategies that enable them to make the best use of the local potential anywhere on the planet.

The available statistics seem to indicate that the number of big tourism companies is relatively small, in all of the more developed tourism countries.

Even so, this handful of majors generally accounts for more than half of total turnover in this sector. Sixty to ninety percent of all companies in the hotel sector, a leading branch of tourism, and also in the travel agency sector, are micro companies, i.e. firms that employ between one and nine persons.

Thanks to standardisation the bigger tourism companies are in a position to offer their clients more attractive services at very competitive prices. They are able to develop new tourism markets and offer new products. This helps them to increase the "customer value" and to reduce their production costs. Many visitors do not want standardised products however. They prefer to tailor the holiday experience to their own specific needs and tastes. They insist on personalised services. Thanks to the multi-optional supply of products and services they are able to offer, destinations are in a position to adapt relatively quickly to the ever changing requirements of the individual tourist.

Dominant Market Structure: Imperfect Competition

Truly perfect competition should be the rule in a world tourism market which has been extensively liberalised, with prices being dictated by the market.

But the fact that the availability and distribution of resources varies greatly from one place to another creates a situation of monopolistic competition in tourism markets. The different natural, cultural and civilisation-related attractions that exist in each country make it possible to differentiate destinations on a geographical basis. Each tourism country, region and place is thus unique and unmistakably individual.

Global Tourism Growth: A Challenge for SMEs

Tourism companies profit from this uniqueness of destinations. Thanks to the customer's increased willingness to pay for these special attractions, tourism companies can set prices that are higher than the market costs. "Value based pricing" allows a wide range of pricing policy measures. Differentiation is the market strategy of destinations. It brings individual SMEs a rent in the form of "brand value". Differentiation strategies work because of the need for variety. This "love of variety" also helps to explain the exchange of tourists between the countries of the industrialised world. The monopoly rent of the SMEs in destinations is returned to the visitors in the form of an increased variety of products and services. Competition in tourism is therefore primarily competition between destinations, and only secondarily competition between individual service providers. Visitors begin by choosing a destination. Only then do they choose the combination of products and services they wish to consume. It is the availability of attractions and the relative importance of each that to a great extent determine a destination's tourism potential.

SME Problem in Developed Countries: Cluster Advantages and Size Problems

Tourism-dependent SMEs benefit greatly from the host destination, which are in almost all cases unique, difficult-to-imitate competitive systems. They can also be described as "clusters". Most tourism destinations have emerged after a long process of specialisation. Companies compete within very narrow confines. They have the benefit of competitive experience, they take advantage of existing test markets, and they can count on reliable suppliers. However these competitive advantages are no longer enough to resolve all the problems of tourism-dependent SMEs. In the industrialised world, where productivity in this labour intensive industry is lower than in less developed countries, SMEs in tourism suffer from the cost disease. They have to increase their prices to compensate for their relative lack of productivity, which in turn harms their ability to compete in the world market. Furthermore the size disadvantage of SMEs reduces their profitability. Bigger companies are able to produce at less cost thanks to economies of scale. Their products and services are more attractive thanks to reduced costs and offer more customer benefits. The bigger firms attract more visitors and produce at lower cost.

Integration and Cooperation: A Necessity for Destination Oriented SMEs

Generally speaking, SMEs in destinations never produce with the most efficient structures. This is one of the drawbacks that result from monopolistic competition, despite its various advantages.

Most producers reduce the quantity and set their prices higher than the costs. It is for this reason that individual tourism is expensive in destinations, with a structure dominated by small businesses. It is also a fact that each service in the chain of services has to be paid for separately, and the cumulative final price is high.

There are few service packages on offer within destinations. The fragmented small business sector that dominates tourism in the destinations often finds it difficult to remain competitive in the international market, as in the factor markets. Subject as they are to fluctuations in demand the capacity of these small firms is often under-utilised and their earning power is limited. They do not have sufficient cash flow.

Global Tourism Growth: A Challenge for SMEs

The way forward for tourism-dependent SMEs is to take far greater advantage of the potential for internal growth. Additional rooms in hotels, more seats in restaurants, these are some of the ways small firms can reduce their average costs. SMEs that make the effort can gravitate towards the optimal size. External growth is also urgently needed however, to overcome the disadvantages that go with insufficient size. At the vertical level of the destination production and marketing need to be increasingly based on partnerships, which would enable SMEs to better position themselves in the markets. Horizontal cooperation is also necessary to increase production and lower costs. Cooperation should only be considered however if it is cheaper than producing in house or buying in the market. The OECD's Centre for Entrepreneurship, SMEs and Local Development is reviewing the organisation and functioning of global value chains for various industries as a way for SMEs to participate more fully in global growth and become more productive.

In the case of tourism, one of the five industries covered in this project, the hotel sector, a leading sector of the tourism industry, consists on the one hand of internationally active hotel chains that are continuing to expand, and on the other of small local hotels. In the worldwide competition to attract visitors with the greatest purchasing power, independent family-run hotels in the SME category are increasingly forced to cooperate at the level of marketing or themselves to become part of a hotel chain of some kind.

State Incentives for Tourism Dependant SMEs

Another question that needs to be asked is whether or not the further development, and indeed the economic survival of tourism-dependent SMEs require any specific state incentives. Tourism policy is basically concerned with the creation of more favourable framework conditions for destinations. It does not specifically address the problems of SMEs.

Support for infrastructures or for marketing efforts does not take company size into consideration. Opportunities are always seized however, in the context of tourism policy, to help overcome the disadvantages that go with insufficient size.

Few measures exist that are specifically aimed at tourism-dependent SMEs. Such measures include state assistance to promote urgently needed efforts in the area of cooperation, as a way of reducing high transaction and organisation costs. It can make sense in this context to promote cooperation projects in order to update existing products and services through innovation. A number of governments do in fact promote innovation and cooperation today.

The differentiation strategy of destinations does not only bring advantages to SMEs however. The development of umbrella brands is difficult and expensive. These promotion efforts have to be borne by the SMEs themselves. Furthermore, brands have to be maintained in quality through constant investment in product improvements and quality assurance systems. For these reasons virtually all governments promote market communication, or destination marketing by their national tourism office. Finally, it should not be forgotten that the multi optional nature of the products and services on offer in destinations is expensive, since a great variety of infrastructures, goods and services has to be provided.

This is why many governments also support tourism-dependent infrastructures. This includes rejuvenation of the accommodation sector and the creation of new companies. There is a real need for policy action in the tourism sector. However, the granting of credits can result in certain market distortions at the expense of SMEs.

The Evolution of Space Tourism from Novelty to Opportunity

At a space business forum in June 2008, Dr. George C. Nield, Associate Administrator for Commercial Space Transportation at the Federal Aviation Administration (FAA), addressed the future of commercial space travel: 'There is tangible work underway by a number of companies aiming for space, partly because of their dreams, but primarily because they are confident it can be done by the private sector and it can be done at a profit.'

Indeed, private companies and entrepreneurs are currently aiming to make this dream a reality. While the current economic downturn will likely slow industry progress, space tourism, currently in its infancy, is poised to become a significant part of the hospitality industry.

Unlike the space race of the 1950s and 1960s between the United States and the former Soviet Union, the current rivalry is not defined on a national level, but by a collection of first-mover entrepreneurs that are working to define the industry and position it for longterm profitability. The race includes and depends on technology firms focused on developing the safest, most reliable, and most economical spacecraft, as well as service firms, or space lines, that will ultimately market and provide space travel experiences to willing "Novanauts."

In this race to send private citizens into space, the first team to cross the finish line will not necessarily win international bragging rights, but can expect to benefit from establishing a name within the space travel industry. Companies that hope to have any chance at success must first establish credibility and demonstrate reliability and safety to a population that may be skeptical of the prospect of commercial space travel.

Specialty firms have announced intentions to develop the technology and/or market commercial space travel to the masses, with some currently collecting deposits for future suborbital flights and, in one instance, lunar missions. Billionaire Charles Simonyi joined a team of astronauts for his second paid visit to the International Space Station on March 25, 2009. While this experience may currently be available to the world's wealthiest individuals, opportunities for the average earthling to experience space travel are on the horizon.

"Space-like" experiences such as the Zero G Jet are currently available, while true space flight opportunities are in development. This article will explore the latest advancements in space tourism and will consider opportunities for this fledging industry. The impact of the current global economic conditions on the evolution of space travel is also considered. We further investigate who the current major players are, review the existing space tourism studies published by industry experts, and provide our expectations for the future of this industry.

Commercial Space Travel: Types of Experiences, Major Players, and Offerings

No longer an exclusive endeavour of the government, space travel is being pursued for commercial gains – enabled by the FAA's Commercial Space Launch Amendments Act of 2004[2] (CSLAA) and further influenced by the $10 million Ansari X Prize. Within the past decade, private citizens have paid large sums to be among the first to experience a variety of space and space-like experiences, including parabolic flights simulating weightlessness, suborbital flights, and higher-altitude weeklong orbital flights to the International Space Station.

The prices associated with these experiences have ranged from roundly $5,000 per person for a parabolic flight to roundly $20 million for a trip to the International Space Station. The following figure provides definitions for space-like and space flight experiences.

Private investors, companies, and the industry as a whole are currently working towards making space travel possible from a variety of "Spaceports," which would be located around the globe. Locations noted during our research include, but are not limited to, the United States (California, Florida, New Mexico, Texas, and Oklahoma), Kazakhstan, French Guiana, Russia, Sweden, Australia, Singapore, and the United Arab Emirates.

As more spaceports are developed, commercial space travel providers anticipate providing point-to-point global travel. Other projects under way include the development of orbital space facilities that would serve as "space hotels."

Ultimately the goal of the industry is to provide a profitable means of offering suborbital, orbital, and possibly lunar-and-beyond expeditions. The development pace of the more complex service offerings (orbital point-to-point flights, space hotels, lunar expeditions, etc.) will be greatly influenced by the initial success of the commercial space tourism industry's first movers, offering suborbital experiences.

Parabolic Flights and Beyond

Established in 1993, Zero G was the first company to market a simulated space experience, offering tickets for parabolic flights based in major tourist destinations in the United States. Zero G offers passengers the sensation of weightlessness without travelling to space. The company's specially fitted jumbo jets perform parabolic manoeuvres to recreate the sensation of Martian and lunar gravity, as well as total weightlessness.

The Las Vegas-based company has flown over 100 flights and currently offers tickets for roundly $5,000 per person, as well as charter flights for groups. In January 2008, Zero G was acquired by Space Adventures, Ltd.

To date, Space Adventures is the only private company to have sent citizens into space – including the "first space tourist,"

Dennis Tito. Space Adventures sent Tito into orbit for nearly eight days in 2001 via the Russian Soyuz shuttle for a reported $20 million.

According to a 2007 article from FOX news, Space Adventures has sold almost $200 million in tourist space flights since 2001. The company is looking to expand its offerings and is currently taking reservations aboard the "first private expedition to the moon" for $100 million per seat.

Others forging their way into commercial space travel include Sir Richard Branson's Virgin Galactic. Virgin Galactic has teamed with X-Prize winner, Scaled Composites, to shuttle private citizens on suborbital flights beginning in 2010. Tickets are currently priced at $200,000, and the company has collected a reported US$30 million as of January 2008.

Other companies collecting money for reservations for suborbital flights include Rocketplane for $250,000 per person and XCOR for roundly $95,000. Another player that has received media attention is Bigelow Aerospace.

Currently the sole manufacturer for several of NASA's key expandable space station modules, the company is developing a family of modules to serve as the first commercial space habitats. Bigelow plans to launch the first "orbital resort" in the near future but currently has no target timeframe for the launch.

A similar initiative is being pursued by Galactic Suite, a Spanish Company with plans to package pre-space training on a remote island, with space travel to the orbital resort by 2012. A 2007 press release indicated a roundly €3 million per person price for this experience.

With the space tourism industry in its infancy, each prospective operator and space technology development firm is working to set the standards for safety, comfort, and the overall Novanaut experience. One thing can be concluded from our research of existing space tourism companies: Multiple organizations and individuals believe that there is a future for us in space travel. The following figures provide details on a selection of players in the space travel industry as of the time of our research.

Understanding the Market Potential

As Space Tourism has yet to establish itself as a viable industry, there is little tangible evidence to conclude that a substantial market exists. However, an in-depth market study was conducted to forecast potential demand and revenues for space tourism activities through 2021 by Futron, a U.S.-based firm specializing in technology management consulting. In 2006, Futron revisited an extensive market study they conducted in 2002, adjusting for the year, ticket prices, and updated population wealth statistics.

The original study was based on a pool representative of those able to purchase such a luxury experience – surveying 450 wealthy individuals to determine their interest in space tourism and willingness to take part in such flights at a number of price points.

Such luxury travellers are estimated as 3% of the total international tourist arrivals worldwide, yet account for 25% of total international travel expenditures – totalling US$180 billion in 2006.

Considering the world population of people wealthy enough to afford space flights, as well as their fitness and interest levels, Futron used a 40-year maturity model to forecast demand and potential annual revenue from suborbital services in 2021 to reach 13,000 passengers and an estimated US$676 million – taking into account declining ticket prices due to economies of scale and applying the Fisher-Pry S-Curve to the potential demand pool. The original study also estimated orbital flights to generate $300 million per year, generating a $1-billion industry by 2021.

While Futron's updated forecasts for 2006 are down from 2002's estimate of 15,000, the study concludes "despite a delayed introduction of commercial passenger suborbital flights, and an increase in initial ticket prices over earlier expectations, demand for suborbital space tourism remains strong." In addition, one should note that the FAA's Office of Commercial Space Transportation has set no specific health or fitness requirements for passengers, suggesting a wider range of acceptability. In addition, the updated study does not take into account any changes in "the public's perception of, or level of interest in, suborbital space tourism," which is likely to have changed since the Ansari X Prize was awarded and companies like Virgin Galactic announced their plans. Although the Futron study cannot provide us with certainties for the future of commercial space travel, the report does give us a sense of potential revenues and scale of the primary demographic. As of the summer of 2008, over 250 people had put deposits down or paid the full price for Virgin Galactic's suborbital flight tickets, while another 600 had signed up to buy tickets once flights begin. As with any new innovation, these individuals will lead the way for the industry's expansion, eventually creating economies of scale, lowering ticket prices, and increasing accessibility to a wider demographic.

Impact of the Current Economy and Future Trends for the Space Tourism Industry

Is there enough demand to warrant longterm success of the commercial space travel industry? Only time will tell. With the current economic recession, technological advances and the launch of regularly scheduled suborbital (and beyond) flights are likely to be delayed.

However, when we consider the forecasts from the Futron study and the inclinations of a large population towards adventure tourism and activities generally perceived as higher risk, or extreme (i.e., skydiving, scuba diving, rock climbing, etc.), the authors foresee the progression of commercial space travel as a viable industry in the long term. While information is limited on the payoff and functionality of each company's plan and proposed operating models, longterm success will rely on basic critical factors such as safety, reliability, service differentiation, and value. As spaceports are built and ticket prices lowered as a result of economies of scale, we predict point-to-point space travel to spur demand and a sustainable source of business. As demonstrated by the cruise industry, combining a destination with the travel experience may justify this mode of travel for some and support repeat purchases, avoiding the possibility of becoming a once-in-a-lifetime experience. In this case, destinations may include "hotels" in space or locations across the globe that can be reached quickly and conveniently. We also predict that existing and new luxury brands will partner with space technology developers to offer upscale service and accommodations for affluent travellers in the first space hotels and hotels located proximate to space training and launching sites. We expect to see tourism centres (hotel accommodations, entertainment, and restaurants) to be developed adjacent to spaceport locations to house guests during space training. These supportive developments will be especially necessary in remote Spaceport locations.

As the first space flights are expected to be affordable to only the wealthiest individuals, who are accustomed to the finest accommodations, we expect that these hotels will be in the luxury segment.

For some, the dream of space travel could be a reality within the next decade. The innovators in the space tourism industry will do much to define the future experiences of prospective Novanauts, setting the standards for safety, creating realistic expectations of the in-flight experience, and developing packages and experiences that will represent the most value for the target market.

The start of the second space race is currently under way, with possibilities that are truly out of this world!

5

Managing Hospitality Information Systems

Whatever the activities of a community or business, the each communicate something about the community or business to consumers. Consumers receive this information through many different sources, or channels. These channels combine to form information systems which are always functioning, regardless of whether you are managing them or not. If you represent a community or business, it is extremely important to know how to manage information systems to make them work for you.

What is an Information System?

In general, an information system consists of all the ways that people communicate with others. Systems are composed of information channels. These channels may be formal or informal, personal or impersonal, and public or private. Information channels are used in different ways and combinations by different people, businesses, and communities. A tourism information system is a specific type of information system. It consists of all the information channels used in a business or community to promote itself as a tourism attraction. These information channels include commercials, ads, brochures, repeat visitors, employees, friends, and relatives.

Characteristics of Tourism Information Systems

There are three characteristics that all effective tourism information systems have:

> *Each channel in the system has its own function. Travellers use different channels to get different kinds of information. An example is deciding where to go on vacation. A person may consult a friend or family member for that decision, but in deciding what to do when he/she gets there, the person may talk with a repeat visitor or employee at the destination site.*

All the information channels used in the system relate to each other. A tourism information system is like a novel because it has many different parts tied together by the theme. Even though a system's channels serve different functions in providing information, they are all tied together by the projected message.

All channels used in the system are interdependent. A tourism information system functions like a puzzle. The different pieces of the system, the channels, are used to communicate with tourists. If any of the puzzle pieces are missing, the puzzle's picture is incomplete. If one or more of the channels used is not dispersing information effectively, or if the information dispersed does not relate to the rest of the system, then the system will not effectively communicate its whole message. If one or more of these characteristics is missing from a tourism information system, then its message will be inconsistent and ineffective.

What are the Parts of a Tourism Information System?

We have covered the fact that a tourism information system is made up of different related and interdependent information channels. But what are these channels? Examples of these channels include:

- State promotional messages,
- Regional tourist associations,
- Travel information centres,
- Individual business promotion,
- Employee knowledge,
- Brochures, signs,
- The community's visual image (appearance):
- storefronts, billboards, etc.

- its hospitality,
- community awareness and pride,
- Other travellers,
- Repeat visitors.

While this list is not exhaustive, it gives you some idea of what can be used as channels. The only limitation is your imagination in how you present your message.

Why Manage your Tourist Information System?

There are three major reasons why it is necessary to manage information systems. The first reason is that travellers need organized information so that it becomes easier to acquire information and make decisions. They do not want to, nor have time to, sort through information that is confusing and disorganized. The easier it is to get information, the more comfortable travellers feel and the more enjoyable the trip will be for them. Travellers who are satisfied with their trip will be more likely to return and to tell others about the good time they had. By managing your information system, you can make it easy for travellers to get the information they want.

The second reason to manage tourism information systems is to present your theme and identify it to travellers in a clear, concise, and consistent manner. By managing your information system, you have some control over what information travellers receive and through what channels. This way you can make sure that all the delivered information relates to your theme, and you are better able to develop continuity and coherence throughout your system.

The third reason why it is important to manage tourism information systems is that they play an important role in community development. This is especially important in tourism because travellers see the community as a whole, rather than as individual parts. People base their image of a community on the information received from the community's information system. A community's image is important because tourists often become future investors and residents in communities that they find attractive. You want to be able to manage your information system so that the image you want is projected.

How can you Manage your Tourism Information System

There are a variety of tools that you can use to manage your tourism information system. Here we want to deal with four that experts believe are the most effective. These tools are most effective when used together, but they can be used individually.

1. Establish a committee or organization to manage your tourism information system. It should control what information is used and how it is distributed throughout the system. It should also be responsible for evaluating the system's effectiveness.
2. Establish a set of standards, or guidelines, for deciding what, how, and through what channels information will be presented. This will help ensure that information used will accurately reflect your community's identity and theme and that it reaches the right target market.
3. Develop community cooperation in the system. Explain the benefits of being involved in the system to local business person and to community residents, and develop community awareness and pride.
4. Consider Zoning-A community's appearance plays a significant role in its tourism information system. A tourist's image of a community is significantly influenced by its appearance. Zoning can be used to make sure that a community's appearance will have a positive influence on it image. Zoning provides the following advantages. It gives you control over "street level environment," meaning such things as side walks, shopping malls and centres, town squares, and the avenues of access and travel to and through each. Zoning gives the control needed to maintain adequate amounts of space for people to move freely in, around, and through these areas.

Zoning can also be used to manage the outward appearance of you "street level environment." All structures constructed, such as storefronts, signs, etc., can be required to reflect your community's identity and theme. Zoning also allows you to save older, historical buildings while allowing the development of surrounding property.

There are two types of zoning: prestated design features, and transfer of rights. Prestated design features can be used as incentive zoning or as mandated design features. With incentive zoning, developers are granted building privileges for including a prestated design feature(s) in the building design. Mandated design features require developers to include a certain prestated design feature in the building. Transfer of rights is used to transfer the rights to development of a particular piece of property from one developer to another.

When using zoning, the zoning commission, or board, must be easily accessible and flexible. Then, when changes in zoning regulations are needed, they can be made.

What Will a Tourist Information System do for You?

A well organized tourism information system will benefit local businesses, the community, and local residents as well as travellers. It helps area residents and travellers locate recreation activities, sites, and service outlets. It helps build community pride and establish long term ties with satisfied visitors. It will also avoid confusion and other problems that can result from poorly oriented, directed, and managed travellers, such as traffic problems.

This bulletin was written to help you understand what a tourism information system is, why it needs to be managed, and to give you some ideas on how to manage it. But managing one is not easy, and it does not happen over night. It takes a lot of long range planning, and foresight, as well as some expertise and being able to stick-to-it to overcome any obstacles encountered.

Sustainable Tourism: A Local Authority Perspective

1. A primary challenge of local governance, both today and in decades ahead, is to steerincreasingly external, global forces on local development so that development achieves the sharedvision of the local population. In cities, towns and villages throughout the world, the primary responsibility for this steering process rests with the institution of local government and its diverselocal authorities.

2. As providers of social services, builders of economic infrastructure, regulators of economicactivity, and managers of the natural environment, local authorities have many direct instruments attheir disposal to influence development. Yet in addition to their direct roles in the development process, perhaps the most important role that local authorities can play in a global economy is that of facilitator among the diverse interests seeking to influence the direction of local development. Only with such a facilitator can a community of diverse interests define a shared vision and actconsistent with this vision.
3. The role of local authorities as facilitators in the development process is reinforced through municipal international cooperation (MIC). With globalization, the governance challenges facinglocal authorities in different parts of the world have increased in their similarities, transcending thenational political and economic systems upon which different communities rely. These shared challenges of governance have instigated thousands of local authorities to establish municipalinter national cooperation projects and to join international local government organisations (LGOs) to advocate for local self-governance and control over the development process.
4. Even prior to the UN Conference on Environment and Development, but particularly since the adoption of Agenda 21, many local authorities and their LGOs have focused on the unique challenges of governance for sustainable development. At the local level, sustainable development is achieved by steering local development activities to simultaneously achieve three objectives:
   - increased local social welfare;
   - greater, and more equitably distributed, local economic wealth; and
   - enhanced integrity of local ecosystems.
5. Thousands of local authorities, in partnership with their communities and supported by MIC activities, have

instigated Local Agenda 21 processes to create a shared vision for local development that is consistent with the sustainable development concept. In response to these visions, local authorities have been adapting their practices and activities to steer local development along the sustainable development path. Local Agenda 21 processes, in conjunction with decentralisation policies originating at the national level, are transforming local governance and reorienting the process of local development in communities throughout the world.

6. Tourism is one of the many external forces influencing the direction and options for local development. The question of whether tourism can be sustainable—that is, whether it can contribute to local sustainable development—is rightfully addressed in the context of the Local Agenda process.

7. A truly legitimate and practical discussion on sustainable tourism must take place in and with the communities that are being influenced by tourist industry development. It must create accountability of the tourism industry to locally-defined development visions. This paper provides an general call for the tourism industry, through both its local and transnational agents, to join and support the Local Agenda 21 processes in communities where tourism is a fundamental development force.

8. The true proof of "sustainable tourism" will be the sustainable development of local communities that serve as tourist destinations. It is time for the sustainable tourism debate to focuson this challenge. Local authorities worldwide welcome the leadership of the UN Commission on Sustainable Development, and the interest of the tourism industry, to reduce tourism's negative impacts and to increase the positive contribution of tourism business and consumption activity to local sustainable development.

Industry Initiatives for Sustainable Tourism

Problems

Tourism is a recognised global industry—one of the largest industries in the world. Likeany global industry, tourist business activities can have considerable impact on local development trends. The local impacts of the tourism industry are diverse and are often unique to the tourism sector.

Tourist activities, as traditionally defined by the tourism industry, fundamentally involve the transportation and hosting of the tourism consumer in a local community, i.e., "tourist destination," where the tourist product is consumed. No other global industry structures itself in such a way that the consumer is brought to the product, rather than the product being delivered to the consumer in his or her own community. This structural difference produces unique social impacts upon the local tourist community, including the interruption of local customs and life styles, the spread of infectious diseases, changes in local demographics, and changes in local housing and labour markets.

The primary product of tourism is not something produced by the industry. The product is often the heritage, wealth, and expected legacy of the community that serves as the tourist destination. The business activity of the tourism industry is to promote the "salable" or appealing aspects of the community, transport non residents into the community, manage the hospitality for and guide the activities of these visitors, and provide them with goods and services to purchase during their stay. If these business activities degrade the community's heritage and wealth, then the community suffers more directly than the consumer, who can return to his or her own community without responsibility for or awareness of the impacts of his tourist activities.

Tourism activities can, in particular, degrade the social and natural wealth of a community. The intrusion of large numbers of uninformed foreigners into local social systems can under mine pre existing social relation ships and values. This is particularly a problem where tourism business is centred in traditional social systems, such as isolated communities or indigenous peoples.

Tourism in natural areas, euphemistically called "ecotourism," can be a major source of degradation of local ecological, economic and social systems. The intrusion of large numbers offoreigners with high-consumption and high-waste habits into natural areas, or into towns with inadequate waste management infrastructure, can produce changes to those natural areas at a rate that is far greater than imposed by local residents. These tourism-related changes are particular lydeleterious when local residents rely on those natural areas for their sustenance. Resulting economic losses can encourage socially deleterious economic activities such as prostitution, crime, and migrant and child labour.

Solutions

Solutions to adverse tourism impacts are to be found in the shared interest of local communities, tourism businesses, and tourism consumers to maintain the natural wealth and social heritage of the tourist destination. In the first instance, therefore, an institutional mechanism must be established, relative to each destination, to articulate and develop this sense of shared interest. To secure the legitimacy of these mechanisms, the participation of all interested local groups orinterests must be guaranteed. Dialogue must take place in an open and transparent way.

Experience demonstrates that if dialogue among interested parties is to have a real impacton development, it must generate accountability among these parties with regards to future investments, practices and policies. Consensus or decisions arising from dialogue must be reflected in institutional action. Only through such accountability can interests maintain a commitment to continued dialogue and a common agenda for local tourism development.

Experience demonstrates that this accountability should be reciprocal between individual or private interests and society or public interests. Without such reciprocal accountability, local communities are typically forced to choose, in conflict, between private and public benefits, even if sample "win-win" development choices `exist. On the one hand, accountability requires that property owners are provided with opportunity to retain the economic value of their property, either through sale or income generating activity. On the other hand, private market relationships, including property ownership, do not provide sufficient basis for social accountability related to "public goods," including ecological integrity and social heritage. Private property titles do not recognise the concepts of ecological integrity or social heritage. Excessive reliance upon private property ownership as a guide in development has in fact contributed to the deterioration of public goods. Within such a framework of accountability, numerous instruments are available to guide local tourist development on a sustainable path. These instruments include:

- Heritage preservation requirements for site developments and building designs;
- Programs to exchange land and development rights from non-suitable to suitable development areas;
- Private heritage and green space stewardship programs;
- Tax benefits accruing to property owners exercising sustainable development practices;
- Tourism taxes and development fees to support construction and maintenance required infrastructure.

However, without true commitment to the sustainable tourism agenda, these instruments are not themselves sufficient to prevent the steady erosion, by legally sanctioned private actions, of local natural wealth and social heritage. Therefore, support from the international, national, provincial and local levels of industry and government, is essential to the success of this agenda.

Agents and Partnerships for Change

Fortunately, in more than 2,000 communities in 64 countries Local Agenda 21 partnership forums already exist to serve as a mechanism for sustainable tourism dialogue. Where these forums are weak or have not yet addressed tourism issues, the tourist industry, local government organisations (LGOs) and concerned NGOs can serve as a catalyst for dialogue. A particular opportunity exists in those countries where Local Agenda 21 national campaigns (in more than 20 countries) or where

National Councils for Sustainable Development (NCSDs-in about 70 countries) have been established. NCSDs can play a key role in providing country-level support to local review of the sustainable tourism agenda. Through their international facilitating body, the Earth Council, a comprehensive effort between industry, NGOs, LGOs and NCSDs can be established.

Of additional interest at the local level is the potential role of local tourism offices or Convention and Visitor Bureaus (CVBs) that have been created through public-private partnerships to promote local tourist attractions. Where motivated to support sustainable tourism development, the CVBs could serve as facilitators of working groups, within the context of Local Agenda 21 activities, on sustainable tourism development. Where CVBs or their related international body (ies) have made no express commitment to sustainable development, local authorities, as primary funders of CVBs, are in an excellent position to mobilise their awareness and support.

Internationally, alliances between LGOs and various tourism industry trade associations, trade unions and consumer organisations can support awareness raising and local demonstration projects that may serve as models for other local communities on a country or regional basis.

Influencing Consumer Behaviour to Promote Sustainable Tourism

Problems

Tourism-related consumption has three stages of impact. First, prior to departure, tourists purchase travel-related clothing and equipment, which may be produced under conditions that undermine the social and ecological sustainability of the producing communities. Second, when tourists travel long distances to tourist destinations, they create considerable atmospheric pollution and other impacts on the global environment. Third, upon arrival at the tourist destination, tourists often continue their accustomed habits of consumption, even though these destinations may not have the infrastructure required to manage those consumption patterns. This paper will focus on the second and third stages of impact.

In addition to high altitude emissions from long distance air travel, air travel produces considerable negative local environmental impacts, including ground level emissions of VOCs and practicalities, disposal of fuel, hazardous chemicals and solid waste, noise pollution, and wildlife and habitat disruption. Marine dumping of wastes from cruise ships is an increasing concern. However, with nearly 600 million international travellers in 1997, surprisingly little public information is available on the environmental and social impacts of long distance travel. For instance, individual travellers receive far greater information about the impacts of their local automobile use than of their air or cruise ship transportation. Motor vehicle pollution is typically more highly regulated than aircraft and ship pollution.

Following arrival at tourist destinations, the tourism industry typically strives to host tourists according to the standards and amenities of their country of origin. These hospitality standards mimic—and encourage—the high consumption lifestyles of developed countries. For instance, luxury hotel rooms, with high levels of energy and water consumption, are given the highest rankings or "stars" in international hotel rankings. These "luxury" consumption standards, using current technologies, are themselves globally unsustainable (i.e., in an equitable world).

The most immediate observable impacts of introducing these high consumption practices into lower consumption communities are:

- Degradation of local water and soil quality, with direct impacts on local health and economies, as a result of the lack of adequate water, drainage, waste water, and waste management infrastructure to manage the higher volumes of waste produced by higher levels of consumption;
- Reduced access by local residents to land, housing and marine resources through, among other things, reallocation of these community resources to foreign tourist residents and inflation of local prices;
- Destruction of traditional sources of income.

Solutions

The most direct way to reduce the adverse impacts of tourism-related travel is to increase opportunities for people to engage in appealing tourism activities in their own cities, regions or countries. In various cities of the world, this local tourism concept is known as "green tourism." Green tourism—in contrast to "ecotourism," which relies on travel to distant locations—seeks to provide recreational attractions and hospitality facilities to local people within their local regions, thereby reducing tourism-related travel.

While green tourism has the positive economic effect of stimulating local economic activity, it reduces the flow of foreign currency to developing nations— and any resulting economic benefits that may accrue to developing towns and cities from these revenue flows. However, short of definitive actions by the tourism industry and host countries/communities to reduce the negative environmental impacts of foreign travel and the negative social impacts of foreign tourist enclaves in developing nations, green tourism advocates will continue to build support among tourism consumers. Solutions to tourism-related pollution in the travel and tourism industry are technologically available. Overcoming economic barriers to their implementation may require government regulation, the development of economic instruments, and industry self-regulation.

The industry has every opportunity to institute voluntary initiatives and self-regulation to address green tourism advocates and those calling for government regulation. The growing effort among international hotel chains, for instance, to offer guests the option of reusing their bedroom towels and linens demonstrates the ability of the industry to respond in one area of impact.

However, more comprehensive efforts are required to tangibly resolve accelerating environmental and social impacts. In this regard, the establishment of formal environmental management systems (EMSs) in each business establishment provides a way for tourism businesses to identify their adverse social and environmental impacts and to institute a programme for continuous reductions of those impacts. EMS registration programmes such as ISO 14001 and European EMAS regimes offer extensive guidance to tourism businesses, and deserve the active support of international tourism industry associations.

Ultimately, the solution to adverse environmental impacts arising from local tourist consumption is the establishment of waste reduction programs and appropriate waste management systems and infrastructure, particularly in developing country destinations. Again a choice exists between voluntary and regulatory measures.

National governments and tourism businesses, which receive disproportional economic benefits from tourism, share an interest in maintaining tourism-related hard currency inflows, and should either directly provide such infrastructure or ensure that funds are made available to local authorities for this purpose.

Without such support, powers should be provided to local authorities to increase local revenues from tourism, through local airport taxes, hotel and service taxes, and development fees, to finance infrastructure construction and maintenance. Only through such economic instruments can the public costs of tourism activity be "internalised" in the local tourist economy.

Local revenue measures need to be carefully coordinated across municipal jurisdictions on a regional basis to ensure coordinated infrastructure development. Without a coordinated regional infrastructure development approach, pollution from communities without infrastructure can undo the environmental benefits of infrastructure investments in neighbouring communities. Where statutory regional planning bodies do not exist to provide coordination, Local Agenda 21 forums may provide a flexible mechanism for multi-jurisdictional coordination.

Tourist businesses can make a significant voluntary contribution to resolving the social costs of tourism by:

- Providing local resident employment and training opportunities, including in traditional trades and crafts;
- Establishing purchasing guidelines that favour local goods and services procurement;
- Making donations and investments in local recreational facilities, parks, cultural facilities and security operations

(which also serve to improve local tourist amenities as well);

- Establishing local profit-sharing arrangements.

Failing necessary voluntary measures, local governments can institute economic incentives and regulatory measures to reward best practices and prevent severe social impacts that need to be resolved at public expense. Ultimately, in the face of private establishments that demonstrate no long-term commitment to maintaining the preconditions for tourism—which include public safety, environmental quality, infrastructure maintenance, and economic justice—local authorities need to use all powers available to protect the cultural and environmental wealth that make an attractive tourist destination.

Agents and Partnerships for Change

A partnership approach to addressing negative impacts of tourism consumption requires, above all, assumption of responsibility and voluntary action by the tourism industry. For example, within the framework of a voluntary EMS approach, partnerships can be established between local governments, airport authorities, regional air quality agencies, airlines, trade unions, NGOs and resident associations to develop an action programme to reduce local airport pollution. Following the model of the "Responsible Care" programme in the chemical industry, these partnerships could be supported by international travel and tourism organisations and related industry associations. Measures to reduce high altitude pollution by aircraft require similar initiatives by the industry and government at the national and international levels.

Of critical importance is the creation of mechanisms to inform and involve tourism consumers in making educated choices about their activities as tourists in distant tourist destinations. Ideally, these efforts would ensure that tourism consumers, as with industry, begin to recognise and understand tourist destinations as living communities that deserve their support and respect. Communications from tourism consumers to tourism industry and to local authorities about their desire to reduce the adverse impacts of their tourism activities can be essential to mobilising changes in industry and government practices. International consumer advocacy organisations and trade unions can play an important role in informing consumers about tourism development activities that violate basic principles of sustainable development. Provision of such information to LGOs can facilitate local authority responsiveness to identified problems. Other actions to reduce the adverse local impacts of tourism consumption at local tourist destinations can be developed within the context of the Local Agenda 21 activities outlined in sections B and D.

Promoting Broad-based Sustainable Development through Tourism while Safeguarding the Integrity of Local Cultures and Protection the Environment

Problems

Many of the technologies and measures required for sustainable development in the tourism sector are clear. Resources exist within the tourism industry-which annually generates hundreds of billions of dollars-to apply these technologies and to make development within the sector more equitable. However, as the experiences of hundreds of local authorities demonstrate, through their engagement in broad-based sustainable development planning through Local Agenda 21, the appropriate application of technologies and resources requires effective and truly accountable development partnerships. If industry and government are to protect and sustain the social, cultural and environmental wealth that attracts tourists, they must build more ambitious and committed partnerships to plan, manage and invest in this wealth.

In this respect, the primary barrier to sustainable development through tourism is an over reliance on market mechanisms to guide tourism development and consumption decisions. The market-which treats cultural and environmental wealth as free, "public goods" and which responds to degradation of this wealth as a "free rider"-provides instruments to guide development, but is insensitive to many requirements of sustainable tourism. Furthermore, in a global market such as tourism, the problem of "leakage", whereby the economic benefits of local tourism activity flow out of the local community and country back to a foreign corporate headquarters, is another indication of the inadequacy of simple market-driven approaches. Sustainable tourism development requires a partnership among the stakeholders of the local tourist destination. This partnership must use both market and non-market instruments to implement a shared sustainable development vision. Without such a partnership, advocacy for sustainable development becomes a conflictive struggle between an industry which seeks to respond only to market forces and a public sector which, when accountable, acts to protect public goods and wealth for future generations. Therefore, the key problem at this stage of the "sustainable tourism" debate is the creation of tangible, working local partnerships. These local partnerships must be encouraged and supported by national governments and industry, and not undermined by "higher level" agreements. To succeed, local residents and their local authorities need to more fully recognise the significant adverse impacts of tourism development and must be informed about opportunities for reduced-impact tourism development. Tourism businesses need to recognise and support the social conditions (e.g., security, public health) and the cultural and environmental wealth that make a community an attractive tourist destination.

Solutions

The UN Commission on Sustainable Development has repeatedly recognised Local Agenda 21 planning as an effective partnership mechanism for implementing Agenda 21 in cities and local communities. Experience with Local Agenda 21 activities in hundreds of communities since 1990 has highlighted a number of principles for effective sustainable development planning. These principles can also provide the basis for effective partnerships for sustainable tourism planning and development in local tourist destinations. These partnerships can be established either within or independent from existing Local Agenda 21 activities.

The principles for Local Agenda 21 planning are as follows:

- Participation and Transparency, that involves local residents, representing all major groups of society, in Local Agenda 21 planning and makes information about sustainable development easily available to the general public.

- Partnerships that build collective responsibility for planning, decision making, problem solving, project implementation and evaluation.
- Accountability that holds all partners answerable for their actions.
- Systemic Approach that addresses the underlying causes of social, economic and ecological problems in an integrated way, focusing on the entire systems that are affected, rather than only problem symptoms.
- Ecological Limits, that are defined by Earth's carrying capacity and that serve as the limits for development.
- Equity and Justice, that are secured locally through the provision of equal opportunities and human rights, and globally through development cooperation partnerships between developed and developing nations.
- Concern for the Future, that requires long-term planning and action that addresses both immediate needs and long-term trends.

These principles can be applied, in working partnerships, to evaluate and improve efforts to address sensitive tourism development issues, such as:

- inequitable distribution of tourism revenues and "leakage" of revenues to foreign shores;
- displacement of preexisting local settlements by tourism developments;
- equal access to local coastal and recreational resources and controversies over uses and long-term protection of those areas;
- concerns related to lack of foreign tourist sensitivity to cultural traditions and sites.

Agents and Partnerships for Change

The primary partnerships for sustainable tourism development will be local partnerships, addressing the unique development goals and needs of each community. Where Local Agenda 21 activities are underway, a Sustainable Tourism Working Group could be established within the existing Local Agenda 21 planning structures to facilitate planning and action.

Notwithstanding the primacy of local partnerships, the trans national nature of tourism requires trans national partnerships to support sustainable tourism planning activities at the local and national levels. The Local Agenda 21 process has established a new mechanism for such trans national partnership, called "Local Agenda 21 Charters." Initiated by the Netherlands Ministry of Foreign Affairs, in cooperation with the International Union of Local Authorities, the International Council for Local Environmental Initiatives, and Towns & Development, the Local Agenda 21 Charters process provides a mechanism for local communities to factor issues of global responsibility within their Local Agenda 21 activities. Two local authorities, typically on a North-South and East-West basis, establish a "Charter" agreement that specifies areas of mutual support to jointly address relevant issues of global equity and sustainability. Presently, 20 local authorities have established the first Local Agenda 21 Charters.

Ultimately, tourism consumers must be rallied to the sustainable tourism agenda, thereby shaping both the market and public policy. Tourism consumers in existing Local Agenda 21 communities may find the Local Agenda 21 Charters mechanism useful in supporting sustainable development in popular tourist destinations. Existing "twinning" or "sister city" relationships with cities that are located in tourist regions can provide the basis for a possible Local Agenda 21 Charters relationship.

Coastal Impacts of Tourism

Problems

Economic development activities in any sensitive natural area pose a particular challenge for sustainable development. Coastal areas host the most productive marine ecosystems and serve as spawning grounds for the oceans. The degradation of coastal areas in many countries, with the resulting impacts upon coastal settlements and fisheries, justifies strict local controls on further coastal development.

Coastal zones are dynamic in nature, responding to daily tidal changes as well as long term events such as sea level rising. This dynamic quality offers a defence from extreme weather events. Rigid infrastructure from coastal development can inhibit the ability of coastal ecosystems to respond to changes.

Since coastal areas are the most highly populated regions on Earth, their protection requires unique attention and the effective management of numerous competing interests.

In many coastal areas, tourism development is destroying or margin alising dwindling habitats for marine animals and spawning fish, as well as the livelihoods of traditional fishing families and villages. Unregulated water sport activities and machinery are adding to this toll. Lack of effective waste water treatment for tourist facilities is making a significant contribution to coastal water pollution. Excessive private tourist development is denying equitable human access to beaches and coastal waters, cutting off local populations from their coastal heritage. Inappropriate development in high risk storm areas is costing families, local economies and governments billions of dollars annually.

Solutions

As a first measure towards the sustainable management of coastal areas, governments at all levels, working in partnership with private foundations and investors, should establish designated coastal areas where development will be forever restricted. Protection of these areas should be stringently enforced. In areas where coastal development can be socially and environmentally justified, tourism development should be designed as a form of low-impact economic activity relative to other development alternatives. The reputation and viability of the sustainable tourism concept depends upon the definition and implementation of clear management objectives for each coastal area. These objectives should clearly designate ecologically and socially/culturally sensitive areas as well as high risk areas. Appropriate tourism uses should be designated for each area according to levels of sensitivity and risk. Education programs should be established to inform tourists about these management objectives. The aims of any sustainable tourism development in coastal areas should be to:

- Recognise the economic value of existing coastal ecosystems, towns and heritage sites by providing opportunity for local revenue-generation through managed tourist use of these areas;
- Design tourism developments, in cooperation with local stakeholders, to suit the unique ecological and social characteristics of each coastal site;
- Use tourism investment to develop and upgrade the watershed, solid waste and waste water management systems for coastal cities and towns;
- Ensure equitable access to coastal areas by all people, with a specific emphasis on using tourism development as a means to upgrade and manage traditional social uses, for example, through the designation of special natural/cultural heritage sites.

In addition sound planning and management to achieve the above aims, the following opportunities for low-impact tourism development could be considered:

- Application of low-impact building and transportation designs, materials and technologies;
- Control of waste production through recycling and efficiency measures;
- Co-investment by the tourism industry, government and local residents to upgrade existing settlements and urban infrastructure, including drainage and sewerage infrastructure.

Agents and Partnerships for Change

The planning and management of coastal development typically requires the cooperation of local stakeholders-including property owners, residents, local business groups, and local authorities-and government agencies at the national and sub-national levels. In general, some institutional mechanism will need to be established to facilitate cooperation and consensus-building among these actors. As coastal areas typically extend beyond the jurisdictions of individual local authorities, regional coastal management agencies are often established through inter-municipal cooperation or sub-national action to provide effective multi-jurisdictional coordination. Alternatively, private foundations or regional/national NGOs have frequently been used as a mechanism for coastal area planning.

Under ideal circumstances, tourism industry representatives, including property owners, will be directly involved in coastal planning and management schemes. In such cases, the tourism industry, in particular trans national businesses, needs to make a good faith commitment not to circumvent local/regional planning and management discussions by directly lobbying national government for special permissions and considerations. Ultimately, actions to reduce the adverse impacts of tourism on coastal areas will reflect the principles of Local Agenda 21 planning outlined earlier

Sustainable Integrated Tourism Planning

The Costs and Benefits of Tourism

As the largest industry in the world, tourism has the potential to help deal with the key issues facing many parts of the globe and therefore can be seen as a positive and negative force. If the costs and benefits of tourism are understood from the outset, strengths and opportunities can be maximized while weaknesses and threats can be minimized. Each tourism planning situation will be different in terms of its tourism characteristics.

The costs and benefits of tourism will vary in each destination, and these can change over time, depending on tourism and other activities in the local and regional context. Tourism can be seen as having the following benefits and costs. Economic Benefits:

* Tourism generates local employment, both directly in the tourism sector and in various support and resources management sectors.
* Tourism stimulates profitable domestic industries-hotels and other lodging facilities, restaurants and other food

services, transportation systems, handicrafts, and guide services.

* Tourism generates foreign exchange for the country and injects capital and new money into the local economy.
* Tourism diversifies the local economy, particularly in rural areas where agricultural employment may be sporadic or insufficient.
* Increased tax revenues from tourists can be reaped if a local sales tax is added to the provincial and federal taxes already in place.
* Employment opportunities will be created in the business communities due to the influx of tourists who will need goods and services.
* Increased entrepreneurial opportunities will provide goods and services not already available in the community and create new tourist products.
* Improved road systems and infrastructure can be financed through tourism attractions.

Economic Costs:

* The jobs created through tourism may be low paying and require few skills.
* Inflated prices may result from local businesses attempting to raise profits or cover the cost of extra employees.
* Inflated property values may occur if the community becomes a tourist 'hot spot'. This will result in higher property taxes that may be unfavourable for local residents.
* If tourism is seasonal at a destination, so too will be the injection of income into the community.
* Health service provision and police services can increase during the tourist season at the expense of the local tax base.
* Affordability and availability of staff housing can be problematic. Social Benefits: The quality of life of a community can be enhanced by economic diversification

through tourism, following the principles of sustainable development.

* Tourism creates recreational and cultural facilities that can be used by local communities as well as domestic and international visitors.
* Public spaces may be developed and enhanced through tourism activity.
* Tourism enhances local community esteem and provides the opportunity for greater understanding and communication among peoples of diverse backgrounds.

Social Costs:

* Rapid tourism growth can result in the inability to meet the capacities of local amenities and institutions; quality of amenity services can be diminished by over use.
* Litter, vandalism, and crime are concerns associated with tourism development that will be the responsibility of the community.
* Tourism can bring overcrowding and traffic congestion. Congestion can result in the perception of inconvenience by the residents, which is interpreted as a negative impact on their quality of life.
* Foreigners bring with them material wealth and apparent freedom. Young members of the host community are particularly susceptible to these economic expectations that tourists bring. The result can be a complete disruption of the traditional way of life in the community.

An increase in crime may result from tourism. The community structure may change (including community bonds, demographics, and institutions).

The authenticity of the social and cultural environment can be changed. Organized events for tourists based on local social behaviour and culture can become distorted in their authenticity, which may not be a valid representation of the local environment. Lifestyles may be disrupted beyond levels acceptable to the host community.

Cultural Benefits:

* Tourism can enhance local cultural awareness, but eventually might distort it.
* Tourism can generate income to help pay for preservation of archaeological sites, historic buildings, and districts.
* Despite many criticisms about alteration of cultures to unacceptable levels, the sharing of cultural knowledge and experience can be beneficial for both the hosts and the guests at tourist destinations, and could result in the revival of local traditions and crafts.

Cultural Costs:

* Youth in the community could begin to emulate the speech and attire of tourists. Loss and damage to historic sites may occur through tourism development and pressures.
* Long-term damage to cultural traditions, and erosion of cultural values, resulting in cultural contamination beyond the level acceptable to the host destination. Environmental Benefits:. Nature tourism encourages productive use of lands that are marginal for agriculture, enabling large tracts to remain covered in natural vegetation. Parks and nature preserves may be created, and ecological preservation supported as a necessity for nature-based tourism.

Improved

waste management can be achieved. Increased awareness and concern for the environment may develop.

Environmental Costs:

* Negative changes in the physical integrity of the area may occur.
* Rapid development, over development, and overcrowding can forever change the physical environment and ecosystem of an area.
* Litter, erosion, overtaxed sewage, and waste management systems may occur.
* Sensitive areas and habitat may be lost.

* Degradation of parks and preserves through over use and poor management may result.
* Excessive waste may be generated.
* Water and air pollution may occur.
* Wear and tear on infrastructure is accelerated.

Sustainable Tourism Defined

With the recent United Nations' directives on sustainable tourism, it is important to begin this section on tourism planning with a definition of some principles of sustainable tourism. These principles will fond the basis for the guidelines and comments in this document.

A definition of sustainable tourism"... the tourism industry must be profitable and environmentally sustainable if it is to provide long-term benefits, but this will not be achieved without a new and different approach to industry planning and development." PATA, Endemic Tourism: A profitable industry in a sustainable environment, Kings Cross, NSW, Australia, 1992.

Clearly, sustainable tourism implies an approach to development aimed at balancing social and economic objectives with environmentally sound management. It is not synonymous with unlimited growth of tourism development. Although we use the phrase "sustainable tourism development", this terminology can be considered misleading because it emphasizes continued and increasing growth rather than the long-term viability or sustainability of tourism, environments, and cultures. Tourism development implies tradeoffs and, in fact, planning for sustainable tourism requires identifying possible constraints or limits for tourism development.

While tourism is welcomed almost universally for the benefits and opportunities it creates, there is a growing recognition of the need to see tourism in its environmental context, to acknowledge that tourism and the environment are interdependent, and to work to reinforce the positive relationship between tourism and the environment. Maurice Strong stated in the 1993 Report of the World Tourism and

Travel Council: "Protecting the environment is both a moral obligation and a business imperative for the Travel and Tourism

Industry. As the world's largest industry it can effectively reach millions of customers with a coherent, compelling environmental message. And the leadership of the industry can and must persuade its members to adopt ecologically sound business practices. After all, a healthy environment is the travel industry's core product. If you can get it right, Travel and Tourism can truly become environmentally sustainable."

The Basis of Sustainable Tourism

Over the past two decades, the intere latedness of all earth systems and human systems has become abundantly clear. We have clearly understood that no human action ever occurs in total isolation from other natural systems, and we have appreciated the reality that humans are dependent on the earth's limited resources. We have realized the fundamental importance of somehow finding ways to live within the carrying capacity of the earth. Over the last twenty years, the global community has been primed for some fundamental changes, including a search for "sustainable development" that is based on new modes of resource allocation and accounting, new attitudes toward the preservation of environmental integrity, and new ways of making decisions in all sectors. Among the imperatives that promote and enhance the vision of sustainable futures, including that of a sustainable future for tourism, are the following: prudent use of the earth's resources within the limits of the planet's carrying capacity; devolution of top-down decision-making responsibilities and capabilities to a broader range of the destination's stake holders; the abatement of poverty and gender inequalities, and respect for fundamental human rights;

* Enhancement of the quality of life through improved health care, shelter, nutrition, and access to education and income-generating skills;
* Preservation of biodiversity and life support systems for all natural habitats; and
* Preservation of indigenous knowledge and ways of living, and respect for the spiritual and cultural traditions of different people. In fulfilling these imperatives, governments and other society agents must struggle to find an appropriate balance between different,

sometimes apparently conflicting needs and value systems. Sustainable development must meet three fundamental and equal objectives, namely:

* Economic: production of goods and services (the overriding criterion in fulfilling this objective is efficiency);
* Environmental: conservation and prudent management of natural resources (the overriding criterion is the preservation of biodiversity and maintenance of ecological integrity); and
* Social: the maintenance and enhancement of the quality of life (equity is the main consideration in meeting this objective) and inter generational, as well as intra generational equity in the distribution of wealth.

Achieving sustainable tourism development requires that the private sector and the public sector cooperate as partners in working toward a sustainable society. Making decisions about sustainable tourism development also requires that governments work within a broader framework than may have been used traditionally, working toward decisions that are:

* Longer-term: to better anticipate and prevent problems;
* Multi-sectoral: to include the full range of functions of the tourism environment;
* Ecosystem based: to recognize the cumulative and synergistic effects of actions;
* Wider: to recognize the impacts of their actions on other sectors, regions, and communities;
* Deeper: to recognize that the causes and consequences of the problems they seek to solve may involve others and other institutions; and
* Full-cycle: to consider the full context of resource use from initial extraction to end use.

Individual tourist resource management decisions will have to be taken with increased understanding of all these dimensions if the goal of sustainable futures is to be attained. Achieving sustainable futures requires the development of appropriate tourism on a continuum where growth decisions, development viewpoints and sustainability issues are balanced with environment and economy. In order to achieve profitability and environmental sustainability in the tourism industry, the tourism industry as a whole must take a different approach to planning and development.

Relationships

We can examine the interdependent relationships between tourism and the environment in terms of the interaction of the visitor, the place, and the host community, using the framework of the tourism system described in Section I. These three elements interact with each other and are affected by external influences. The relationships are essentially two-way and can be either positive or negative.

Intends of visitors, we are aware of the range of impacts that growing numbers of visitors and their growing demands have on the places and host communities where tourism opportunities exist, and we know that an increasing number of visitors are searching for higher quality and more satisfying experiences. These trends can bring positive results if there is appropriate and sustainable tourism development in order that the health and wellbeing of visitors and local residents is ensured, so that communication, education, awareness, and understanding grow from tourism opportunities provided by a community and its location. If tourism is poorly managed, negative results-such as scarred landscapes from overuse, crowding, and traffic problems-will reduce the quality of the tourism experience and quite possibly lead to a hostile and/or exploitative host community.

The concept of sustainability can be interpreted in a number of ways, for example, as a philosophy, as a set of principles and/or values to guide development, or as criteria or tests for determining sustainability. Sustainability is possible only if tourism resources (natural, human-made or cultural) can be maintained over time. The idea of stewardship/trusteeship-to hold the resources of a country in trust for future generations and the responsibility to pass them on in good condition-is applicable here. This means that we want to achieve a situation that can be maintained without depleting the resource, cheating the visitor or exploiting the local population. Achieving sustainability (economic, political, Q social, cultural, and environmental) requires an ability to accept and accommodate change. It implies, also, that mechanisms are in place to mediate between different interests, which mayor may not be true in any particular setting or situation. In general, the terminology associated with sustainable tourism is inconsistent and frequently confusing. In spite of this variability in terminology, various actors, and interests have attempted to define their perspectives on goals, practices, effects, and expectations of tourism.

Principles for Sustainable Tourism

Many destinations are now pursuing strategies that aim to ensure a sensitive approach when dealing with tourism. Many of these strategies are based on a formal expression of principles for sustainable tourism. Planners and others can use these principles as basic guidelines when attempting to incorporate the broad vision of sustainability into local policies and practices.

The list of principles provided below are important for destinations and organizations that wish to be guided by the ethic of sustainable and responsible tourism. Residents of a community must maintain control of tourism development by being involved in setting a community tourism vision, identifying the resources to be maintained and enhanced, and developing goals and strategies for tourism development and management. Equally important, community residents must participate in the implementation of strategies as well as the operation of the tourism infrastructure, services, and facilities. A tourism initiative should be developed with the help of broad-based stakeholder input. Tourism development must provide quality employment.

The provision of fulfilling jobs has to be seen as an integral part of any tourism development. Part of the process of achieving quality employment is to ensure that, as much as possible, the tourism infrastructure (hotels, restaurants, shops, etc.) is developed and managed by local people. Experience has demonstrated that the provision of education and training for local residents and access to financing for local businesses and entrepreneurs are central to this type of policy. Broad-based distribution of the benefits of tourism must occur at the tourism destination. Local linkages and resident participation in the planning, development, and operation of tourism resources and services will help to ensure that a more equitable distribution of benefits will occur among residents, visitors, and other service providers. Sustainable tourism development has to provide for inter generational equity. Equitable distribution of the costs and benefits of tourism development must take place among present and future generations.

To be fair to future generations of tourists and the travel industry, society should strive to leave a resource base no less than the one we have inherited. Sustainable tourism development must, therefore, avoid resource allocation actions that are irreversible. A long-tend planning horizon needs to be adopted by businesses and destination tourism organizations to ensure that destinations are not used for short-tend gain and then abandoned as visitor tastes and business interests move elsewhere. A longer-tend horizon encourages the use of pro-active strategies to ensure destination sustainability and the establishment of local linkages over time.

Hannony is required between the needs of a visitor, the place, and the community. This is facilitated by broad stakeholder support with a proper balance between economic, social, cultural, and human objectives, and a recognition of the importance of cooperation among government, the host communities, and the tourism industry, and the non-profit organizations involved in community development and environmental protection. Tourism strategies and plans must be linked with a broader set of initiatives and economic development plans.

A need exists for more coordination at both policy and action levels among the various agencies involved and among different levels of government. This is particularly relevant to tourism and environmental policies. Service provisions such as transportation, parking, and water and sewer capacities must also be considered in conjunction with tourism plans and developments. Cooperation among attractions, businesses, and tourism operators is essential given that one business or operation can be directly affected by the performance or quality of another.

There is a definite need for impact assessment of tourism development proposals. The capacity of sites must be considered, including physical, natural, social, and cultural limits and development should be compatible with local and environmental limits. Plans and operations should be evaluated regularly with adjustments as required.

Guidelines have to be established for tourism operations, including requirements for impact assessment. There should be codes of practice established for tourism at all levels-national, regional and local. There is also a need to develop indicators and threshold limits for measuring the impacts and success of local tourism ventures. Protection and monitoring strategies are essential if communities are to protect the resources that form the basis of their tourism product.

Tourism planning must move away from a traditional growth-oriented model to one that focuses on opportunities for employment, income and improved local wellbeing while ensuring that development decisions reflect the full value of the natural and cultural environments. The management and use of public goods such as water, air, and common lands should include accountability on behalf of the users to ensure that these resources are not abused. Sustainable tourism development requires the establishment of education and training programmes to improve public understanding and enhance business, vocational and professional skills.

Sustainable tourism development involves promoting appropriate uses and activities that draw from and reinforce landscape character, sense of place, community identity and site opportunity. These activities and uses should aim to provide a quality tourism experience that satisfies visitors while adhering to the other principles of sustainable tourism. The scale and type of tourism facilities must reflect the limits of acceptable use that resources can tolerate. Small-scale, low impact facilitiec and services should be encouraged, for example, through financing and other incentives. The tourism process must also ensure that heritage and natural resources are maintained and enhanced using internationally acceptable criteria and standards.

Sustainable tourism marketing should include the provision of a high quality tourist experience which adheres to the other principles outlined above, and whose promotion should be a responsible and an ethical reflection of the destination's tourism attractions and services. These principles are ambitious, and it is fair to say very difficult to achieve so that tourism developments that will always adhere to all of these principles. However, these principles must be seen as targets for all tourism planning.

Crategic integrated sustainable tourism planning The nature of sustainable tourism development requires a process of planning and management that brings together a series of interests and concerns in a sustainable and strategic form of planning and development. Tourism planning continues to be contentious and somewhat nebulous, because most government officials and tourism industry practitioners harbour their own definitions and parameters of the task. By its very nature, planning is multidimensional and is purposely integrative. Even in the less complex circumstances of some Asian and Pacific countries at early phases of tourism development, it is necessary for those with the responsibility to oversee-or administer tourism planning in the public interest to be cognizant of two special dimensions: strategic planning and integrated planning.

Need for integrated tourism planning Although there is evidence that some tourism destinations have been developed without conscious, strategic and integrated planning, many of them have experienced unforeseen consequences that have led to their deterioration.

The Need for Planning

Some managers and decision-makers argue that we are overwhelmed with plans and planning processes. Others argue that we require more regulation and planning in order to ensure that the goals of sustainable tourism can be met. There are others who maintain that we require less planning and possibly less regulation. There is no right answer to the level of planning that a particular situation calls for and clearly every society context will determine what is appropriate. Similarly, though sustainable tourism calls for a high level of local involvement in planning and developing tourism, the amount and quality of resident participation will vary depending on the cultural and political factors in the destination.

It is obviously useless to develop a sophisticated planning system if there is no political or community support for it. In these cases, one might first have to create an appropriate setting or structure for a planning process that avoids the failures of past planning practices.

The failures of traditional planning

Many people are sceptical about the effectiveness of planning. They see it as a waste of time since most plans never see the light of day and end up on a shelf. In many cases, planning in the past has tended to be very much based on developing regulatory procedures as opposed to creating suitable mechanisms for achieving the goals and objectives developed within the planning process. The failure of traditional and rational approaches to planning can be attributed to a number of factors as discussed below.

Lack of Flexibility

The logical, rational approach to planning, it has been argued, has made plans far too rigorous and unable to adapt to changing conditions. Unless the external environment is perceived to be quite static, a detailed step wise approach that is rigorously adhered to could make it very difficult for the organization or destination to create an optimal fit between its resources and the forces influencing tourism in its setting. A dynamic approach as provided through strategic planning principles enables a dynamic planning process, better able to adapt to changes.

Lack of Strategic Thinking and Vision

A major criticism has been launched against traditional, rational planning approaches by some researchers who argue that such plans lack leadership vision in the process of formulating strategies. The inclusion of "strategic vision" by leaders and decision-makers (not technical planning experts) ensures that the plan is not merely an operational plan, but provides direction and concepts for achieving the organizations broad goals and interests.

Ineffective top-down planning

Planning by the destination's planning officials or by retaining planning experts from outside the destination results in a plan which is unable to effectively represent the diverse opinions, needs and attitudes of a range of tourism stakeholders. The chances of successful implementation of such a top-down plan is further inhibited by the lack of community support and involvement in the process, particularly in political systems where residents seek greater participation in the decision-making of their community direction.

Poor Linking of Formulation and Implementation

Another major impediment to planning has been the inability to link formulation of the plan to the outcomes of implementation so as to ensure accountability and to measure the success of the planning exercise. The lack of clear, easy to implement actions and responsibilities to ensure accountability for carrying out the actions, has been a deterrent to effective implementation. A clearly deemed relationship between the planning and implementation of action steps must be present to ensure effective delivery of both the tourism experience and the sustainability of the destination's assets and resources. Strategic tourism planning-an action planning approach

A strategic planning approach is essential for sustainable tourism, where by the disparate planning and development activities related to tourism are linked to an overall, broad strategic tourism plan to provide an integrated framework for directing tourism. Strategic planning seeks an optimal fit between the system and its environment.

Hence, it: is long-term; contains vision; specifies goals (ends); specifies major actions (means) to achieve goals; specifies the major resource allocations to arrive at (ways); is dynamic, flexible and adaptable; ensures that formulation and implementation of the strategic plan are not discrete, but linked closely through constant monitoring, environmental scanning, evaluation and adjustment; and is not a linear process (e.g., constant environmental scanning occurs throughout the process to enable pro-active response and adjustment; monitoring can start as soon as target indicators and levels are established to provide base line information). A strategic approach to a sustainable community tourism plan also requires: close coordination with local and regional legislative and political structures; community participation and support; a new role for planners as educators and providers of technical expertise, but not solely plan designers; the plan is designed primarily by those who have a stake in the outcome; an innovative and inclusive organizational structure for joint planning; a learning community that is informed, educated and aware; applying the principles of sustainable tourism development to ensure the long-term sustainability of the ecology, the local economy and the sociocultural values of the host community, while distributing the benefits equitably among the stakeholders.

The Nature of Strategic Tourism Plans

Sustainable tourism planning requires a strategic planning approach, which seeks an optimal fit between the system and its environment through the creation of a long-term direction (vision), goals and strategies for the allocation of resources and monitoring impacts, and detailed action plans. This is achieved through dynamic, flexible and adaptable planning, where: The fonnulation and implementation are closely linked through constant environmental scanning, monitoring, evaluation and adjustment of the strategic plan. The plan is created by a broad and diverse group of actors (stakeholders) whose needs, attitudes and values are closely reflected in the plan's philosophy, vision and contents. There is a clear recognition of the interdependence among the various components of the plan, which is considered in the creation and implementation of goals and strategies. Planning approaches span a broad spectrum, ranging from a rational, lock step approach all the way to strategic, broad-based plans. Despite this proliferation, a good plan generally contains the following elements and action steps:

* Vision and/or mission statement.
* Situation (issues) analysis.
* Strategic goals.
* Evaluation of strategic alternatives to achieving these goals.

* Strategies Implementation of strategies (measurable objectives and detailed action plans).

Monitoring and evaluation of implementation strategies and action plans Adjusting the strategic and operational plans based on information feedback from evaluation and constant scanning of the external environment.

Strategic Planning Principles

Strategic tourism planning requires careful consideration of the goals and principles of sustainable tourism. Some of the goals and principles that should be considered in tourism planning are: Economic:

* Development which takes into account the full costs and benefits of the alternatives and decision embarked upon, from an overall economic and social perspective.
* Broad-based distribution of benefits among all stakeholders.
* Provision of a quality visitor experience that is compatible with the destination's goals and values.
* Ensure that fiscal costs of infrastructure provision and marketing do not outweigh the benefits (for example, residents may end up paying higher taxes to subsidize tourism development but may not benefit from improved income, social services, use of or access to the publicly constructed infrastructure, education and training opportunities, etc. Socia:
* Steady employment avoids the underemployment and unemployment associated with seasonal hiring for peak tourism periods.
* Better employment opportunities than the low pay positions typically associated with tourism services.
* Quality jobs that encourage the use of local knowledge, skills and traditions, and offer a sense of fulfilment and satisfaction to the residents.
* Improved standard of living and equitable distribution of benefits within (and between) generations in the present and future.

Ecological:

* Maintenance of essential ecological processes, biological diversity and non-renewable resources for future generations (through preservation or conservation strategies).
* Planning at a scale and pace that enables effective and ongoing monitoring and mitigation of long-term impacts.
* Full-cost accounting of environmental resources in cost-benefit analyses.
* An environmental and cumulative impact that analyses important prerequisites to development, and environmental management systems needs to be implemented by businesses and organizations.

Cultural:

* Tourist activities and behaviours should be respectful of cultural activities, sites and values.
* Designs should be compatible with national and local heritage and character and should foster the community's identity or sense of place.

Tourist types and activities should match the needs and expectations of the local people, with protection of sensitive and indigenous cultures against any adverse impact.

Political:

* Compatibility between overall economic development goals of regional and community interests and tourism goals.
* Integration of plans and planning with other relevant community and regional plans and processes.
* Balance top-down planning with resident input and participation in planning and development.

Strategic Tourism Planning-an Action Process

The major steps in a strategic planning process for tourism for a community-based destinat. Note that while the steps appear sequential, the process is an iterative one, with feedback loops connecting the various stages. It is also important to note that this is a recommended process-each nation/destination may need to tailor this process to suit its own requirements, norms and values.

Means of Achieving Strategic Action

Oriented Integrated Tourism Policy

Tourism planning can operate at many levels:

* The individual site. (Examples include a beach, heritage site, park or theme park.)
* The destination. (In some cases the site and the destination may be the same, but usually it refers to the larger geographical setting where the site is situated.)
* A region within a country. (This can be a geographic or political boundary or it can be based on tourism attraction factors.)
* The nation. (Especially true in the case of smaller island countries.)
* Several countries. (A good example is the area around the Making River that is being presented as a theme-related destination involving several countries.)

There can be little argument that there should be integration within each of the levels and across all levels, so as to achieve balance, aesthetic harmony, cooperation, confidence (for investment), efficiency, identity, sensitivity and most importantly sustainability. These aspirations of integration can be achieved through preparation of a tourism policy, which is a policy for tourism following a systematic process.

Developing a Tourism Policy

Policies can help guide a government and other stakeholders' programmes of action and provide a frame of reference for the tourism industry's actions.

If we are to achieve sustainable tourism, it is always preferable that a set of tourism policies be developed either as a set of distinct tourism objectives or better still that all levels and areas of policy formation integrate tourism directives in their decision-making process.

Such a Policy Should

* Provide a set of guidelines for the actions of all stakeholders;
* Specify the broad objectives to be achieved;
* Specify action plans; and
* Identify areas of responsibility and power for policy implementation.

Tourism objectives should be the product of stakeholder participation and recognize the complexity of tourism development and management. It is rare where there will be a classic policy development process. Political priorities, power realities, economic development requirements and industry pressures will very much influence what occurs in the policy development process. Ideally at least, the role that tourism should play in the overall national as well as regional development should be clearly articulated and understood. Only then can other areas of public and private development reflect tourism objectives and priorities. The officials responsible for economic development, environmental protection and tourism are just examples where the policy and decision-making areas of activity meet or should meet.

Each objective should be tested for its general applicability and contribution to broad objectives related to overall sustainable development with specific attention to:

* Energy and water conservation;
* Employment;
* Economic growth;
* Infrastructure plans; environmental and resource conservation; urban and rural revitalization; heritage conservation; consumer protection; community welfare; business creation.

A commitment to the achievement of a satisfactory tourism policy requires a set of objectives that focus on the following issues: Economic:

It is necessary to optimize the contribution of tourism and recreation to economic prosperity, full employment, regional economic development, and improved international balance of payments.

Sociocultural

It is essential to contribute to the personal growth and education of the population and encourage their 'appreciation of the local geography, history, and ethnic diversity. Social policy should also seek to avoid activities that have the potential to indamine or denigrate the social and cultural values and resources of the area and its traditions and lifestyles.

Market Development Oriented

Policies must encourage the free entry of foreign visitors, while balancing this goal with the need to monitor persons and goods entering the country with laws protecting public health.

Resource protection and conservation: Policies must protect and preserve the historical and cultural foundations as a living part of community life and development and to ensure future generations an opportunity to enjoy the rich heritage of the area. These policies will also ensure the compatibility of tourism, recreational, and activity policies with other broader interests in energy development and conservation, environmental protection, and judicious use of natural resources.

Hwnan resource development: It is important to ensure that tourism has an adequate supply of professionally-trained skilled and managerial staff to meet future needs. Hwnan resource policies should also ensure that the education and training programmes and materials are available to meet the needs of tourism. Government operations concerns: Policies must help to coordinate government activities related to tourism while allowing the public sector to take a leadership role by supporting the needs of tourists, residents and tourism businesses with appropriate legislation and administration. Most countries will have developed their own style of policy-making.

It is important that the policy for tourism be consistent in its general aim and orientation and be readily integrated with other policy areas. Lateral (with other policy areas) and vertical (internal) linkages must be integrated. A policy process progresses to strategies, plans, programmes, legislation and regulations. It is important that each stage at any level (national/regional/local) be carefully integrated laterally and vertically.

Developing the Tourism Plan

There is no single model of tourism plan or one process. There are many variation sin content, style, approach and emphasis, and some possibilities are identified here.

Alternative Plan Approaches

A master plan is the principal in strwnent of planning for tourism. Such a plan may be comprehensive and wide-ranging, or it may focus on one or a combination of:

* Physical/environmental issues;
* Economic issues;
* Promotion and marketing;
* Conservation (of environment or heritage resources);
* Sociocultural issues;
* Investment;
* Human resources development.

On a temporal scale, the master plan may focus on a short-term time scale (five years, perhaps to coincide with the cycles of the national economic strategy), or it may focus on an indeterminate scale with indications of preferred end-states or achievements, not associated with particular time periods. Other differences in approach may cover:

* Attitudes to spontaneous development (strict or flexible planning);
* Degree of incentives and technical assistance;
* Apportionment of benefits; integration with tourism-related activities; certainty of site prescription;

An important element in any tourism plan is the degree to which it is integrated with the nationwide or region-wide economic, welfare and physical development plan. Tourism plans prepared in recent years, and those to be prepared, should include specific reference to:

* Ecological sustainability;

* Environmental conservation;
* Heritage (built environment) and cultural heritage conservation;
* Sustainable development of heritage resources.

Content

For any particular nation, the plan could adopt a particular focus, perhaps for only one of the review phases. However, a generalized prospectus of contents would include:

* The institutional or organizational framework, setting out:
* The principal organizations;
* The principal responsibilities;
* The legislative framework;
* The roles and functions of the private and public sectors.
* The principal plan elements, such as:
* Infrastructure;
* Facilities and services;
* Visitor attractions.
* Development implications-economic, environmental, and sociocultural;
* The principal means of securing implementation, including:
* Financing and investment;
* Incentives;
* Marketing;
* Promotion;
* Tourism information systems;
* Tourism awareness programmes;
* Human resources development.

The plan of any nation may refer to regional cooperation in the various aspects of tourism planning and development, and the contribution which can be made to the regional circumstances. In some cases, the emphasis of the plan may direct the considerations away from the physical dimensions of the tourism development. This would be unfortunate, because no matter what form the development takes, the tourism experience of the visitor will take place in a region, in a destination, at a site. Therefore, it is important that these particular aspects of tourism planning are given due attention.

The form and Structure of Physical Plan Elements

Tourism planning may focus on the nation, the region, a destination, or a site. Integration of all these will achieve the most satisfactory outcome. In the context of physical development, tourism planning at any level can be conducted with attention to spatial form and structure.

Regional

There are various operational issues linked to the principal determinants of regional form and structure. Experimentation is ongoing, but there are some constant principles. The basic options include:

* Using existing developments as magnets and regional control factors;
* Creating new developments;
* Creating a hierarchical network of tourism destinations by devising a balanced strategy;
* Developing a region-wide strategy, eliminating those areas that have little tourism potential, devising a destination-focused strategy, devising a tour or circuit strategy; and
* Developing a strategy of complementary tourism destinations, with each destination specializing in focus or market segment.

The basic fond and structural patterns include:

* Concentration of tourism development and cot Tidors linking:
* Major resorts;
* Tourism destination areas; and
* Base camps on the threshold of a tourism region. Gateways or points of entry into the destination areas.

Variants on this basic spatial formula exist in tourism planning literature and in many case studies worldwide. The dilemma for the Asian and Pacific region is to reinterpret the land-based concepts of regional form and structure into a region specific idiom.

Destination Area

The destination area contains the critical mass of resources, facilities and amenities that contribute to the satisfaction of tourists. The basic elements of a tourism destination area or zone are:

* One or more communities to supply the utilities, services and facilities; one or more attraction complexes; transportation linkages between the communities and the attractions; and
* An entrance or gateway at the destination. An important principle in the planning and design of tourism destinations is that they be distinctive places with unique internal relationships between the various parts (other places and the various facilities and services). The destination is what attracts the tourist. To be successful, the tourism destination should be planned to maximize:
* The locational advantage;
* The product advantage (in comparison with competitor destinations);
* The advantage of proximate cultural resources and natural resources; transport linkages; and hospitable host attitudes.

There is no single formula for successful destination tourism, but there are planning and design principles appropriate to the destination scale. These include:

* The destination should be integrated into a region-wide strategy;
* The destination should attract (or create) a distinctive image;
* Successful destination planning will involve:
* Public-private partnership;

* Integration; and progressive accumulation of the critical mass of attractions, services, facilities, amenities, and transport linkages-all within carrying capacity limits.

Site Scale

The scale of this tourism planning is a particular challenge, because at this scale a single, functional or aesthetic problem can seriously disrupt the image of a tourism destination. If the tourism business on any site fails, it becomes a monwnent to bad decision-making that may affect an entire destination by association. At this level, "place" takes on a particular important meaning. It is not only the contribution each place makes to the entire destination, but also a geographical reference point and landmark. It is at the site scale that regional and destination tourism planning yield concrete outcomes, and at this level the projections and predictions of demand for facilities, services and experiences materialize. Therefore, a special understanding of the site characteristics, their potential and constraints, and the contribution of the site to the wider destination area become crucial. It is also critical that the planning, management and monitoring processes be efficient at this scale. In order to avoid the repetition of inappropriate design and development, post-development evaluation should become an integral part of the planning process, especially to determine the validity of the pre development design decisions.

Physical Development Strategy

In order to implement the tourism development proposals examined at the various levels (national, regional, destination and site), it is necessary to provide a suitable physical development planning strategy. An important element of any physical development strategy is land use planning. It is important to recognize that many countries may have land use strategies but they are unevenly enforced and lack support at local levels. In some cases, there may not yet be a policy.

There are four different approaches to land use planning:

Blueprint: planning, which is based on the expectation that the full plan as prepared will be implemented exactly and in its entirety. Such an expectation is unrealistic, because no plan ever starts with complete information and functions within a completely controlled operational environment. Such a plan type is too inflexible.

Regulatory: planning, which relies upon the application of development performance standards with the possibility of all development eventually conforming to previously set model codes and standards. While easy to implement, the built environment may become monotonous and repetitive. Even so, some fond of regulatory planning is inevitable.

Market-driven: planning, which is best suited to individual projects, rather than to planning strategies for entire communities or regions.

A systems-driven approach to planning which is becoming more common, especially as planning functions are needed to address increasingly complex situations involving threats to the environment and as development is increasingly scrutinized according to ecologically-sustainable principles. This approach provides for review, monitoring and adjustment as circumstances change in the plan. The land use planning system most likely will combine the compatible elements of the systems-driven methodology and the regulatory approach to planning. In many cases, the system of land use planning control is derived from standard European or North American codes of planning practice and then modified to meet the needs of national governments and administrative systems. Usually, a land use planning control system in force for the planning system is backed by appropriate legislation which provides for control over land use and development, specified administrative procedures, and necessary infrastructure development. F or tourism development, the most important issues in land use planning and development will include:

* Location of tourism uses;
* Accessibility to and travel within tourism districts/zones;
* Development standards;
* Design standards;
* Traffic problems;

* Quality of the built environment;
* Landscaping of tourism developments;
* Freestanding major developments;
* Tourism attractions in rural environments;
* Location of the major transport interchanges such as airports, and bus/coach terminals; and
* Impact of tourism development on local architectural styles and important areas of heritage.

To achieve a good standard of land use development, the planning system should: coordinate development-related infrastructure requirements; implement appropriate concepts and ideas in order to achieve acceptable, conventional standards of aesthetics, health, convenience and diversity (of interest, experience, and culture); promote development where and when appropriate; provide the developer with prior knowledge of the development requirements (in the form of performance standards); prevent prejudicial development (by type, location, timing, or quality); reflect acceptable changes in standards and fashions; and facilitate innovation. It may be claimed that the best plans and developments have been the outcome of deliberate planning using a systematic planning and decision-making process, but there are examples of successful plans and developments which have not emerged from the application of a systematic process. Such development may be considered to have been fortuitous, fragile, or both. In any case, the pursuit of a systematic process should offer the best chance of successful and harmonious tourism development.

Implementation of a Tourism Plan

It is preferable to consider the planning process as a continuum that integrates the steps of plan creation with its implementation. Stages of implementation can include the following:

* Preparing and putting into practice guidelines, regulations and policies necessary to bring the plan to fruition;
* Undertaking development in accordance with the plan;

* Supervising that development; preparing the community for the impact of tourism development; preparing and providing training facilities for those intending to work in the tourism/travel/hospitality industry;
* Collecting information to monitor the progress of the plan as it is put into practice;
* Undertaking marketing and promotion to ensure that the tourism destination is known and appreciated for what it has to offer.

A tourism plan is a tool to guide development. Little, if anything, will happen without: a suitable legislative and administrative structure; suitable sources of finance; suitable entrepreneurial interest; evidence of demand for the tourism product at the destination; and certainty of access by visitors.

In addition, a tourism plan At any level, especially at national and regional levels, will need desegregation so that the various resource needs-land/water, labour and capital-are seen in their spatial, temporal, financial, infrastructure, and social interrelationships. An additional consideration is the likely impact of forces external to the destination area, especially the impact of decisions, international airlines that service the region, and the international tour operators who facilitate the arrival of tourists.

Institutional Framework

There is considerable evidence of the need for an effective institutional framework if tourism development is to be coordinated, efficiently supervised, monitored and integrated into the overall scope of national economic, environmental and social planning. It is important that the institutional framework encompasses organizations from both the public and the private sector. A coordinated framework is necessary because of the fragmented nature of the tourism industry. The tourism plan using process provides the catalyst for inputs from the various stakeholders with the outcome of decisions affecting tourism development. Even after the preparation of a tourism development plan, the final outcome is dependent upon the integrated realization of a series of independent development decisions based upon the pursuit of individual opportunities.

The public sector, the private sector, non-profit organizations, the community, and tourists play important roles in tourism planning and development. In each case, there will be particular perspectives on tourism development, the need for tourism planning, and the shape of that planning. The principal perspective of the public sector is to manage development to achieve community goals in the public interest. For the private sector, the principal function is to provide facilities and services to tourists while maximizing returns on investment. The private sector has also come to accept that it has social and environmental responsibilities. It is recognized that entrepreneurial flair may create tourism development opportunities beyond those identified in the prepared tourism plan. The formal plan should be composed with sufficient flexibility to accommodate such initiatives, especially if it is responding to shifts in tourist preferences. Some changes in preferences may be identified through the constant monitoring and evaluation of tourism activity by consultants, market research investigators, design professionals and project managers. Financial institutions and corporate lending agencies will have a particular interest in the changes of fashion and the dicates of the tourism market. The World Tourism Organization (WTO) has described the distinct roles of the public and private sector by the principle that governments should not seek to do what the private sector is able and willing to do. However, in many cases of large-scale development, the private sector and government may work in a partnership. Other partnerships may develop where governments assist indigenous landowners to start an enterprise that will be managed eventually by indigenous communities.

The perspective of the tourist on tourism planning is different from the other stakeholders. The interests of every tourist cut across the various independent decisions made by governments and the private sector, and the tourist is concerned with the experience that can be gained. One of the main purposes of tourism planning is to create a harmonious balance between the different interests of the various stakeholders. This balance may be achieved through the establishment of an appropriate multifaceted institutional framework. In some tourism development plans, an effective institutional framework is considered to be one of the principal determinants of successful tourism development.

Back country Tourism Perspectives on Shared Decision Making in B.C. Land use Planning.

Little doubt exists that British Columbia's tourism industry is dependent on the province's Crown lands for its market appeal and long-term sustainability. The province's motto "Splendour Without Diminishment," its vehicle license plate slogan "Beautiful British Columbia," and its well-established tourism brand "Super, Natural British Columbia" all highlight the importance that successive governments have attached to the region's Crown lands as a backdrop for tourism activity. Comprised of about 92 percent of the province's 95-million hectare landscape, these lands contain some of the world's most majestic mountains, extensive forests, wildest rivers, and outstanding biodiversity. In combination, these resources helped to advantageously position British Columbia on the international tourism stage.

Concurrently, these lands have traditionally been a source of revenues and livelihood for communities and businesses engaged in forestry, mining, oil and gas development, power generation, fisheries, and agriculture. With an economy built by industries that depend on secure access to natural resources, it is not surprising that integrated land use planning in British Columbia is both challenging and critical.

Prior to the early 1990s, B.C.'s land use planning initiatives were forest-centric in their emphasis. Primarily conducted by the province's Ministry of Forests, planning focused on expanding timber extraction opportunities for industry, almost to the exclusion of other resource industries including tourism. In the early 1990s, excluded stakeholders highlighted inequities in the existing planning process and demanded a more inclusive approach. After much heated debate, B.C.'s government instituted an innovative land planning program guided by shared decision-making (SDM) principles. This more inclusive approach to planning was systematically applied in the 1990s via two province-wide planning processes: the Commission on Resources and Environment (CORE), and the Land and Resource Management Planning (LRMP) process. These SDM processes were designed to integrate the land use needs of all potential stakeholders. The two programs offered unprecedented opportunities to incorporate non traditional resource use values into B.C.'s land planning decisions. One stakeholder group with such values that seized the opportunity to participate in these SDM programs was the back country tourism sector. The perspectives of these tourism stakeholders concerning SDM mechanisms and outcomes are the focus of this paper.

SDM in LRMP Planning Processes

SDM approaches to LRMP planning emphasized "the importance of equal access to information and equal opportunity for input and scrutiny of issues and concerns by all participants, thereby creating a constructive environment for problem solving". Facilitated participation, consensus building, collaboration, interest-based negotiation, and mediation are SDM principles that are designed to generate more inclusive, representative, and respectful resolutions to disputes. While not suited to all situations, SDM is appropriate in circumstances where conventional approaches to conflict resolution have failed and alternative techniques are needed. Such situations are often associated with land use disputes involving multi stake holder interests and conflicts over natural resource allocations. Such disputes were particularly prevalent in B.C. through out the 1990s, and SDM mechanisms were employed to address these conflicts in the context of the province's CORE and LRMP initiatives. SDM mechanisms were believed to be suited to creating process and planning outcomes that were more creative and reflective of public interests. They were also thought to be capable of increasing the planning capacities of the participants. (A more detailed summary of the principles and guidelines associated with SDM processes as well as the potential outcomes they may produce is provided in Tables 1 and 2). The extent to which these are implemented in SDM processes, and subsequently provide benefit, offer a useful basis for assessing the efficacy of such procedures in land use planning situations.

B.C.'s Tourism Land and Natural Resource Needs

Tourism is strategically important to B.C. Over the past decade and a half, it has been one of the largest and fastest growing sectors in the B.C. Economy. In 2001, tourism supported an estimated 112,000 jobs and $9.2 billion in revenues. These contributions were spread throughout the province, providing needed economic diversification to rural areas (BC MRSM 2001).

The foundation of B.C.'s tourism industry is the province's spectacular beauty, landscapes, and natural resources. Targeted promotional programs and unsolicited testimonials attest to the importance that B.C.'s natural landscape plays in shaping opportunities for tourism growth: "there is a dynamic at work in B.C. that makes it unique not just in Canada but possibly in the world. It has to do with the almost mystical allure of B.C.'s physical environment". Scenic view scapes, intact wildlife habitats, pristine forested landscapes, and unaltered shorelines are the core ingredients for many of the province's outstanding adventure, cultural, and nature-based tourism products. Without protection of these tourism resources, the industry's sustained contribution to the province's welfare is questionable. These circumstances reinforce the importance of incorporating environmental and cultural tourism values into provincial land use planning initiatives.

Past Tourism Land Use Planning Initiatives

Despite the perceived importance of tourism to the province's economy, the industry's natural resource needs had not been systematically incorporated into most land use planning initiatives. Traditionally, government organizations had focused primarily on marketing tourism, as opposed to developing the legislative capability or technical systems needed to effectively integrate tourism resource requirements into regional land use plans. As a consequence, restricted land use access and limited crown land tenure possibilities stymied many opportunities for back country tourism development in British Columbia. More recently, as recognition of tourism's natural resource requirements has grown, so has the need to incorporate the industry's resource requirements into land use planning decisions. This imperative has been reinforced by a diminishing provincial dependence on natural resource extraction industries for economic development, and the escalating demand for nature-based tourism opportunities. As a consequence, many of the province's recently completed LRMPs have included tourism values in their management directives.

Research Focus and Method

This paper examines tourism stakeholder perspectives concerning the application and outcomes associated with using SDM responses in the development of British Columbia's LRMPs. Perspectives on these issues were collected via a survey of respondents who participated in LRMP processes undertaken between 1995 and 2002. Through several targeted questions, the survey probed their views concerning:) the degree to which SDM process principles and guidelines were implemented during the LRMP initiatives;) the extent to which potential SDM outcomes were realized via the LRMP processes; and) those factors considered most critical to the success of SDM processes.

Stakeholder responses to these questions were recorded on a Likert-type scale ranging from 1=strongly disagree to 4=strongly agree. Mean scores for responses to each question were tabulated.

The greater the mean value recorded, the more strongly the respondents agreed with the statement examined. For reporting purposes mean scores were interpreted as follows: 1-1.50= strong disagreement, 1.51-2.25=disagreement, 2.26-2.75=undecided, 2.76-3.50 =agreement, 3.50-4.00=strong agreement. This paper describes the perspectives of the thirty-one tourism stakeholders who participated in the survey. The collective viewpoints of these stakeholders are then compared with the combined responses of all other survey participants. Unless statistically significant differences ([varies]=0.05) in the responses of tourism and nontourism stakeholders are apparent based on Student tests, only the perspectives of tourism stakeholders are described.

Findings

The following section is divided into four parts. First, an overview is presented of the extent to which tourism values were recognized in the province's completed LRMPs. Then, tourism stakeholder perspectives are described concerning the extent to which the SDM process principles and guidelines were applied in the LRMPs. Third, their opinions are reported concerning the extent to which the potential benefits associated with the use of SDM processes were realized in the LRMPs. Finally, tourism stakeholder viewpoints are identified concerning the most important factors influencing the success of SDM processes.

LRMP Recognition of Tourism Values

As of March 2003, tourism stakeholders had engaged in twenty-one LRMP processes throughout B.C. (B.C. LUCO 2003). These LRMPs provide strategic management and resource allocation directives for over 80 percent of the province's Crown lands. Fourteen of them have been approved by the government and are now being implemented. Tourism values are incorporated to varying degrees in each of these LRMPs.

A tangible measure of the ability of SDM processes to incorporate tourism values is reflected in the amount of LRMP land designated to tourism use. LRMP lands most inclusive of tourism values are designated as special management zones (SMZ) and protected area zones (PAZ). The percentage changes in PAZ and SMZ land use areas designated for potential tourism use as a result of individual LRMP decisions. The figures also reveal that while there are substantial variations in the amount of land allocated for tourism use within the LRMP regions, each planning process resulted in a significant increase in areas available for tourism use. This suggests that SDM processes were effective in integrating the perspectives of tourism stakeholders into the LRMP processes.

Tourism Stakeholder Involvement in LRMP Processes

Tourism respondents' perspectives concerning their participation in the province's LRMPs are described in this section. In particular, results are given on their overriding reasons for participating, and their viewpoints concerning how their involvement influenced the planning processes employed.

Motivations for Involvement

Tourism respondents indicated that they were participating

in LRMP processes because their constituency felt that it was the best way to achieve their land-use goals. They suggested that they entered these processes with clear goals in mind, and had a strong commitment to making the processes work.

Planning Process Influences

Overall, the tourism respondents felt that their participation in the process had made a difference in the outcomes of the LRMP(s). They believed their involvement had helped shape the design of planning processes. They claimed they were able to offer clear direction to the process based on input derived from their constituencies. They also felt that the planning processes used had helped them to effectively communicate with, and gain support from, their constituencies on LRMP planning matters.

Despite these positive perspectives, they were less sure about their ability to shape the ongoing activities of these SDM processes. For instance they expressed uncertainty about: 1) the extent to which the processes had provided them with the training needed to participate effectively; as well as, 2) the degree to which the process mechanisms had helped them be accountable to their constituency. While they felt that they had not received the level of funding needed to fully participate in the planning activities, this perspective was statistically less pronounced ([varies]=0.05) than it was for nontourism respondents.

Integration of SDM Process Principles and Guidelines Into LRMPs

Tourism stakeholders expressed their views on whether or not overriding SDM process principles and management guidelines were integrated into LRMP planning procedures. This section describes their opinions on the extent of such integration in terms of structural dimensions such as process organization, process tools, and process staffing as well as equity considerations related to inclusiveness and power balance.

Structural Characteristics

Process Organization Tourism respondents' perspectives about the integration of SDM organizational processes into LRMP procedures were mixed. From a positive perspective, they suggested that the processes offered: a focus on significant and timely issues for resolution; deadlines for moving the process along; clear procedural ground rules; enough flexibility to accommodate new information and changes as needed; and, a clear notice of the government's authority to impose a decision if consensus among the stakeholders was not reached.

On a more negative note, they expressed greater ambivalence concerning the presence of several other SDM organizational elements. In particular, they were uncertain about the extent to which the organization of the LRMP processes allowed participants to: collectively identify and agree on goals and objectives for the LRMPs; establish clear roles for the participants; and facilitate communication with the general public.

Process Tools Several SDM process tools were developed to facilitate the development of the province's LRMPs. For the most part they were designed to provide the information needed by stakeholders to make informed land and resource planning decisions. Overall, tourism stakeholders were uncertain about the extent to which these process tools provided the quality of information needed for effective decision making. Those tools deemed to be especially useful to the tourism stakeholders included overlay mapping technologies, and multiple account procedures for evaluating land use options. In contrast, respondents were uncertain about the strength of the communication and negotiation tools available to participants.

Process Support Staff Tourism stakeholders agreed that the staff provided to administer the development of their LRMPs were effective in facilitating smooth running processes. They also believed that the agency managing their planning processes acted neutrally and without bias. This sentiment was particularly strong with respect to the role facilitators played in these processes.

Equity Characteristics

Process Inclusiveness Tourism respondents agreed that the LRMP processes ensured that all appropriate interests and values were included at the LRMP planning tables. They also acknowledged that the processes encouraged open communications as well as teamwork. However, they were uncertain that all LRMP participants had a clear understanding of the varying stakeholders' interests at the planning tables.

Process Power Balance Tourism respondents expressed ambivalence concerning the extent to which the processes had been able to effectively address potential power imbalances at the LRMP planning tables. They agreed that the process staff acted in a neutral and unbiased fashion. They also felt that the LRMP participants had opportunities to adjust the process as needed. However, they were ambivalent concerning how committed the LRMP participants were to making the SDM process work. They felt that LRMP participants were still primarily accountable to their constituents for the decisions they made.

Tourism Perspectives on LRMP Process Outcomes

Tourism stakeholders were asked for their opinions concerning the outcomes associated with participating in LRMP planning processes. In particular, their views were examined regarding the extent to which the processes produced satisfactory LRMP outcomes, helped reduce conflict, as well as increased social capital and other beneficial second-order effects.

Satisfaction with LRMP Outcomes

Tourism respondents reported several beneficial effects associated with the use of LRMP processes. Overall, they expressed clear agreement that the processes used in the development of the LRMPs provided the best way of developing such plans. More specifically they felt that the LRMP procedures used: represented an effective method for making land use decisions, generated creative ideas for action, and served the public interest.

On a more personal level, they suggested that they their involvement in the process was a positive experience and that they would be willing to get involved in similar processes in future. They also agreed that their organizations' needs had been better accommodated through the LRMP processes than would have been the case under other planning approaches.

Despite their positive views on the worth of the LRMP processes, respondents were not convinced of the value of the end results generated. On average, the tourism stakeholders expressed only marginal agreement that the LRMP processes had been a success. In this regard, they were undecided as to whether or not the processes had actually provided: satisfactory LRMP outcomes, a clear strategy for plan implementation, and a shared commitment to plan implementation. They were even less certain that the resulting LRMPs had actually addressed the specific concerns of the tourism industry. Tourism stakeholder views on all of these outcomes were statistically similar ([varies]=0.05) to the collective perspectives of all other nontourism respondents in this study except with respect to the worth of LRMP approaches in land use planning contexts. In that case, tourism stakeholders were significantly more convinced ([varies]=0.05) that LRMP processes were the best way of developing such land use plans.

Conflict Reduction

Tourism respondents generally agreed that the processes employed in the development of the LRMPs helped to reduce potential conflicts. This agreement was strongest with respect to the role such processes played in improving respondents' understanding of the interests of other participants, and building better working relationships with other LRMP members. They also felt that the processes helped to build stronger relationships among other LRMP table members, as well as to change the behaviours of some of these stakeholders. However, they were undecided as to whether the processes had actually decreased conflict over land uses.

Social Capital and Second-Order Benefits

Beyond the direct outcomes generated through the use of LRMP processes, the tourism stakeholders suggested several other indirect effects associated with the application of these planning approaches. In particular, they felt that as a result of the processes they had developed a stronger awareness of: their region, government land use management responsibilities, and contacts important to themselves and their constituents.

They also agreed that the information they had acquired would be of value to them and their tourism organizations in the future. Indeed, they indicated that they had already used some of this information for purposes beyond the LRMPs. However, they were less certain about the existence of any spin-off partnerships or new collaborative activities that had occurred as a result of these processes.

SDM Success Factors

Based on their past involvement in LRMP planning programs, tourism respondents reported their views on the importance of specific factors in generating successful collaborative planning processes and outcomes. In particular, the importance of various aspects of stakeholder inclusion, process management, and process design was examined.

Stakeholder Inclusion

Tourism respondents strongly agreed that several internally and externally focused inclusion factors were important to the success of SDM processes. From an internal decision making perspective, they rated the inclusion of all relevant stakeholders, and the presence of mutual respect and trust amongst these groups as being essential to the ultimate success of SDM processes. They also felt that it was important that participating groups have a clear understanding, not only of their own interests, but also the interests of the other stakeholders. They believed that developing such understanding was dependent on not only all groups having access to high quality information, but also possessing equal availability of support resources for data collection and planning purposes. Tourism stakeholders placed significantly more importance ([varies]=0.05) on the availability of such support resources than did their non-tourism LRMP counterparts. From an external support perspective, the tourism respondents felt that ensuring the process was accountable and open to the public, as well as to stakeholder constituents was imperative. They felt that a commitment to both the internal and external flow of information and ideas was especially important the success of these processes.

Process Management

Tourism respondents were clear that having an effective management process in place was critical to the success of SDM planning initiatives. From their perspective, the management tools and mechanisms needed to ensure success included: clear rules and procedures, a clearly defined purpose and objectives, and a requirement for achieving consensus agreements.

They felt such processes worked best when there were clearly defined timelines for reaching agreements, and the alternatives of not doing so were clearly understood. They placed significantly more importance ([varies]=0.05) than their nontourism counterparts on the use of independent facilitators or mediator to effectively manage such processes.

Process Design

Tourism respondents firmly supported SDM processes that were designed to ensure that the plans developed were implemented and monitored. They also felt that it was very important to select participants who were committed to making the SDM processes work. They expressed significantly more agreement ([varies]=0.05) on the need for this factor than their nontourism counterparts. Despite believing that clear guidelines were needed for the management of such processes, they also firmly felt that the process designs should be flexible and adaptive, and based on voluntary participation.

Management Implications

The preceding findings reveal that tourism stakeholders were generally satisfied with the way that SDM processes facilitated their involvement in the development of British Columbia's LRMPs. However, they also identified areas where these processes could be strengthened to generate more positive and lasting results for tourism stakeholders. Their suggestions are reflected in the following recommendations.

* Increase Support for Stakeholder Participation For tourism stakeholders to play ongoing and contributive roles in current and future LRMP-related programs, they must receive greater support from government agents. Such support might be provided not only in the form of financial resources to subsidize participants for the time and energy taken from normal business activities, but also in the form of high quality technical and research support. Such support would provide the incentive for

stakeholders to participate more robustly in such decision making processes.

* Increase Equity in Stakeholder Participation To address perceived imbalances in the representation of tourism interests in LRMP processes, ensure that this sector's representation is equivalent to that of other resource sectors. As with forestry, the tourism industry has a variety of stakeholder groups with distinct interests related to land use as well as several areas of common concern. When selecting sector representatives, process facilitators should include enough tourism representatives to reflect the varying land use needs of this diverse industry. Depending on the planning context, potential participants might include stakeholders associated with urban, back country, cultural, and nature-based tourism. Of course, decisions concerning the number of tourism representatives to be included should be balanced with those assigned to other interest groups. This approach would help to address real and perceived power imbalances in LRMP planning.
* Provide More Training to Process Participants While the tourism stakeholders supported the use of collaborative processes in LRMPs, they were not necessarily satisfied with the outcomes that were produced for their constituents. Being able to persuasively present the "tourism case" in an SDM context requires considerable skill and high quality information. More specialized training in communication, data interpretation, problem solving, and negotiation would help tourism stakeholders to more effectively shape the outcomes of LRMP processes.
* Encourage Stakeholder Participation in LRMP Implementation Tourism stakeholders invested considerable time and energy in the development of their LRMPs. Through this involvement they developed an in-depth appreciation of the context and intent of their LRMP's management directives. At the same time they expressed some skepticism concerning the extent to which the directives established in LRMPs might

eventually be implemented. Resources should be provided to facilitate the ongoing involvement of these tourism stakeholders in the implementation and monitoring phases of such planning programs. In this manner the legacy of ideas, perspectives, and intents—which participants in the planning processes created—can be maintained and consistently interpreted during the LRMP implementation phases.

Conclusions

This research suggests that tourism stakeholders believe SDM principles and guidelines have been incorporated into LRMP processes, and that this is generating a range of positive outcomes for the public at large. They also feel that the growing inclusiveness of these processes is opening the door for greater integration of tourism interests and values in the outcomes produced. For instance, despite having access to limited training, financial, and technical support, these stakeholders convinced their respective LRMP planning tables to designate an increased level of land and resources to tourism uses. Tourism values are also more prominently reflected in the overriding management directives that drive the long-term implementation of many LRMPs.

As a result of these recent land use triumphs, and the unfavourable outcomes for tourism associated with previous planning approaches, it is not surprising that tourism stakeholders believe that engagement in these SDM driven processes is "the best way to go." Indeed, tourism stakeholders express optimism for the outcomes these processes can create and a real interest in participating in future endeavours of this type.

Despite their stated commitment to making such processes work, tourism stakeholders are generally not satisfied with the extent to which the LRMP outcomes to date have met the needs of their constituents. They express considerable ambivalence concerning how well their voices are being heard and understood by their non tourism planning counterparts. Consequently, they suggest that future SDM processes must place added emphasis on creating mechanisms that heighten stakeholder awareness and appreciation of their tourism values. Such mechanisms involve creating communication systems that facilitate both internal and external information sharing.

While SDM approaches are perceived to be a useful vehicle for increasing the voice and influence of tourism interests in the province's LRMP decisions, many tourism respondents are also concerned that their hard-won, land-use management advances will not necessarily be secure in subsequent implementation programs. They express this concern in the reality of ongoing cutbacks in government staff and resources allocated to managing the implementation of the LRMPs. They are particularly concerned that, outside of these LRMPs, few land use policy instruments exist that are capable of securing tourism's ongoing presence on B.C.'s Crown lands. Many of them feel the need for ongoing SDM processes that will ensure the integration of tourism values in future implementation programs associated with LRMPs.

6

Management of Hospitality Marketing

The marketing mix-the 4 Ps-target audience-segmentation-objectives-evaluation. These and other terms are all used in the process of "marketing." In tourism and tourism related industries, success means understanding this process. This bulletin is designed for those in the tourism industry who may not be completely familiar with marketing or who may simply wish to refresh their basic marketing skills. Covered will be important concepts used in marketing, the relationship of marketing to tourism, and a process for developing a marketing plan for tourism/recreation businesses and/or communities. It will be impossible to cover in detail all the aspects of marketing within the scope of this bulletin. There are, however, other bulletins in this series that will provide more in-depth information on the different components of a marketing plan.

What is Marketing

People hold a variety of misconceptions about marketing. Most common is its confusion with selling and advertising. Selling and advertising are actually types of promotion which is only a component of marketing. Marketing involves much more, including product/service development, place (location and distribution), and pricing. It requires information about people, especially those interested in what you have to offer (your "market"), such as what they like, where they buy and how much they spend. Its role is to match the right product or service with the right market or audience. Marketing, as you will see, is an art and a science. According to the American Marketing Association, marketing is "the process of planning and executing the conception, pricing, promotion, and distribution of ideas, goods, and services to create exchanges that satisfy individual and organizational objectives." Simply stated it is creating and promoting a product (ideas, goods or services) that satisfies a customer's need or desire and is available at a desirable price and place. Modern marketing is a way of doing business, heavily based on the "marketing concept" which holds that businesses and organizations should:

(1) design their products/services to meet customer needs and wants;

(2) focus on those people most likely to buy their product rather than the entire mass market; and

(3) develop marketing efforts that fit into their overall business objectives.

By adopting this concept you not only provide your customers with better products, you will avoid wasting valuable time and money developing and promoting a product or service nobody wants.

Recreation and Tourism Marketing

Earlier it was mentioned that a product can be "ideas, goods, or services." Since tourism is primarily a service based industry, the principal products provided by recreation/tourism (R/T) businesses are recreational experiences and hospitality. These are intangible products and more difficult to market than tangible products such as automobiles. The intangible nature of services makes quality control difficult but crucial. It also makes it more difficult for potential customers to evaluate and compare service offerings. In addition, instead of moving the product to the customer, the customer must travel to the product (area/ community). Travel is a significant portion of the time and money spent in association with recreational and tourism experiences and is a major factor in people's decisions on whether or not to visit your business or community. As an industry, tourism has many components comprising the overall "travel experience." Along with transportation, it includes such things as accommodations, food and beverage services, shops, entertainment, aesthetics and special events. It is rare for one business to provide the variety of activities or facilities tourists need or desire. This adds to the difficulty of maintaining and controlling the quality of the experience. To overcome this hurdle, tourism related businesses, agencies, and organizations need to work together to package and promote tourism opportunities in their areas and align their efforts to assure consistency in product quality.

The Marketing Plan

One of the most important steps a business or community can take to improve the effectiveness and efficiency of their marketing efforts is to develop a written marketing plan. This plan will guide their marketing decisions and assist them in allocating marketing resources such as money and personnel time. The plan should include:

(1) the overall business objectives—what you want to accomplish;

(2) an assessment of the market environment—what factors may affect your marketing efforts;

(3) a business/community profile—what resources are available,

(4) market identification (segmentation)—the specific groups or clientele most interested in your product;

(5) the marketing objectives for each segment;

(6) the marketing strategies (or mixes) for different markets you target—the best combination of the 4 Ps (product, price, place, promotion) for each segment;

(7) an implementation plan—how to "make it work;"

(8) the marketing budget-how much you have to spend; and

(9) a method for evaluation and change.

A framework which can be used to develop a marketing plan. Each component will be briefly discussed in the remainder of the bulletin. For more information regarding different components of the plan be sure to consult other bulletins in this series.

Overall Business Objectives

Businesses, agencies, and communities should develop overall objectives and regularly monitor their progress. The objectives should provide guidance for all decisions including finances, personnel and marketing.

They should be quantitative and measurable statements of what the business or community wants to accomplish over a specified period of time.

Business objectives are often stated in terms of sales, profits, market shares and/or occupancy rates. Communities frequently establish objectives relating to such things as increasing the number of tourists, developing or changing their image, facility and activity development, cooperation among tourism related businesses and increasing length of stay and local expenditures.

It is important that the objectives be reasonable given the market conditions and the firm's or organization's resources. Establish a few reasonable objectives instead of a long, unrealistic "wish list." This is especially true for new businesses or communities which do not have much experience in tourism development and/or marketing.

Market Environment Analysis

The next step in developing a marketing plan is to assess the impact of environmental factors (such as economic, social and political) on present and future markets. Changes in these factors can create marketing opportunities as well as problems.

Demographic and Lifestyle Trends

Changing demographics and lifestyles are having a major impact on R/T participation. An assessment of these trends is important to understand how they will likely affect your business or community. Some of the important trends that bear watching:

(1) population growth and movement;

(2) rural community growth compared to metropolitan areas;

(3) number of adult women employed outside the home;

(4) the number of households is growing, especially non family and single parent households, but family size is decreasing;

(5) the impact of two wage earner households on real family income;

(6) the number of retired persons with the financial ability to travel;

(7) better health to an older age; and

(8) continued aging of the population (we are becoming a middle aged society).

Economic Conditions

Overall economic conditions can have significant impacts on recreation and tourism markets. A marketing strategy that is effective during periods of low unemployment rates may have to be significantly adjusted if unemployment increases.

Businesses and communities should monitor and assess the likely impact of factors such as unemployment rates, real family income, rate of inflation, credit availability, terms and interest rates. Consideration should also be given to the prices of complementary products, such as lodging, gasoline and recreation equipment.

Laws and Government Actions

As a complex industry, tourism is significantly affected both positively and negatively by laws and by actions of governmental agencies. For instance, rulings on such things as liability issues or decisions regarding building and health codes may change or possibly prevent the construction of a proposed facility. If a public facility changes the prices of its services, this could affect the service offerings of associated private businesses. These actions may have both positive and negative effects on the marketing efforts of the business and community. To avoid wasting valuable resources it is important that R/T businesses, agencies, and communities continually monitor and evaluate governmental actions.

Technology

Technological developments are increasing rapidly. New

recreation products, such as all-terrain vehicles and wind surfers, provide new ways for people to satisfy their recreational preferences. New production technologies and materials offer recreation and tourism businesses ways to reduce costs and improve the quality of their products/services. Advances in telecommunications have and will continue to create new promotional opportunities. Technological innovations, in relation to jobs and the home, have resulted in increased leisure time for many people.

Competition

Businesses and communities must identify and analyse existing and potential competitors. The objective of the analysis is to determine the strengths and weaknesses of the competition's marketing strategies. The analysis should include the competition's:

(1) product/service features and quality;

(2) location relative to different geographic markets;

(3) promotional themes and messages;

(4) prices; and

(5) type of customer they are attracting.

Business and Community Profiles

Too many communities attempt to market themselves as tourist destinations without accurate information about their resources (facilities, services, staff), image (projected vs. Actual), and how well their customers are satisfied. Without this information, it is difficult to make other decisions in the planning process. Included should be such things as recreational and entertainment facilities, cultural and historic sites, overnight accommodations, restaurants, shopping opportunities, special events and activities, staff size, and transportation. Each item of the "inventory" should also be assessed in terms of quality and availability.

Market Segmentation (Identification)

Recreation and tourism businesses and communities often make the mistake of attempting to be all things to all people. It is difficult, and risky, to develop marketing strategies for the mass market. Strategies designed for the "average" customer often result in unappealing products, prices, and promotional messages. For example, it would be difficult to develop a campground that would be equally attractive to recreational vehicle campers and backpackers or promote a property to serve both snow mobilers and nature oriented cross country skiers.

Marketing is strongly based on market segmentation and target marketing. Market segmentation is the process of:

(1) taking existing and/or potential customers/visitors (market) and categorizing them into groups with similar preferences referred to as "market segments;"

(2) selecting the most promising segments as "target markets;" and

(3) designing "marketing mixes," or strategies (combination of the 4 Ps), which satisfy the special needs, desires and behaviour of the target markets.

There is no unique or best way to segment markets, but ways in which customers can be grouped are:

(1) location of residence—instate, out-of-state, local;

(2) demographics—age, income, family status, education;

(3) equipment ownership/use—RV's, sailboats, canoes, tents, snowmobiles;

(4) important product attributes—price, quality, quantity; and

(5) lifestyle attributes—activities, interests, opinions.

To be useful, the segment identification process should result in segments that suggest marketing efforts that will be effective in attracting them and at least one segment large enough to justify specialized marketing efforts. After segments have been identified, the business or community must select the "target markets," those segments which offer them the greatest opportunity. When determining target markets, consideration should be given to:

(1) existing and future sales potential of each segment;

(2) the amount and strength of competition for each segment;

(3) the ability to offer a marketing mix which will be successful in attracting each segment;

(4) the cost of servicing each segment; and

(5) each segment's contribution to accomplishing overall business/community objectives. It is often wiser to target smaller segments that are presently not being served, or served inadequately, than to go after larger segments for which there is a great deal of competition.

Marketing Objectives for each Segment

Marketing objectives which contribute to the accomplishment of the overall business objectives should be established for each target market. Objectives serve a number of functions including:

(1) guidance for developing marketing mixes for different target markets;

(2) information for allocating the marketing budget between target markets;

(3) a basis for objectively evaluating the effectiveness of the marketing mixes (setting standards); and

(4) a framework for integrating the different marketing mixes into the overall marketing plan.

The target market objectives should:

(1) be expressed in quantitative terms;

(2) be measurable;

(3) specify the target market; and

(4) indicate the time period in which the objective is to be accomplished.

For example, increase the number of overnight stays by people from the Chicago market over the next two years by five percent. Remember, rank objectives by priority and carefully evaluate them to ensure that they are reasonable given the strength of the competition and resources available for marketing.

Marketing Strategy (Mix)

The marketing strategy, or mix, should be viewed as a

package of offerings designed to attract and serve the customer or visitor. Recreation and tourism businesses and communities should develop both external and internal marketing mixes for different target markets.

External Mix

The external marketing mix includes product/service, price, place/location, and promotion.

Product

Earlier we said the principal products that recreation and tourism businesses provide are recreational experiences and hospitality.

The factors that create a quality recreational experience often differ among people. A quality experience for one skier might include an uncrowded, steep slope. To another it might be a good restaurant and a chance to socialize. Decisions on what facilities, programs and services to provide should be based on the needs and desires of the target market(s). They should not be based on the preferences of the owner/manager or necessarily on what the competition is providing.

Recognize that a recreational/tourism experience includes five elements: trip planning and anticipation; travel to the site/area; the experience at the site; travel back home; and recollection. Businesses should look for ways to enhance the quality of the overall experience during all phases of the trip.

This could be accomplished by providing trip planning packages which include maps, attractions en route and on site, and information regarding lodging, food and quality souvenirs and mementos.

Recreation and tourism businesses should also view their service/product in generic terms. Thinking of products/services in this manner helps focus more attention on the experiences desired by customers and also the facilities, programs and services that will produce those experiences. For example, campgrounds are the business of providing recreational "lodging" not just campsites to park an RV or set up a tent. Marinas should provide recreational "boating" experiences, not just slippage.

Location and Accessibility—Place

Too many tourism businesses and communities fail to recognize their role in improving travel to and from their areas. They focus instead on servicing the customer once they arrive at the site/community. A bad experience getting to or leaving an R/T site can adversely affect a person's travel experience. Ways to help prevent this include:

(1) providing directions and maps;

(2) providing estimates of travel time and distances from different market areas;

(3) recommending direct and scenic travel routes;

(4) identifying attractions and support facilities along different travel routes; and

(5) informing potential customers of alternative travel methods to the area such as airlines and railroads.

Potential businesses should also carefully assess alternative locations for:

(1) distance and accessibility to target markets;

(2) location of competitors with respect to target markets;

(3) modes of travel serving the area; and

(4) other attractions and activities that might induce travel to the area.

Pricing Price is one of the most important and visible elements of the marketing mix. When setting prices it is important to take into consideration all of the following:

(1) business and target market objectives;

(2) the full cost of producing, delivering and promoting the product;

(3) the willingness of the target market to pay for the product or service you provide;

(4) prices charged by competitors offering a similar product/service to the same target market(s);

(5) the availability and prices of substitute products/services;

(6) the economic climate (local and national); and

(7) the possibility of stimulating high profit products/services (such as boats) by offering related services (such as maintenance) at or below cost.

When establishing prices, R/T businesses should give attention to pricing strategies which may encourage off season and non-peak period sales, longer stays, group business, and the sale of package plans (combination of room, meals, and recreational facilities). For additional information on pricing, see Extension bulletin E-1999.

Promotion

Promotion provides target audiences with accurate and timely information to help them decide whether to visit your community or business. The information should be of importance and practical use to the potential or existing visitor and also accurate.

Misrepresentation often leads to dissatisfied customers and poor recommendations. Don't make claims you cannot live up to. Developing a promotional campaign is not a science with hard and fast rules. Making decisions regarding which type or combination of promotion types to use (personal selling, advertising, sales promotions, or publicity) is not always easy. If, however, you follow a logical process and do the necessary research, chances for success will be improved. It will be necessary to make decisions regarding:

(1) Target audience—the group you are aiming at;

(2) Image—that which your community or business wants to create or reinforce;

(3) Objectives—those of the promotional campaign;

(4) Budget—the amount of money available for your promotion;

(5) Timing—when and how often should your promotions appear;

(6) Media—which methods (television, radio, newspaper, magazine) will most effectively and efficiently communicate your message to the target audience; and

(7) Evaluation—how can the effectiveness of the promotional campaign be determined.

More detailed information on tourism promotion is contained in Extension bulletins E-1939, E-1957, and E-2005.

Internal Mix

As stated, marketing services such as recreation and tourism differ from marketing tangible products. Recreation and tourism businesses must direct as much attention at marketing to customers on site as they do to attracting them. In this respect, internal marketing is important because dissatisfied customers can effectively cancel out an otherwise effective marketing strategy.

The success of internal marketing is dependent on creating an atmosphere in which employees desire to give good service and sell the business/community to visitors. To create such an atmosphere requires the following four important elements:

(1) Hospitality and Guest Relations—An organization wide emphasis on hospitality and guest relations, including a customer oriented attitude on the part of the owners and managers as well as the employees. If the owner/manager is not customer sensitive, it is unlikely the lower paid employees will be.

(2) Quality Control—A program which focuses on improving both the technical quality (the standards associated with what the customer receives) and the functional quality (the standards associated with how the customer receives the service). All employees who come into contact with customers should receive hospitality training.

(3) Personal Selling—Training the staff in the selling aspects of the property (business) or community. This also includes rewarding them for their efforts. By being informed about the marketing objectives, and their role in accomplishing those objectives, they can help increase sales.

(4) Employee Morale—Programs and incentives aimed at maintaining employee morale. The incentives can be both monetary and nonmonetary.

A customer oriented atmosphere usually results in customers that are more satisfied, do less complaining and are more pleasant to serve. This helps build employee morale, their desire to provide good service and their efficiency.

Marketing Budget

Successful marketing requires that sufficient money and personnel time be made available to implement activities comprising the marketing strategy. A marketing budget is a financial plan which shows the total amount to be spent on marketing during different times of the year and how it is to be allocated among alternative activities. Separate marketing budgets should be developed for each marketing mix strategy. The separate budgets should then be aggregated to develop an overall marketing budget. If the total amount is too great it will be necessary to modify the overall objectives and the target market objectives, narrow down or drop target markets, or adjust marketing mixes. The final budget should be realistic given your objectives. When deciding on a marketing budget, consideration should be given to the job that needs to be done as defined by the objectives. Basing marketing budgets on some percent of sales or what the competition spends usually leads to over spending or under spending. Decisions should also be based on the costs, projected revenues, and desired profitability of different activities, not just costs alone. Successful marketing activities will generate additional revenues which can be projected based on the marketing objectives (such as increase off season stay by 5%).

Although budgets should be viewed as flexible plans, every effort should be made to adhere to them. Revisions in the budget should only be made after careful consideration of the likely impact of the change on the marketing mix and accomplishment of your objectives.

Implementation

Many well designed marketing plans fail because they are poorly executed. Businesses, agencies, and communities can increase the likelihood of successful implementation if they:

(1) Identify specific tasks which must be accomplished;

(2) Assign people or departments specific responsibility for different tasks;

(3) Provide employees with information on the marketing plan (rationale, objectives, strategies);

(4) Develop time lines and deadlines;

(5) Adhere as much as possible to the budget; and

(6) Regularly monitor and evaluate progress.

Evaluation

It is important that marketing efforts be continually evaluated. This will improve the effectiveness of marketing strategies by quickly identifying differences between actual results and expected performance and determining likely reasons for the success or failure to realize objectives.

A framework for evaluation would include:

(1) Determining which elements of the different marketing mixes are most important to evaluate.——It is rarely possible or cost effective to evaluate all elements;

(2) Establishing performance standards to compare against actual results.—Marketing objectives, if properly formulated, should serve as performance standards;

(3) Development of formal and informal methods for collecting data on actual results.—There are many ways different elements of the marketing mix can be evaluated. For example, promotions can be evaluated with money off coupons. Special information request forms, telephone numbers to call or post office box numbers to write to can identify the area the request is coming from. Also, formal (written) and informal (face-to-face) surveys can be used to determine the promotional material the customer used in planning the trip;

(4) Comparison of results with objectives;

(5) Determination of needed change(s).

Customer satisfaction in tourism is greatly influenced by the way in which the service (hospitality) is delivered and the physical appearance and personality of the business. It is critical that these elements be communicated in the best possible manner to convince people to come and experience what your business or community has to offer. Equally important is the ability to generate repeat business because of your efforts. Thus, marketing becomes the method to reach potential visitors. It is a vital part of tourism management and can be done effectively and well, with sophistication and tact, or it can be done poorly in a loud, crass and intrusive manner. Hopefully, this bulletin has given you the basics for the former rather than the latter. Remember that to do an effective job at marketing:

(1) Adopt a strong customer orientation which includes regular research and assessment of their needs, wants and attitudes;
(2) Allocate sufficient resources and time to marketing;
(3) Assign formal responsibility for marketing to one person or department; and
(4) Develop and regularly update a marketing plan.

Information Supply in Tourism Management

Operators in tourism management, compared to other management sectors, are confronted with a vast field of complex aims, requiring different plans of action. The special working requirements of the services sector are a result of its business peculiarities. Problems instrategic, and frequently operational planning, are characterized by their complexity, often being intermingled, non-transparent, individualistically dynamic and requiring the achievement of multiple goals. The vast amount of information or complex weighting of the different sectors can present an insurmountable problem for human resources. As are sult there are high expectations of decision-makers' trouble-shooting abilities.

In order to solve complex problems, decision-makers need to have a factual knowledge of the industry (declarative knowledge) and the methodology used (procedural knowledge). The wealth of knowledge is drawn from two pools; that obtained from the "storage" of already existing experiences, and by generating knowledge in the respective field. Com-bining these two pools creates an arena for problem solving.

Declarative Knowledge – Decision Basis in Tourism Planning

Currently, information gains more and more importance, leading legitimately to the development of a fourth economic sector – the information sector. Information also plays a vital role in tourism for entrepreneurs and managers who spend the whole day involved in information processing. In the tourism industry there is no lack of market research data, on the contrary, there is a rather uncontrolled growth of various data sources, each having different survey purposes and survey designs. Tourism surveys of national and international market research institutes are published in ever shorter intervals and the level of itemization of market data increases rapidly. Information collected by these means has indicated data which can be organized into the following groups:

1. Information on markets and environment,
2. Information on customer behaviour,
3. Information on competition in the industry, and
4. Internal information for executive boards.

The first three information groups are predominantly non-discretionary from a manager's point of view as the information can very rarely be directly influenced by an individual company. Information from these groups are similar in nature and scope for most sectors represented in the tourism industry (hotel trade, restaurant trade, tour operators, travel agents, common carriers, pressure groups, etc.). In the fourth group however, there is a larger scope for variety. Due to high costs for primary market research many tourism managers abandon market research in general. Even the larger businesses and tourism organizations lack market research departments and employees rarely work exclusively on market research items. This results again in an inconsistent development of marketing aims and strategies, as businesses as often as not grope in the dark for their direction.

In Europe the most frequent or highly recognized of the commissioned tourism studies are either publicly financed, directly by national or local authorities, or indirectly by government agencies. This method of procuring market research, is important and often a condition for its development, as the expensive primary studies cannot be financed by the numerous small or medium-scale businesses. The resulting obligation to pass on information, created by the above mentioned research financing, has lead to a wider search-inregional tourism organizations, and other bodies representing tourism-to find means of successfully sharing and communicating information.

Traditional data resources in tourism market research are reports, records and statistics which may be presented either in printed format or are electronically driven (CD-ROM). Computer-based information systems (databases) are currently a rarity, but usually can be found either in connection with the official statistical data of a country or a region or international institutions. The information available by this method is rarely used since it ignores the special information requirements of the end-user (managers), or is simply inaccessible due to high fees, complicated application procedures or is simply not user friendly.

The lack of practical relevance, of these information systems, can be explained by their bias toward representing the economic interest of the sponsors and data collectors and/or by the universal requirements the systems have to meet in the collection, storage and search of statistical data from other industries. Market research results are mainly available in print and they can be obtained either in bookshops, online or directly from the author. From the consumer's perspective this way of passing on secondary information has a number of disadvantages:

- Due to the complex design of market research reports the surveyed data is not up to date any more.
- Data from different sources cannot be easily compared especially if it has been surveyed for different purposes.
- Information contained in reports is often of limited relevance for the particular problem.
- Presentation of data is either not detailed enough, not significant enough, or supplementary information is missing which prevents a faultless interpretation of results.
- Often only very specific data from a more comprehensive study is required and thus the cost-benefit-ratio becomes unattractive.

There is usually an overabundance of available information leaving managers to cope with determining which is the best source. Often the entrepreneur has to rely on external consultants and market research specialists resulting in additional costs.

Procedural Knowledge – Decision Basis in Tourism Planning

"The big problem with management science models is that managers practically never used them." More than 20 years ago John Little described the discrepancy between the scientific development of planning instruments, models, level of itemization and the fact that, when available, the knowledge gathered is rarely put into practice. This is caused by the numerous, often poorly documented assumptions of model architects, which was denoted as model plutonism by Hans Albert. As a response to this problem Little suggested that the manager is included in the model. He postulated in his article on the Decision Calculus, aniline models with the following features: robustness, ease of control, simplicity, completeness of relevant detail and suitability for communication.

The communication problem is of vital importance in the every day life of managers' daily events. It is still common practice to employ various levels of change rather than continue-ally observe the changes in market share and volume. Many entrepreneurs do not even know terms such as market segmentation or market positioning and they do not regard them as essential. They keep on looking for measures to expand seasonal business but lack knowledge of methods that will measure their success. Corporate planning only takes place if external financing is required and supporting documents have to be submitted to the lender. Heuristic forecasting methods are hardly ever used, accordingly quantitative methods are never used. Models of strategic market plan-ningportfolio analyses and analyses of the lifestyle of a product-employed in other industries are hardly ever used in tourism management. The grounds for the poor employment of methodological processes in tourism management can be divided into two groups; technological development and insufficient training. Issues related to the technological development of existing information processing and transmission systems are:

- Data required for the application of tourism models is either not up-to-date or unsuitable.
- Standard software is not able to support the relatively complex tasks in tourism management.
- Specially developed software is too expensive for single tourism businesses. Issues related to the insufficient training of tourism managers are:
- Managers have little knowledge of existing methods or available data.
- Managers are confronted with various data sources and different results and they do not know how to cope with this situation.
- Managers do not know which data sources and models are suitable.

The Transmission of Market Research Data in the Internet

Due to the vital role of tourism in many countries and regions in Europe a number of programs concerning tourism promotion have been installed. Government and private tourism organizations have been established in order to strengthen a tourism destination. Usually the aim is to increase the added value of a region. The major tasks of these bodies are:

- To provide consumers with information about the destination,
- To coordinate and implement sales promotion measures,
- Tourism advertising,
- Support in sales and distribution, and
- To coordinate and implement market research projects.

For most of their tasks (except the coordination and implementation of market research projects) these tourism promoting bodies provide efficient methods. The actual effect of the last item mentioned has been lost in the past due to inefficient instruments relating to the transmission and utilization of declarative and procedural knowledge. Now with the development of cheaper hard-and software many tourism organizations are reconsidering their promotion policy.

In almost all industries systems are being developed in order to support investment and marketing planning. Also the tourism industry has developed decision support systems and the most important applications are: (1) systems supporting marketing decisions in national tourism organizations, (2) travel counselling systems for shipping clerks, (3) systems supporting regional planning regarding the optimal selection of locations in which to invest (4) systems providing tourism portfolio analyses, (5) simulation tools for forecasting travel behaviour in certain regions. In Austria in 1982 the Austrian Society of Applied Research in Tourism (ASART) started a project aiming at the development of a marketing information system for the national tourism organization in Austria (Austrian National Tourist Office). The first version of the tourism marketing information system (TourMIS) consisted of a database installed in a host system of the Scientific Computer Centre Vienna and an optimization programme for the advertising budget of the Austrian National Tourist Office. Though the programmes were adapted in 1991 in favour of PC-software, and hence became accessible for a greater number of people (mainly employees of tourism organizations in the federal provinces), the area-wide information supply for top managers in the tourism industry did not begin until 1999 when the internet version was introduced.

Tourism Marketing Information System

The major aim of Tour MIS is an optimal information supply and decision support for the tourism industry. The first step is to provide aniline tourism survey data, as well as evaluation programmes to transform data into precious management information. Tour-MIS predominantly comprises:

1. A database containing tourism market research data (declarative knowledge),
2. Various program modules (method-base, procedural knowledge) converting acknowledged methods/models into simple surfaces, and
3. Various administrative programmes which assist the maintenance of the database and track and control the information search behaviour of users.

The internet supports the transport and presentation of animated and unanimated pictures, sound and video recordings and text and numerical data and is expandable. A high-performance SQL-database and a functionally designed user interface for Tour MIS based on hypertext and Perl permits the development of interactive applications. The programme modules contained in the method-base are developed according to the specific requirements of tourism managers. The internet offers a number of advantages against the old PC-solution. Since changes in the database have immediate worldwide effect the speed of information transmission can be reduced to the availability of the information source. For example, Tour MIS makes the monthly projections of Statistics Austria available within only a few seconds to all regional managers of the Austrian National Tourist Office regardless of whether they are located in New York, Sydney, Tokyo or Madrid. Anybody provided with access to the internet and entitled to use Tour MIS may access data and information, make calculations or simulations send or receive data – without tiresome postal procedures, danger of loss, delays and costs. All these advantages have led to a significant expansion in the number of users.

Conditions for the use of the System

In the beginning Tour MIS was provided with strict access control and used to be only accessible to certain users. In this respect the application did differ from traditional internet offers. However, the present concept is also not an Intranet. Unlike the Intranet which supports internal information management systems Tour MIS is not owned by a certain organization but is open to all authorized tourism organizations, societies, tourism consultants, companies, tourism training centres, pressure groups, etc. in Austria and abroad. By covering the maintenance costs, a consortium of 12 of the most important initiators of market research projects in Austria (Austrian National Tourist Office, nine provincial tourism organizations, the two special interest associations for Hotel Trade and Restaurant

Trade of the Federal Chamber of Commerce, Federal Ministry for Economic Affairs and Labour Tourism and Recreational Commerce Section) guarantee the continuous updating of the comprehensive database. Since 2000 this initiative has provided the Austrian tourism industry with free access to overall data and functions (with some exceptions) of Tour MIS. The necessary hardware resources are situated at the Institute for Tourism and Leisure Studies at the University of Economics and Business Administration in Vienna where a major part of the necessary maintenance work is carried out.

The Tour MIS Database

In the beginning Tour MIS contained data that was strongly influenced by the internal interests of its commissioner, the Austrian National Tourist Office. In this respect international tourism statistical data, empirical tourism studies and economic indicators for the most important markets of origin for the Austrian tourism industry have been collected in Tour MIS. The PC-version, developed in the early nineties, contained more than 10,000 time series. The periodicity of information was generally based on annual data, however the most significant time series have also been recorded for periods of less than a year. Over the years the database has continually expanded. Due to the increasing importance of overseas markets further information has been required. Unequal needs of provincial tourism organizations led to additional statistics regarding the federal provinces and Vienna, being city and federal province at the same time, acquired an exceptional position. Furthermore data on the Austrian and international city tourism has been added. This information was collected at the branch offices of the Austrian National Tourist Office, transmitted by fax and data was entered manually into the marketing information system in order to be available to users. Later based on international cooperation (European Cities' Tourism, European Travel Commission) the first online maintenance agreements with local tourism organizations were initiated. The most important available data sources of Tour MIS are indicated in. Besides the basic information search functions the method-base has also been continually upgraded. In this respect the system more and more meets the requirements of an efficient decision support tool. In the next paragraphs the most important data sources and the facilities for analysis and reporting are discussed.

National Tourism Statistics Austria

One of the first data sources which was installed in Tour MIS was the official tourism statistics in Austria. Data generated from the registration with accommodation suppliers is one of the fundamental supports of the official inbound tourism statistics in Austria. Accommodation statistics are divided into two different kinds of survey: the accommodation for inbound travel and the accommodation capacity. The data on arrivals and over nights are surveyed for 50 generating countries related to 13 different accommodation types and 1,600 municipalities (= report communities) on a monthly basis.

Thus the official travel survey offers 25 million data points per annum which can be transformed into precious information for tourism managers. From the data material important information on tourism development, trends in markets of origin and accommodation types, evaluation of the competing situation can be derived. For example, for each of the 1,600 municipalities the database allows the user to regularly monitor the development of the average duration of stay, the seasonality, market shares, guest-mix structure, and, in connection with the capacity statistics, the occupancy rate.

Tour MIS presently offers official tourism statistics only at the provincial basis which nevertheless requires maintenance work of 11,700 data sets per month. The necessary data transfer from the host system of Statistic Austria (ISIS) to Tour MIS takes place automatically each time after the arrival of new data segments and in accordance with various maintenance routines.

The information supply of Tour MIS users takes place by means of predominate tables and reports created for the user in real time operations. The content and design of tables or reports plays an important role in the user's perception of the system's usefulness and usability. Only if the information supply meets the users' needs will the system achieve its aim of providing a high-performance usage of market data and improve the information supply in tourism management.

Source Feature Evaluation Period Update Data

Statistic Austria bed nights, arrivals, capacity (suppliers and beds) 50 countries of origin (markets), 13 types of accommodation – for Austria and her 9 provinces since 1960 monthly secondary data in time series format

Austrian Guest Survey 250 variables incl. intention to revisit, guest satisfaction, type of travel, means of transport, duration of stay, travel motive, expenses, selection of accommodation, activities, net income of the household, profession, education, etc. 16 countries of origin (markets) – for Austria and her 9 provinces since 1991 each third year primary data ETC (European Travel Commission) bed nights, arrivals, capacities (beds) 21 countries of origin (markets) – for 33 destinations (countries) in Europe since 1990 annually secondary data in time series format ECT (European Cities' Tourism) bed nights, arrivals, capacities (beds) 21 countries of origin (markets) – for 80 European cities since 1983 annually secondary data in time series format

Number of visitations in Austrian attractions (Austrian National Tourist Office) number of visits for 240 Austrian attractions federal provinces of Austria since 1998 annually secondary data in time series format Austrian Hotel and Restaurant Panel 60 variables incl. net product, fixed and working assets equity and debt capital,, cash flow, profitability-ures, etc. location, size, category and type of business. Since 1982 annually primary data.

- No particular database knowledge is required by the user,
- The data transformations and calculations implemented in the method-base of Tour MIS allow for adequate problem reporting, and
- The user interface refers to a familiar technical terminology.

Especially for the requirements of the managers in the provincial tourism organizations. The table compares the seasonal results of one federal province (Carinthia) with the results of all other federal provinces in Austria. The comparison with the developments in other (competitive) destinations permits an evaluation of the market share development in Carinthia.

The analysis in indicates for example that Carinthia could defend its position regarding the three most important markets

(Germany, Netherlands, Italy), shown in the increase of market shares, despite the fact that Carinthia experienced a severe loss in bed-nights. On the other hand an apparent success regarding the increased demand of American guests (+ 7,7%) has to be put into perspective since the other federal provinces outperformed Carinthia in this segment. Due to the comparative analysis and a simple and informative presentation of the statistics (using sorting features and different colours to distinguish between market share gains (green) and losses (red)) the data material is upgraded. The analysis presented in may be used for historical or current data, for each Austrian province, based either on arrivals or bednights for each of the 13 different accommodation types.

Competitive Analysis for Austrian Regions

The opportunities for implementing tools which use official tourism statistics for bench-marking analyses, the implementation of early warning systems and forecasting tourism trends is obvious. Due to the refinancing interests of data collection authorities and the lack of financial resources in the tourism industry, however, the data analysis for smaller tourism regions or report communities has been prevented in the past. This factor must be regretted since it can be assumed that the evaluation of key success factors in tourism marketing will significantly improve when they are measured in smaller regional units. Also tourism managers, especially those operating on a regional level, usually have only very little influence in the organization of nationwide surveys. Therefore, many of the statistical series are based on administrative regions that are not always congruent with actual regional use and by tourists and subsequent flows.

Number of Visitations in Austrian Attractions

The collection of statistical data on leisure-time activities and especially the measurement of visitor arrivals in attractions is a rather complex project. It is rarely executed internationally on a systematic or continuous basis. The major problems lie in the delimitation of the study object and the methods of measurement. Since the early 90's the Austrian National Tourist Office has collected and distributed information on the visitation numbers in Austrian attractions. In close collaboration with the nine provincial tourism organizations a list of 240 Austrian attractions is checked for completeness and updated on an annual basis.

Number of Visitations in Austrian Attractions

Since 2001 this maintenance procedure is carried out online in Tour MIS. Here the market research specialists at the respective provincial tourism organizations enter their information into the system. Due to the newness of the database the reporting facilities are still very limited. The present tables either provide simple time series for a single attraction or list all attractions for one or more federal province(s) arranged according to frequency of visits.

Austrian Guest Survey

Since 1988 alternating each third year a comprehensive visitor survey in Austria has been carried out. The Austrian Guest Survey is one of the most important sources of information in tourism market research. It provides vital information on guest profiles, customer satisfaction, information and booking behaviour, type of travel, destination, means of transport, accommodation, activities, visitor expenditures and other current topics. The Austrian Guest Survey is financed and coordinated by a consortium of authorities responsible for tourism promotion in Austria (Austrian National Tourist Office and nine provincial tourism organizations), the Chamber of Commerce and the Federal Ministry for Economic Affairs and Labour (Tourism and Recreational Commerce Section). Since the Austrian Guest Survey is a primary study it presents some features which complicate the information diffusion in Tour MIS compared to the above mentioned secondary data sources. The main reasons for these additional difficulties are:

(1) The much wider scope of the study,

(2) The required data analyses are more demanding, and

(3) Interpretation possibilities are limited by the sample size and characteristics.

The Austrian Guest Survey has more than 200 features which are partially modified for each survey. Considering the scope of the study and that only descriptive evaluation is possible the Austrian Guest Survey offers more than 1 million findings per survey. Traditional forms of report (market research report, press releases etc.) cover just a small part of the real investigation and evaluation potential. Thus important questions managers would raise remain unanswered although theoretically the answers exist. Data of primary analyses are available unprocessed (disaggregated data format). Regarding the Austrian Guest Survey there are 10,000 interviews per survey, all of the features being available in quantitative form. However, information processing requires the application of analytical methods ranging from calculating simple mean values to complicated data mining procedures.

The necessary methodological knowledge has to be obtained from statistics experts who create costs which, in most cases, cannot be covered by the tourism industry. Therefore, due to a lack of know-how or lacking financial support, many questions managers raise remain unanswered although data actually would be available. Contrary to a census, as found in official statistics, sample surveys do not integrate all elements of the whole picture into the study. The major aim in statistics is to draw reliable conclusions regarding to the totality from a limited number of elements. The previously mentioned evaluation procedures take more effort and interpretation depends on the features of the sample (sample size and sampling technique).

Automatic Selection of Analysing Methods

In addition the user may select only a certain part of the overall data set for evaluation (i.e. data of a certain province or market). In order to prevent interpretation errors due to unreliability of results, those values based on a small sample are only indicated after informing the user about the problem.

The analysis takes place in real time. Tour MIS provides the facilities to evaluate more than one survey, at the same time offering two alternatives: longitudinal and cross section analyses. The first application informs the tourism manager about changes in the guest behaviour over a specified period of time. Query support is provided by offering only variables surveyed unmodified over the overall selected period of time (i.e. the standard questionnaire programme). The latter application increases the sample size (for 4 surveys more than 45,000 interviews) which makes answers to detailed questions possible (assuming a particular time invariance, of course). This function permits for example reliable results about the share of side expenses of Italian guests in the federal province of Salzburg during a particular season.

Comparison of Hotel and Restaurant Groups

The database supports regional planners and tourism managers in their decisions as well as managers in the hospitality industry. The results of the past 10 years of a project which has been executed by the Austrian Society of Applied Research in Tourism and commissioned by the Austrian Hotel and Restaurant Association situated within the Austrian Federal Chamber of Commerce are presented in Tour MIS. In this project operating data and annual financial statements for hotels and restaurants in Austria are compared on an annual basis. Information collected directly from the businesses with a high level of itemization is supplemented with comprehensive, compressed data stored at cooperative industry related organizations such as the Wirts chafts för derungs institute der Austrian Federal Economic Chamberund Tourism us bank and Bürges Förder ungsbank of the Austrian Federal Ministry of Economic Affair and Labour. In connection with the design and evaluation of continually repeated surveys a number of new approaches for the diagnosis and comparison of industry groups are developed. Tour MIS presently provides the following applications:

- Industry information for more than 1,300 hotels and restaurants per year since 1991.
- Various functions supporting key ratio analyses in the hotel and restaurant industry.
- The chance for hotel and restaurant managers to participate online in the most significant hotel and restaurant panel survey in Austria.

Information about more than 50 different key ratios is provided in the form of arithmetic mean and median values for 30 distinguished industry groups. Within the industry groups additional evaluations for businesses of excellent profitability (best practice enterprises) are available. For the hotel and restaurant panel database Tour MIS users are provided with the following query and analysing facilities:

- Evaluation of a key ratio for all industry groups referring to a certain year.
- Comparison of all key ratios for a particular industry group.
- Development of a key ratio uncovering the main industry developments.
- Benchmarking analysis for a particular hotel or restaurant (only provided when managers are actively participating in the study).

The quality of information based on the results of the survey is strongly influenced by the number of participating businesses. Due to the chance for interaction in the internet the first results may be obtained straight after entering business data. In this context the problem of how to prevent participants from entering incorrect data occurs. Tour MIS offers a number of plausibility controls during data entry and records data in a second, temporary database. At regular intervals experts determine which records are qualified to be stored in the general database.

Analysis of the user Behaviour of Tour MIS

How do we know that we have successfully implemented a system? Researchers have not really agreed on an indicator for successful implementation. One appealing approach is a cost-benefit study. In this evaluation, one totals the costs of developing a system and compares them with the benefits resulting form the system. In theory, this sounds like a good indicator of success, but in practice it is difficult to provide meaningful estimates. Obtaining the cost side of the ratio is not too much of a problem if adequate records are kept during the development of the system. However, an evaluation of the benefits of a computer-based information system is difficult. How can the value of improved information processing be measured? With transactions processing and some operational control systems, it is usually possible to show tangible savings. For example, many transactions systems have resulted in increased productivity in processing paperwork without a proportional increase in cost. Operational control systems, such as those used to control inventories in large hotels and restaurants, may reduce inventory balances, saving storage and investment costs while maintaining existing service levels. For systems that aid a decision maker, it is much more difficult to estimate the benefits.

For a marketing information system, like Tour MIS, use of the system is voluntary. A manager or other user receives a report but does not have to use the information on it or

1. Council of the European Union, Council Directive 95/97/ EEC of 23 November 1995 on the collection of statistical information in the field of tourism, Official Journal. L291 of 6 December 1995.
2. Commission of the European Communities Report to the Council, the European Parliament, the Economic and Social Committee and the Committee of Regions on the Application of the Directive of the Council 95/97/EEC on the compilation of statistical data in the field of tourism, 17 January 2001, even read the report.

In particular systems that provide aniline retrieval of information from a database can be classified as voluntary since the use of such a system is frequently at the discretion of the user. For this type of system where use is voluntary, it is generally accepted that high levels of use is a sign of successful implementation. In this case the economic or personal success of its users is indirectly measured by the frequency of usage. Several authors have shown that the frequency of usage is determined by the perceived usefulness (textual component) and the ease of use (technical component).

The acceptance of Tour MIS can be determined by means of constantly updated and aniline available access statistics. Contrary to other internet applications the accesses to websites is not counted but the number of virtually answered queries is. Results of the Tour MIS statistics are therefore not influenced by website characteristics (number of graphics or distortions due to the application of window techniques), but do represent the 'genuine user acceptance'. In addition, the comprehensive protocol system permits the analysis of queries broken down into various user groups, information sources and the type of query.

The community of Tour MIS users has continually developed. In 1998 there were only 50 registered users at the Austrian National Tourist Office and at the end of 2001 more than 1,000 registered Tour MIS users have been counted. The distribution of user groups indicates that Tour MIS is not only favoured by tourism managers (44.6%), but also by employees, students and pupils of education and research institutes (31.6% of all queries) and other non-tourism professionals or private persons (23.8%). The distribution of various user groups is present. The average number of queries per user in 2001 and therefore indicates the frequency of use for a specific Tour MIS user group. The employees of provincial tourism organizations use Tour-MIS most (92 queries per user) due to the comprehensive data material available on the federal provinces. The students, as the largest user group, show a relatively low number due to only temporal interest (for a seminar paper or a diploma thesis they need access to data material only once). The number of accommodation providers and F&B managers using the system is, considering the number of existing businesses, very low. A reason for this is probably that the most interesting information source for this user group (the Austrian hotel and restaurant panel database) is a relatively new data set that is simply not known by the managers. Overall, 34.538 queries have been processed in 2001, signifying an increase of 35.5% in comparison to the previous year (25,492 queries).

About half of all queries are made regarding the official tourism statistics in Austria. The industry appears to be very interested in the development of the major markets of origin and accommodation types in the federal provinces (on average approx. 50 queries per day). Regarding the official statistics for Austria most queries are made in connection with information concerning monthly statistics (20% of all queries). The international data sources ECT and ETC gained 18.7% respectively and they rank behind the official Austrian statistics. The significant increase of queries regarding these two international data sources as well as the tendency towards English queries, however, indicate a growing international interest in Tour MIS.

The assessment of demand of information certainly needs a more detailed investigation than simply monitoring the current use of market research resources. However, in Tour-MIS 'demand of information' not only refers to the principal (statistical) sources, but also to the sort of data transformations (analysis) and formats of automatically generated reports available to the users. The functional characteristics and the design of the system have always been developed in close collaboration with the affected managers. For instance, concerning the development of the decision support tools part of the international data sources in the system, the developers have met more than 20 times in form of working group meetings and seminars with representatives (CEOs and research directors) of European Cities Tourism and the European Travel Commission. The involvement of the managers in the design and operation of the information system resulted in favourable user attitudes and perceptions of the information system and led to higher levels of use. In the beginning only a few members were able and willing to actively contribute to this project by entering their data on a regular basis. Today, more than 100 managers working in different tourism destination marketing organizations, based in more than 30 different European countries, and speaking more than 15 different languages, are obviously convinced by the significance of the project and the value of the system as they regularly and voluntarily enter their data into the system.

Generally speaking tourism managers benefit from access to the internet in two ways: the internet provides the opportunity to communicate and serves as a platform for new distribution channels. The present article does not deal with new distribution channels and new booking systems in the tourism industry. This undoubtedly important topic has been discussed in an number of publications and symposia. The present article introduced Tour MIS, an aniline accessible decision support tool for tourism and hospitality management which has been successfully used by more than 1,000 users for three years. According to Ritchie and Ritchie for the development of an industry supported destination marketing information system, information must be both generally accessible and widely advertised so that managers are aware of the benefits it offers.

In lieu of a more preferable cost-benefit analysis, the success of Tour MIS was analysed by studying actual system use observed from various log files generated by the system. The merits of this form of evaluation lie in the objectivity of the findings, the cost-effective procedure, and the comparability of the estimates when the analysis are performed on a regular basis.

The major reason for the poor application of management science models and methodologies in tourism management is the insufficient education of practitioners and the inadequacy of problem solving features of standard software solutions. The development of simple, affordable (shareware) programs, downloadable for every tourism manager, is the first step into a new era of dialogue between research and practice. Within a short time, for internal diagnosis, forecasts and simulations on the net there will be high-performance computer languages available which are now being developed by major international software producers.

Technological progress will also offer benefits for the electronic transmission of tourism market research data. Interdisciplinary research projects will be challenged with tourism research, research in statistics and commercial information technology. For example there are still a number of problems to be solved in order to be able to jointly use ecoscopic and demoscopic tourism data within a marketing information system. These combination options require a constant standardization of information sources as well as new approaches towards the methodological processing of data gained from various studies. Another vital research initiative will be the development of information systems about themselves? Optimizing the knowledge presentation of 'service quality in information services' has been neglected in the past. By applying and accepting decision support systems the significance of this field of research will increase. Another important factor will be the role system imminent? Protocol presentations play, which are continually improved. Thus data on the user behaviour offers not only information on necessary improvements in the data processing of tourism market research results, but also on the future focus of tourism market research. The sudden explosion of data and the growing need for information challenges basic research as far as data reduction and decision support methods are concerned. Therefore existing concepts for qualitative forecasts and market reaction models and their calibration options in a marketing information system have to be reconsidered. In this respect projects which aim at a systematic and regular compilation of experiences experts made with regard to various technical subjects (i.e. short-term development of singular markets of origin) are considered to be promising. It is their aim to provide an improved evaluation of future market developments and eventually to integrate the findings into the strategic planning of national and regional tourism organizations and businesses. Another necessary development regards already existing data collections and the processing of the European cities' statistics. In this respect this author has observed many shortcomings relating to the international comparability of the data. The improved communication possibilities provided by the new medium stimulates critical discussions and behavioural learning among all participants. Within European Cities Tourism, among other things, new initiatives to evaluate one city's major competitors have been released due to the managers' increased awareness of the importance of this problem.

The trend towards globalization in research, where the internet plays a vital role, refers also to tourism research. To those critics who refer to the internet as uncontrolled growing, complicated and in its applications too playful, supporters used to point out that one day smart and profitable applications would be found. That is where we stand now. The new areas of responsibility regional and national tourism managers are confronted with today, not only suggest shortcomings in education but also promise new opportunities for the next manager generations to acquire status.

Tourism Planning

Tourism is one of many activities in a community or region that requires planning and coordination. This bulletin provides a simple structure and basic guidelines for comprehensive tourism planning at a community or regional level. Planning is the process of identifying objectives and defining and evaluating methods of achieving them. By comprehensive planning we mean planning which considers all of the tourism resources, organizations, markets, and programs within a region. Comprehensive planning also considers economic, environmental, social, and institutional aspects of tourism development.

Two Sides of Tourism Planning

Tourism planning has evolved from two related but distinct sets of planning philosophies and methods. On the one hand, tourism is one of many activities in an area that must be considered as part of physical, environmental, social, and economic planning. Therefore, it is common to find tourism addressed, at least partially, in a regional land use, transportation, recreation, economic development, or comprehensive plan.

The degree to which tourism is addressed in such plans depends upon the relative importance of tourism to the community or region and how sensitive the planning authority is to tourism activities.

Tourism may also be viewed as a business in which a community or region chooses to engage. Individual tourism businesses conduct a variety of planning activities including feasibility, marketing, product development, promotion, forecasting, and strategic planning. If tourism is a significant component of an area's economy or development plans, regional or community-wide marketing plans are needed to coordinate the development and marketing activities of different tourism interests in the community. A comprehensive approach integrates a strategic marketing plan with more traditional public planning activities. This ensures a balance between serving the needs and wants of the tourists versus the needs and wants of local residents. A formal tourism plan provides a vehicle for the various interests within a community to coordinate their activities and work toward common goals. It also is a means of coordinating tourism with other community activities.

Steps in the Planning Process

Like any planning, tourism planning is goal-oriented, striving to achieve certain objectives by matching available resources and programs with the needs and wants of people.

Comprehensive planning requires a systematic approach, usually involving a series of steps. The process is best viewed as an iterative and nagging one, with each step subject to modification and refinement at any stage of the planning process. There are six steps in the planning process:

1. Define goals and objectives.
2. Identify the tourism system.
   (a) Resources.
   (b) Organizations.
   (c) Markets.
3. Generate alternatives.
4. Evaluate alternatives.
5. Select and implement.
6. Monitor and evaluate.

Step One: Defining Goals and objectives. Obtaining clear statements of goals and objectives is difficult, but important. Ideally, tourism development goals should flow from more general community goals and objectives. It is important to understand how a tourism plan serves these broader purposes. Is the community seeking a broader tax base, increased employment opportunities, expanded recreation facilities, better educational programs, a higher quality of life? How can tourism contribute to these objectives?

If tourism is identified as a means of serving broader community goals, it makes sense to develop plans with more specific tourism development objectives. These are generally defined through a continuing process in which various groups and organizations in a community work together toward common goals. A local planning authority, chamber of commerce, visitors bureau, or similar group should assume a leadership role to develop an initial plan and obtain broad involvement of tourism interests in the community. Public support for the planning process and plan is also important. Having a good understanding of tourism and the tourism system in your community is the first step toward defining goals and objectives for tourism development. The types of goals that are appropriate and the precision with which you are able to define them will depend upon how long your community has been involved in tourism and tourism planning. In the early stages of tourism development, goals may involve establishing organizational structures and collecting information to better identify the tourism system in the community. Later, more precise objectives can be formulated and more specific development and marketing strategies evaluated.

Step Two: Identifying Your Tourism System When planning for any type of activity, it is important to first define its scope and characteristics. Be clear about exactly what your plan encompasses. A good initial question is, "What do you mean by tourism?" Tourism is defined in many ways. Generally, tourism involves people travelling outside of their community for pleasure. Definitions differ on the specifics of how far people must travel, whether or not they must stay overnight, for how long, and what exactly is included under travelling for "pleasure". Do you want your tourism plan to include day visitors, conventioneers, business travellers, people visiting friends and relatives, people passing through, or seasonal residents?

Which community resources and organizations serve tourists or could serve tourists? Generally, tourists share community resources with local residents and businesses. Many organizations serve both tourists and locals. This complicates tourism planning and argues for a clear idea of what your tourism plan entails.

You can begin to clarify the tourism system by breaking it down into three subsystems:

(1) tourism resources,

(2) tourism organizations, and

(3) tourism markets.

An initial task in developing a tourism plan is to identify, inventory, and classify the objects within each of these subsystems.

Tourism Resources are any (1) natural, (2) cultural, (3) human, or (4) capital resources that either are used or can be used to attract or serve tourists. A tourism resource inventory identifies, and classifies the resources available that provide opportunities for tourism development. Conduct an objective and realistic assessment of the quality and quantity of resources you have to work with.

Tourism Organizations combine resources in various proportions to provide products and services for the tourist. It is important to recognize the diverse array of public and private organizations involved with tourism.

The most difficult part of tourism planning is to get these groups to work toward common goals.

You should develop a list of these organizations within your own community and obtain their input and cooperation in your tourism planning efforts. Setting up appropriate communication systems and institutional arrangements is a key part of community- tourism planning.

Natural Resources

* Climate-seasons.
* Water resources-lakes, streams, waterfalls.
* Flora-forests, flowers, shrubs, wild edibles.
* Fauna-fish & wildlife.
* Geological resources-topography, soils, sand dunes, beaches, caves, rocks & minerals, fossils.
* Scenery-combinations of all of the above.

Cultural Resources

* Historic buildings, sites.
* Monuments, shrines.
* Cuisine.
* Ethnic cultures.
* Industry, government, religion, etc.
* Anthropological resources.
* Local celebrities.

Human Resources

* Hospitality skills.

* Management skills.
* Seasonal labour force.
* Performing artists-music, drama, art, storytellers.
* Craftsman and artisans.
* Other labour skills from chefs to lawyers to researchers.
* Local populations.

Capital

* Availability of capital, financing.
* Infrastructure-transportation roads, airports, railroads, harbours & marinas, trails & walkways.
* Infrastructure: utilities water, power, waste treatment, communications.

Tourism Management Organizations and Services

Off-Site: Coordination, planning, technical assistance, research, regulation:

* Federal & state departments of commerce, transportation, & natural resources.
* Federal, state, regional, & local tourism associations.
* Educational organizations & consultants, e.g., Travel & Tourism Research Association; U.S. Travel Data Centre; Travel Reference Centre, Univ. of Colorado, Boulder; Travel, Tourism, & Recreation Resource Centre, Michigan State University.
* Travel information & reservation services On-Site: development, promotion and management, of tourism resources:
    - Federal agencies, NB. departments of commerce, transportation, & land management agencies.
    - State agencies, NB. departments of commerce, transportation, & land/facility management agencies.
    - Local government organizations, e.g., visitor information, chamber of commerce, convention & visitor's bureaus, parks.

* Businesses: Accommodations: Hotels, motels, Lodges, resorts, bed & breakfast cabins & cottages, Condominiums, second homes, Campgrounds-Food & Beverage: Restaurants, Grocery, Bars, nightclubs.

Fast Food, Catering Services

- Transportation: Air, rail, bus; Local transportation: taxi, limo, Auto, bicycle, boat rental; Local tour services.
- Information: Travel agencies, Information and reservation services, Automobile clubs.
- Recreation Facilities & Services: Winter sports: ski, skating, snow mobile areas; Golf courses, miniature golf; Swimming pools, water slides, beaches; tennis, handball, racquetball courts, bowling alleys; Athletic clubs, health spas; Marinas, boat rentals and charters; hunting & fishing guides; Horseback enterprises; Sporting goods sales & rentals.
- Entertainment: Nightclubs, amusement parks, spectator sport facilities; Gambling facilities: casinos, horse racing, bingo; video arcades; art galleries and studios, craft shops, studios, demonstrations; performing arts: theatre, dance, music, film; historic & prehistoric sites; museums: art, history, science, technology; arboreta, zoos, nature centres.
- Special festivals and events-Support services: Auto repair, gasoline service stations; boat & recreation vehicle dealers and service; retail shops: sporting goods, specialties, souvenirs, clothing; health services: hospitals, clinics, pharmacies; laundry and dry cleaning; beauty & barber shops; baby-sitting services; pet care; communications: newspaper, telephone; banking and financial services.

Tourism Markets: Tourists make-up the third, and perhaps most important subsystem. Successful tourism programs require a strong market orientation.

The needs and wants of the tourists you choose to attract and serve must be the focus of much of your marketing and development activity. Therefore, it is important to clearly understand which tourism market segments you wish to attract and serve. Tourists fall into a very diverse set of categories with quite distinct needs and wants. You should identify the different types of tourists, or market segments that you presently serve or would like to serve. This may involve one or more tourism market surveys. A visitor survey identifies the size and nature of the existing market and asks the following questions:

* What are the primary market segments you presently attract?
* Where do they come from?
* What local businesses and facilities do they use?
* What attracted them to the community?
* How did they find out about your community?
* How satisfied are they with your offerings?

A market survey (usually a telephone survey) also can be conducted among households in regions from which you wish to attract tourists. This type of study helps identify potential markets, and means of attracting tourists to your area.

Tourism Market Segments

In a general tourism plan, some clear target tourism market segments should be identified. You might begin by defining the market area from which you will draw most of your visitors. The size of your market area depends upon the uniqueness and quality of your "product", transportation systems, tastes and preferences of surrounding populations, and your competition. Identifying the market area will help target information and promotion and define transportation routes and modes, competition, and characteristics of your market. Next, divide your travel market into the following trip length categories:

* day trips from a 50 mile radius,
* day trips from 50 to 200 miles away,
* pass-through travellers,
* overnight trips of 1 or 2 nights (most likely weekends), and
* extended overnight vacation trips.

After you have an idea of your market area and kinds of trips you will be serving, begin defining more specific market segments like vehicle campers, downhill skiers, sightseers, family vacationers, single weekenders, and the like. These segments can be more clearly tied to particular resources, businesses, and facilities in your community.

What kinds of products and services are likely to attract each of these groups? Tourist needs as well as their impact on the local community are quite different for day tourists versus overnight tourists. Areas catering primarily to weekend traffic will experience large fluctuations in use. In deciding the relative importance of these different segments, communities need to assess both their ability to provide required services (do you have enough rooms?), as well as the demand for different types of trips relative to the supply and your competition.

The Environment: A tourism plan is significantly affected by many factors in the broader environment. Indeed, one of the complexities of tourism planning is the number of variables that are outside of the control of an individual tourism business or community. These include such things as tourism offerings and prices at competing destinations, federal and state policy and legislation, currency exchange rates, the state of the economy, and weather. These factors are discussed more fully in Extension bulletin E-1959 as part of the market environment analysis.

Local populations also must be considered in tourism planning. As they compete with tourists for resources, they can be significantly affected by tourism activity, and they are an important source of support in getting tourism plans implemented. A survey of local residents can be conducted to assess community attitudes toward tourism development, identify impacts of tourism on the community, and obtain local input into tourism plans. Public hearings, workshops, and advisory boards are other ways to obtain public involvement in tourism planning. Local support and cooperation is important to the success of tourism programs and should not be overlooked.

Tourism Market Segments

I. Geographic market areas.

II. Trip categories.

Day Trips:

* short-within 50 miles.
* long-up to 200 miles.

Pass through traffic:

* day visitors.
* overnight stays.

Overnight Trips:

* weekend.
* vacation.

III. Activity or trip purpose Outdoor Recreation:

* Water-based Activity:
  - Boating: sail, power, cruise, row, canoe, water ski.
  - Swimming: pool, beach, sunbathing, scuba.
  - Fishing: charter, sport, from pier, boat, shore, ice.
* Land-based Activity:
  - Camping: back packing, primitive, developed.
  - Hiking: climbing, beachcombing, spelunking.
  - Hunting.
  - Skiing: downhill, cross country.
  - Snowmobiling.
  - Bicycling.
  - Horseback riding.
  - Picnicking.
* Air-based Activity:
  - Aeroplane rides, hang gliding, ballooning, parachuting.
* General:
  - Nature study.
  - Photography or landscape painting.
  - Viewing natural scenery.

Sightseeing & Entertainment:

* Visiting particular sites or areas:
  - historic or prehistoric.

- cultural.
- amusements.
- scenic.

* Attending particular events, shows, or demonstrations:
  - ethnic festivals.
  - sporting events.
  - performances.
  - agricultural fair or festival.
  - boat show.
  - shopping.

Other Primary Purpose for Trip:

* Visiting Friends & Relatives.
* Convention & Business/Pleasure.

Step Three: Generating Alternatives. Generating alternative development and marketing options to meet your goals requires some creative thinking and brainstorming. The errors made at this stage are usually thinking too narrowly or screening out alternatives prematurely. It is wise to solicit a wide range of options from a diverse group of people. If tourism expertise is lacking in your community, seek help and advice outside the community. Tourism planning involves a wide range of interrelated development and marketing decisions. The following development questions will get you started:

* How much importance should be assigned to tourism within a community or region?
* Which general community goals is tourism development designed to serve?
* Which organization(s) will provide the leadership and coordination necessary for community tourism planning?

What are the relative roles of public and private sectors? Tourism marketing decision questions include:

* *Segments:* Which market segments should be pursued; geographic markets, trip types, activity or demographic subgroups?

* *Product:* What kinds of tourism products and services should be provided? Who should provide what?
* *Place:* Where should tourism facilities be located?
* Promotion: What kinds of promotion should be used, by whom, in which media, how much, when? What community tourism theme or image should be established?
* *Price:* What prices should be charged for which products and services. Who should capture the revenue?

Step Four: Evaluating Alternatives. Tourism development and marketing options are evaluated by assessing the degree to which each option will be able to meet the stated goals and objectives. There are usually two parts to a systematic evaluation of tourism development and marketing alternatives: (1) Feasibility analysis, and (2) Impact assessment.

These two tasks are interrelated, but think of them as trying to answer two basic questions: (1) Can it be done?, and (2) What are the consequences? A decision to take a specific action must be based both on feasibility and desirability.

Feasibility Analysis: First, screen alternatives and eliminate those that are not feasible due to economic, environmental, political, legal, or other factors. Evaluate the remaining set of alternatives in more detail, paying particular attention to the market potential and financial plan. Make a realistic assessment of your community's ability to attract and serve a market segment or segments. This requires a clear understanding of the tourism market in your area and how this market is changing. Also carefully identify your competition and evaluate your advantages and disadvantages compared to the competition.

Plan toward the future because it takes time to implement decisions and for your actions to take effect. Therefore, look at the likely market and competition for several years to come. Review forecasts for the travel market in your area, if available. Careful tracking of tourism trends in your own community can help identify changes in the market that you will have to adapt to.

Impact Assessment: When evaluating alternative

development and marketing strategies it is important to understand the impacts, both positive and negative, of proposed actions. A classification of economic, environmental, and social impacts associated with tourism development. The types of impacts and their importance vary across different communities and proposed actions. Generally, the size, extent, and nature of tourism impacts depend upon:

* volume of tourist activity relative to local activity.
* length and nature of tourist contacts with the community.
* degree of concentration/dispersal of tourist activity in the area.
* similarities or differences between local populations and tourists.
* stability/sensitivity of local economy, environment, and social structure.
* how well tourism is planned, controlled, and managed.

Look at both the benefits and costs of any proposed actions. While tourism development can increase income, revenues, and employment, it also involves costs. Evaluate benefits and costs of tourism development from the perspectives of local government, businesses, and residents.

Impacts of Tourism

Economic Impacts:

* Sales, revenue, and income.
* Employment.
* Fiscal impact-taxes, infrastructure costs.
* Prices.
* Economic base & structure.

Environmental Impacts:

* Lands.
* Waters.
* Air.
* Infrastructure.
* Flora & fauna.

Social Impacts:

* Population structure & distribution.
* Values & attitudes.
* Education.
* Occupations.
* Safety & security.
* Congestion & crowding.
* Community spirit & cohesion.
* Quality of life.

Impacts on Local Government Local government provides most of the infrastructure and many of the services essential to tourism development, including highways, public parks, law enforcement, water and sewer, garbage collection and disposal. Evaluate tourism decisions with a clear understanding of the capacity of the local infrastructure and services relative to anticipated needs, and take into account both the needs of local populations and tourists.

A fiscal impact analysis evaluates the impact of tourism on the community's tax base and local government costs. It entails predicting the additional infrastructure and service requirements of tourism development, estimating their costs, deciding who will pay for/provide them, and how. Will tourism generate increased local government revenue through fees and charges, local sales or use taxes, increased property values or property tax rates, or larger local shares of federal and state tax revenues?

Impacts on Business and Industry Businesses that are directly serving tourists benefit from sales to tourists. Through secondary impacts, tourism activity also benefits a wide range of businesses in a community. For example, a local textile industry may sell to a linen supply firm that serves hotels and motels catering primarily to tourists. A local forest products industry sells to a lumberyard where local woodcarvers or furniture makers buy their supplies. They in turn sell to tourists through various retail outlets. All of these businesses benefit from tourism. If most products and services for tourists are bought outside of the local area, much of the tourist spending "leaks" out of the local economy. The more a community is "self-sufficient" in serving tourists, the larger the local impact.

Impacts on Residents

Local residents may experience a broad range of both positive and negative impacts from tourism development.

Tourism development may provide increased employment and income for the community. Although tourism jobs are primarily in the service sectors and are often seasonal, part time, and low-paying, these characteristics, are neither universal nor always undesirable. Residents may value opportunities for part time and seasonal work. In particular, employment opportunities and work experiences for students or retirees may be desired. Residents may also benefit from local services that otherwise would not be available. Tourism development may mean a wider variety of retailers and restaurants, or a better community library. It may also mean more traffic, higher prices, and increases in property values and local taxes. The general quality of the environment and life in the community may go up or down due to tourism development. This depends on the nature of tourism development, the preferences and desires of local residents, and how well tourism is planned and managed.

Steps Five and Six

Implementation, and Monitoring and Evaluation. We will not attempt a complete discussion of decisionmaking, plan implementation, and monitoring, but these are critical steps in the success of a tourism plan. A set of specific actions should be prescribed with clearly defined responsibilities and timetables. Monitor progress in implementing the plan and evaluate the success of the plan in meeting its goals and objectives on a regular basis. Plans generally need to be adjusted over time due to changing goals, changing market conditions, and unanticipated impacts. It is a good idea to build monitoring and evaluation systems into your planning efforts.

Concluding Remarks

Successful tourism planning and development means serving both tourists and local residents. The bulletins in this series stress the importance of a market orientation for attracting and serving tourists. This market orientation must be balanced with a clear view of how tourism serves the broader community interest and an understanding of the positive and negative impacts of tourism development.

Remember, tourism should serve the community first and the tourist second. Tourism development must be compatible with other activities in the area and be supported by the local population. Therefore, the tourism plan should be closely coordinated with other local and regional planning efforts, if not an integral part of them.

Tourism Development Simulation Model

Tourism industry development has its greatest impacts at the community level. These impacts reach far beyond jobs, wages, and revenues. Social and environmental consequences such as crime, congestion, and water pollution also can have serious impacts on the quality of life of residents as well as on the quality of vacations for tourists. Community leaders and planners have indicated a need for information about these impacts.

Since 1980, researchers at a number of universities in the Northeast and elsewhere have worked toward developing a framework and a database with which any locality could make "ball-park" estimates of the impacts of typical types of tourism development. A major research finding has been that it is not easy to define typical communities, typical developments, or average impacts.

Another finding has been that the complex interactions between residents, tourists, industry, and government make it difficult to justify a simple framework for analysis. On the other hand it is difficult to present the correct framework (assuming one exists) in a simple manner. In order to test our preliminary research hypotheses, a tourism-planning computer game has been developed which pits the player against the development pressures of a hypothetical small New England community.

In addition to meeting our objective of illustrating our long-term research goals in a palatable format the game has been used successfully in the classroom and, in fact, has taken on a project status of its own.

Project Background: A Game?

The Tourism Development Simulation Model (TDSM) is a computer program developed in conjunction with a series of projects on the impacts of tourism development. The emphasis in the earliest project was on the development of a methodology that could be used by individual municipalities and state agencies to estimate and project impacts caused by alternative tourism product mixes at the local level. A follow-up project focused on the fiscal impact portion of the model.

In the early stages of design and development of this model, it became readily apparent that the scope of the work was very broad-too broad to produce the quick and comprehensive results users wanted. It was, in fact, difficult to describe the goals of the project or its potential value to targeted users. It was decided, therefore, that a simplified version of the model could provide the basis of a computer game, and that this game concerning tourism development in a hypothetical community could provide an alternative means of describing the usefulness of the major project objectives. The production and distribution of the game has been so successful that it has taken on a project status of its own. Priced at cost, it was initially distributed as an amusing "think piece" for researchers and planners, and as an palatable introduction to related research projects. The game is loosely based on the impact assessment framework developed in a study of the impacts of tourism on thirteen coastal communities in the Northeast. A typical small New England community was characterized using some empirical results and some "best guess" approximations to relationships between major variables. The relationships were then refined to reflect the "reality" exhibited in recent community case studies.

In addition to providing the intended introduction to long-term project goals, the processes of designing and constructing the game and using it as a community behaviour simulator have taught us much about the implications of "reality" and "reasonableness" on mathematical representations of community behaviour. These lessons have had a considerable impact on our primary goal of developing a tourism development simulation model.

Designed to illustrate the principles of community budgeting and planning in the context of tourism industry development, the game has been used as an educational tool for students of tourism planning at the graduate and undergraduate level, and non-degree participants in leadership development programs in both the U.S. and Canada. For all audience types, the educational vehicle provided by the computer game is accepted enthusiastically. As with others, we have found this approach to have definite advantages over traditional seminar presentations. This paper describes the details of the game's design and describes the importance of the "reasonableness" criterion used in the development of the underlying model. It also attempts to persuade the reader that a computer game, based on a "best-guess" model, can provide a useful research and educational tool.

The Tourism Industry Focus

The tourism industry has many dimensions of concern to community researchers. It is recognized to include a wide range of business types whose activities impact a broad cross-section of the host community.

Tourists are of many types as are the residents of the affected community. In conducting community-based tourism research it is therefore important to identify and measure impact generators and recipients by their types so that policies can address specific problems and needs. In the model underlying this game, however, all tourist-related businesses are represented by an industry average, and all non-tourist-related businesses are represented by another average. In a similar way, residents are grouped and tourists are grouped. In contrast to the research \approach, the emphasis here is on the general dynamics of the tourism industry as it relates to other society components in a typical community setting.

The community is viewed as a circle whose outer ring is the natural resource base. Within that is the social system which provides the context for all community activities. Finally, in the centre are the four major components of the model: the tourism industry, "other" industry, local government, and the residents. Outside the community are four factors that influence and are influenced by community activities: exports, nonresident capital, nonresident labourers, and tourists. The arrows that connect the components and outside factors illustrate the major linkages assumed by the model that underlies the game.

Specific adjustments in behaviour of tourism businesses, "other" businesses, residents, and tourists are determined by equations relating causal factors to specific actions. This follows the basic econometric approach of meddling market systems. By sacrificing the behavioural differences of different types of producers and consumers, the simulation-game goes beyond equations that are typically estimated in research projects and speculates about a very complex set of important interactions within the community. Of particular interest were the social and environmental impacts of development that can change the "quality of life" for residents, the "bottom line' for businesses, and the "quality of the vacation" for tourists. Such impacts are well documented in the literature. Finally, the game recognizes the political nature of the decision-making process, the budget-balancing skills required by individual community officers, and the unpredictable disturbances to the planning process caused by unforeseen events.

A Community Setting

In order to simulate tourism development in the most realistic way possible, the model centres on the decisions made by an administrative officer of a typical small town in New England in the late 1970's. At the beginning of a game there are 20,000 residents in 10,000 households, and the population is growing at 1% per year. Half the population is considered to be in the labour force. 7500 of these are employed by the tourism industry, 2250 are employed in the "other" industry of the local economy, and the unemployment rate is initially 2.5%. Wage rates are $ 10,000 per year in the tourism industry and $20,000 per year in the other industry. Although average firms in both tourism and "other" industries begin the simulation breaking even, profits earned in the subsequent years are distributed to the residents of the community as additional income. Consequently disposable household income averages $11,255 per year in year 1. The natural resource base of the community is assumed to be a major recreation area, thus the draw for tourists and a major factor in the quality of life in the community. This resource might be a park or beach that is valued by the community and attractive enough to draw tourists to town, but fragile in the sense that increased use, in the absence of preventative investment, will result in a reduction in its aesthetic qualities. A number of works report on such impacts on recreational resources.

In the initial year of the simulation 200,000 tourists visit the community, staying an average of 7 days each, and visiting the natural resource recreation site on every day of their stay. Residents each make 10 visits per year to the recreation site. Residents and tourists pay the same price per visit to the recreational site, which is managed by the industry, however the tourists pay a visitor's fee to the town.

The town administrator has the authority to invest these and other town revenues in the protection/enhancement of the natural resource base. Year-to-year variation in weather is one example of the unpredictable nature of the community environment. The model assumes that changes in the average seasonal temperature from its norm of 75 degrees F will influence use of the recreational resource by residents as well as tourists. Each year of the simulation, average seasonal temperature is assigned a random value from 70 to 80 degrees. When temperatures drop below 75 degrees, visits to the site decrease, and when temperatures exceed 75, they increase.

As residential and tourist populations increase they are assumed to impact the social and environmental characteristics of the community as well as its economy. These are manifested in crime and congestion rates and water quality measures known to the community, reported as social and environmental indexes and as headlines in the local press. Thus, the quality of life in the community is assumed to be reflected in indexes for three basic community qualities: economic, social, and environmental.

The environmental index is assumed to reflect the quality of the recreational resource. The geometric mean of the three indexes, weighted by the population of the community, is used as an overall measure of community well being. Such quality of life indexes have been pursued for a number of years, with varying degrees of success. This well being measure might also be thought of an indicator of the economist's social welfare function. In addition to the raw indexes, the game player is presented news headlines that correspond to the severity of the index above or below their initial, equilibrium position. For example, when the social index drops 30% below its initial value the player is informed "Crime and Congestion at Record Levels. Police Frustrated." And when the environmental index rises 30% above its initial value the player is informed "National Task Force Adopts Local Environmental Plan as Model."

The Game Player

The game player assumes the role of an unusually potent town administrator who must guide development using tourism promotion and three other types of expenditure programs: "other" industrial development programs, social programs, and environmental projects. These expenditure categories are assumed to include all major expenditure items in a town's budget except for administration, which is ignored by the model. In order to balance the town's budget the player must adjust tax rates for residential and business property and decide upon daily tourist fees. The player's objective is to achieve balanced economic, social, and environmental development as measured by their respective indexes. At the end of each year of office the player is presented with quantitative and qualitative assessments of performance, and given the opportunity to change any of the seven fiscal controls. The game ends after 10 years of service or when the player quits or is fired, which ever comes first.

The Tourism Development Model

Model Structure

Some 40 equations containing more than fifty parameters characterize the components of community activity and development in the small hypothetical town. Most of these (19 equations) characterize the tourism industry and "other" industry behaviour. These include basic supply and demand relationships for the tourism product and the "other" product produced in the town, as well as derived demands for labour and supplies and business relocation.

The multi-market model framework is common to macro meddling efforts. Supply and demand equations are logarithmic and contain a lagged dependent variable. This formulation characterizes behaviour as "partially" adjusting toward some distant equilibrium value. The amount of the adjustment declines each year following the initial change in the independent variable. The rate of adjustment is determined by the size of the lag coefficient. Such models are frequent in econometric research studies since their coefficients are directly interpretable, and the implied dynamics is intuitively appealing.

The logarithmic specification implies that the coefficient of each explanatory variable is a short-run elasticity (the percentage change in the dependent variable in the first year resulting from a 1% change in the independent variable). Long-run elasticities (the ultimate percentage change in the dependent variable after a 1% change in the independent variable) are computed as the ratio of the short-run elasticity to (1-lag coefficient).

Random Events

As described above, weather is an important cause of random variations in visits to the recreation site and has important implications for the tourism industry. Part of the change in export sales by the "other" industry in the community is also generated as a random event. The model assumes the percentage deviation of current from previous export sales is randomly selected in the range from-5% to +5%. Early in the administration of the town it is unlikely that any unforeseen event will alter the outcome of control decisions. By the fifth year of the administration, however, there is a 60% probability that some such unforeseen event has occurred. These events are announced as "Important News Flash(es)." Five types of random events are built into the model:

The percentages and the dollar amount indicated by the News Flashes are also determined randomly. The percentages range from 25 to 100%, and the dollar amount of the deficit can range from 0 to $250,000. The choice of the five events was meant to correspond to five of the major uncertainties facing tourism community administrators: unexpected catastrophes in tourism and the "other" industry, a direct threat to tourism attractiveness because of pollution, unforeseen (and unplanned) rapid growth in tourism, and a personal threat to the job security of the administrator.

The player is given the opportunity to respond to these events before the impact is levied on the social, environmental, and economic indexes. The successful planner will take corrective actions given this opportunity.

The probability of a subsequent event is low for the immediate future after an event, but increases as the years pass. This may be an unrealistic representation of the planner who spends considerable time responding to crises. The game events may be repeated or not and the severity of the events, as measured by the percentage or dollar amount, will vary from occurrence to occurrence and game to game. It is very unlikely that any two games will be similar.

Community Impacts

Population Change

The 20,000 or so residents of the game community work either in the tourism industry or the "other" industry. There is a natural growth in the population of 1% per year as well as migration into and out of the community depending on the difference between the percentage of unemployed workers and an assumed "frictional" employment level of 3%. If the unemployment rate is above the frictional level there will be population migration out of the community; if the unemployment rate is less than 3% there will be some migration of population into the community.

Income Generation and Wealth

Residential income is the sum of wages paid to workers and profits earned by owners in the tourism and "other" industries. It is assumed that the major portion of current income is expended on necessities purchased from the "other" industry and luxuries including recreation-days purchased from the natural resource managers, the tourism industry.

The wealth of residents is characterized by the value of residential property (broadly defined). Residential property values are influenced by the number of residents; with more residents, demand for property rises and property values increase. Property taxes are the only taxes paid by residents, and they are controlled by the rate set by the game player.

Town Finances

The town derives revenues from five sources: daily tourist fees, residential property taxes, tourism industry property taxes, "other" industry property taxes, and interest income on any accumulated budget surplus from previous years (at a 10% annual rate). The town allocates its budget to five categories of expenditures: tourism promotion, "other" economic programs, social programs, environmental programs, and an automatic interest expense deducted for any accumulated deficit from previous years (also at a 10% annual rate).

The Quality of Life

Economic, Social and Environmental Impacts

In addition to the income generated for residents by the tourism and "other" industries in the communities, there are a host of other economic, social, and environmental characteristics that constitute the quality of community life. All these characteristics are assumed be represented by a set of four indexes. The economic index rises with the average wage rate and falls with unemployment. The social and environmental indexes rise with expenditures on social and environmental programs and fall with increases in the numbers of tourist-days and residential recreational visits.

A social-environmental index, which is also used as a measure of tourism attractiveness in the demand equation for tourist visits, is provided by the geometric mean of the social and environmental indexes. A quality of community life is provided by the geometric mean of the social-environmental index and the economic index. This index is assumed to be the objective function for the community and determines the annual game score.

Game Play and Use of Controls

Active Play

The first active screen of the game requests that the player provides three initials for identification. These are later used to record the player's final score for comparison with other scores. The player is asked at once whether the seven economic controls should be changed from their initial settings. As soon as the player is "Ready for the next year to begin," a community overview screen is shown such as the one in this screen provides current and past values for tourism industry revenue, "other" industry revenue, real disposable household income, the unemployment rate, and the accumulated town surplus or deficit. This screen also presents up to five news headlines determined by the indexes described above and the player's current and cumulative score. The following sequence of screens afford the player the opportunity to view five detailed informational screens including:

- "Local Government Financial Statements,"
- "Social Environmental Statistics,"
- "Tourism Business Statistics," and
- "other Industry Statistics."

When the player is finally satisfied that enough information has been viewed and that the appropriate adjustments to the seven controls have been made, the next year begins, and the model calculates changes to the community and its industries. Overview results for the next year are presented summarizing these calculations. When a player chooses to change one or more of the economic controls, a screen is presented that indicates the current level of each of the controls and how controls can be changed When all controls have been changed to the desired values, the player begins the next year of the administration.

Player Performance

The first informational screen of each year provides the annual score for the player based on the overall wellbeing index. However, the player (administrator) also must attempt to balance the budget in order to keep from being fired. If the deficit (or surplus) exceeds more than a few percent of the total budget the planner is defamed in the press. If the deficit (or surplus) is greater than about 10% the player will be fired despite the overall wellbeing of the community. Thus, the relative size of the town's budget deficit or surplus

The Game

You have been hired as the town planner for a community with an important tourism industry, it generates 55% of local income. The town budget is currently $11.9 million. Town revenues last year were generated from a $1 daily tourist tax ($1.4 Million last year), and property taxes from residents ($8 M), tourism businesses ($2 M),and other businesses ($0.5 M). The last administration allocated $5.5 M to social programs, $1.5 M to tourism promotion, $4.5 M to environmental programs, and $0.4 M to other economic development programs. Your task is to adjust tax rates and expenditures to achieve:

The End of The Game and Scores

The game ends when the planner quits, is fired, or survives 10 years in office. The score consists of the average of the community well being index weighted by the residential population and summed over the number of years in office normalized so that 100 points per year reflects maintaining the initial levels of all indexes. The distribution of scores generated from 100 plays where the only criterion was to balance the budget is given in the scores underlying the illustration ranged from 402 to 1072 with only thirteen scores above the norm of 100 points per year for the entire ten-year period.

The distribution of scores obtained when following a specific decision rule has been a major aide in assessing the performance of the model. The rule that each year the tourist fee would be changed by exactly the ratio of the current deficit (or surplus) to the current number of tourist days. We have adopted this budget-balancing, status-quo type decision rule as our base line distribution of scores. In this distribution, the major cause of variation was games in which the player was fired prior to the ten-year maximum. The secondary cause of variation was the influence of random events on community well being. As the bimodal distribution of the figure suggests, a typical game involved two events. When the first event was serious, the budget-balancing, status-quo player could not compensate and was fired between the fourth and seventh year as reflected in the cluster of scores between 400 and 700. The second event occasionally resulted in a firing, but because of its timing late in the game most players reached the tenth year. Every game ends with the opportunity to view a listing of the ranked scores from the previous 100 games played. These results identify the players by initials, and the individual games played by the score earned, the number of years the office was held, and the nature of the "NEWS FLASH" events that occurred while in office. These are indicated by the initial letter of the news flash (F, G, 0, U, or B) and provide a basis to evaluate the specific events that have most dramatically affected the well being of the game community. This list of scores has been useful to teachers for evaluating uses of the game and relative success of individual students in dealing with hypothetical community problems.

It is of particular interest to note that a major problem with the model was uncovered by students who figured out how to "beat the game." Property taxes, in the model, are treated as reductions in income prior to its allocation to leisure and non-leisure goods. As such, the model predicts no social outrage following rapid property tax increases that are put back into social and environmental programs. Accordingly, students have found that extremely high scores can be earned by raising property taxes and spreading the proceeds across social programs. This result has lead to revisions in the game as well as the identification of new topics for tourism research.

In Research

As suggested by the distribution of scores shown in the game acts as a stochastic simulation model when a specific decision rule is adopted. A research version of the game offers the player the opportunity to change behavioural parameters and automatically restart with specific decision rules. This enables the study of the influence of individual parameters and identification of behavioural relationships that lead to extreme scores. This is the basis for an ongoing study of the model, its parameters, and future refinements of the model.

Summary and Conclusions

It has been the purpose of this paper to present the details of a project that started toward a research objective, later became an educational project, and is currently on going as a combined research and educational program. Based in research findings from a variety of studies, a "straw-man" computer game was constructed to help in the presentation of a difficult concept in a new research effort: the dynamic and stochastic nature of tourism community behaviour. This game was "borrowed" for use in the classroom and subsequently revised for educational purposes. We are convinced that game play is a very exciting way of teaching tourism planning. We have also found that students and others playing the game can provide us with an unexpectedly rich source of research assistance'. In our quest for a "reasonable" characterization of tourism community behaviour. We have therefore altered our research procedures to explicitly account for the research-education interaction. It has been to our great delight that, on more than one occasion, students have identified inadequacies in the model by their ability to "beat the game." The future for this type of project is bright. The model has been used by over 50 researchers and 500 students, and feedback from its use has suggested a wide range of revisions. These include adding more sectors of the economy toward the goal of a Leontief model of transactions, adding more types of tourists and residents, and adding more specific impacts thus far only generalized as social and environmental impacts. It has also been suggested that more of the complexities of community government be included such as the role of zoning on development. Many of these suggestions could result in major improvements to the model; however, the game's simplicity would need to be sacrificed. In the process of deciding upon such improvements, it will be our overriding concern to maintain a balance between the model's usefulness as an educational tool and as a research vehicle.

7

Market Segmentation in Hospitality

Goals

This discussion paper has three key goals:

- For tourism operators and planners to better understand Market Segmentation;
- To provide an indication of trends in the market, with special focus on emerging segments; and
- To provide a useful backdrop of information for the Product Club Advisory Board to assist in the development of new or enhanced product lines.

Market Segmentation

Market segmentation can be defined as the process through which people (both tourism providers and consumers) with similar needs, wants and characteristics are grouped together so that a tourism business/organization can use greater precision in serving and communicating with these groups (marketing). There are associated benefits of segmentation (e.g. identifying partnerships to promote networking and guiding research and development) but the bottom line is that it enables better marketing decisions, and promotes more viable operations.

In more general terms, segmentation comes down to ties that connect two or more individuals (or businesses) together; it could be their age, their love of certain music, the magazines they read, or what their son or daughter is doing in school. The possibilities are endless.

Approaching Segmentation

Market segmentation can be approached from two broad directions: supply side (e.g. grouping similar products together) or the demand side (e.g. demographics and behavioural patterns of tourists). The objective is consistent: trying to reach out to potential customers in a more cost effective manner. The levels of segmentation can be broad (e.g. businesses offering an 'outdoor' experience) or narrow (e.g. a segment of the population in a set geographical boundary, who have a certain medical condition, with children, in a particular income bracket).

The approach to segmentation is important however. There is debate about 'Product Push' versus 'Market Pull'. The former is designing a product and packaging it and hoping that there is a market for it, while the latter attempts to find a niche market, identifying the needs and wants of individuals within that market, and designing a product to meet those needs. Generally it is more effective to undertake the market pull approach,1 but at the same time it is important to understand the strengths of a region's product. This is especially important when it comes to developing partnerships and products that fit with local community and cultural values. A mixed approach-market pull and 'manipulated or value-added' product push-is likely to be valuable when developing new product lines.

The following comments focus on the three main bases for market segmentation: product related, demographic and behavioural. Generally the more defined a market segment, the easier it is to reach out to individuals. Whichever approach is used, the segments (or niche markets) should be at least one of two things-*Focused* or *Targetable*-preferably both.

Focused: the stronger the ties that link people together the better; not just age and income but expectations, passions, habits, affiliations etc. The niche market does not have to be small to be focused, but usually the larger the market the weaker the ties.

Targetable: The easier it is to reach people in a niche market, the better. If they are all receiving the same newsletter or visit the same location on a regular basis, the better. An example of a focused market is 'ringers' (i.e. those who ring birds for counting and monitoring purposes) within the bird-watching segment. This niche is also targetable because it has its own specific newsletters, associations and conferences. An example of a niche market that is not particularly focused but is targetable is the 'David Thompson' segment. (This idea arose at a recent TASK meeting-to have a retreat inviting only those called David Thompson!). It is not focused as the only connection is the name; individuals are likely to have disparate interests and passions. With today's technology, however, it is a targetable audience. [Suggestion for a key note speaker: David Thompson, past president of Whistler Tourism Association!]

Product Related Segmentation

- Without listing all the subgroups, typical product-related segmentation may be along the lines of the following:
- Adventure Operators/Organizers *(from family adventures and motorcycle tours to* hunting and bird-watching)
- Attractions *(from museums and theme parks to sports clubs and festivals)*
- Transportation and Services *(from train and van tours to restaurants and gas stations)*

Another product-related segmentation strategy is based on seasons, for example grouping Winter or Fall activities. The Product Clubs of the Canadian Tourism Commission (CTC) are diverse, from focusing on Greek or Aboriginal businesses to particular styles of accommodations, such as 'charming inns'. For those with an outdoor theme the product segmentation is often similar to the above, or even broader. One promotes the four choices of:

- Land Travel
- Water
- Winter
- Mixed Activities

The use of technology, and more specifically websites, can be very beneficial for segmentation and steering potential customers to their particular vacation interests. Websites can quickly lead consumers to the same tourism package/business via different 'routes'. For instance, a cat skiing operator can be reached via 'Adventure Seekers', or 'Winter Activities'. The use of technology should also be utilized in segmenting the market into further subgroups.

For many years there has been a movement from mass production (and marketing) to customized production (e.g. with a computer manufacturer, customers can choose online their preferred specifications and have it 'built to order'). So too, with the tourism product. Given the consumers' limited time (and tendency to book last minute vacations), they may choose a vacation with a variety of outdoor activities, even offered by different operators. The message here is not to offer consumers what the operators *think* they want, but to provide a wide array of choices, ask them what they want and then organize it for them.

Nature-Based Tourism

The Kootenay region as a whole can largely be viewed as a nature-based tourism product given the plethora of national and regional parks, small communities, lake systems, mountain ranges and truly outstanding natural beauty.

Cultural and heritage tourism will continue to play a strong role, but the major draw will be the natural surroundings. Segmentation has already occurred with the creation and naming of the new Product Club.

Explorers of the Western Canadian Wilderness Product Club. Aside from the geographical identifier, there are two key words: *Explorers* and *Wilderness.* These conjure up an image of unspoilt natural beauty and outdoor activities – it is a nature- based tourism product. The nature-based tourism industry has grown so much in recent years that it now contains four broad sub-markets or segments:

Eco-Tourism: Travel for a learning experience about natural environments, using tourism products and services that are sustainable and sensitive to its surroundings. It should be noted that one recent local project 3 identified a regionally useful definition of Ecotourism within the nature-based tourism segment:

"Ecotourism is responsible travel to natural areas which conserves the environment and improves the welfare of local people"

Adventure Travel: *Personal accomplishment though thrills of dominating dangerous* environments.

Wilderness Travel: *Personal recreation through travel in natural environments which are devoid of human interference.*

Car Camping: *Family travel, providing a safe interface between wild and civilized.* All of these descriptions or definitions are open to interpretation. At one end of the spectrum for 'wilderness travel', for example, may be a tourist on a mountain-bike traversing a logging road though a planted forest. Others may believe that wilderness is non-existent in South-East BC because there are few mountain ridges where there is absolutely no visual human intrusion. This is an important aspect with regards to marketing (and product development) as it is important that the region does not attempt to 'sell' something it does not have. It is equally important not to put off potential visitors because they perceive that the area as too wild and rugged. When undertaking product enhancement or development it should be recognised that these four subgroups are at different stages of the typical life cycle. Broadly speaking, wilderness travel is likely nearing the peak of its business life cycle. This is because true wilderness areas are diminishing and only a limited number of tourist activities can take place in wilderness settings before the product can no longer be categorized as wilderness.

Car-camping too, on a global scale, is either approaching the peak of its life cycle or even started the down-ward slide. One component of 'vehicle camping' is still on the rise, however, and that is RV travel. Nearly one in twelve (or seven million) vehicle owning households in the USA own an RV, exhibiting nearly an 8% increase in the last four years. There is expected to be a further 15% increase over the next decade. Baby boomers are fuelling this growth and many have yet to reach the prime purchasing age of RV ownership. The rising cost of gasoline and the continuing weakness of the Canadian dollar might provide opportunities for South Eastern BC to offer alternatives to the 'Alaskan experience'.

Both eco-tourism and adventure travel are likely to have greater growth potential and are still on the upward curve of the life cycle. Eco-tourism was recently identified in a series of local community consultations as "the greatest opportunity for tourism growth in the region". 4 Sustainable tourism should not be confused with eco tourism. The latter is a sub sector of sustainable tourism and is a more narrowly defined segment within nature- based activities. Sustainable principles, on the other hand, can apply to all types of tourism activities.

Examples of Segmentation of Outdoor and Learning Travellers

Outdoor travellers and learning travellers are reviewed in more detail given the nature- based local tourism product and the, as-yet-untapped, potential of learning vacations.

Outdoor Segment

Even though a large part of the local tourism product is based on the outdoor experience and natural beauty, this does not mean that all tourists regularly participate in outdoor activities. The graph below provides a picture of the outdoor segmentation of the US market. As seen, a large component of the segment is categorized as 'outdoor inactives' (36%). There are many market segments that overlap. The pie chart above provides the segmentation split for outdoors travellers. Another market segment, the 'Learning Traveller' was identified as an emerging market. The learning Traveller may overlap with a number of above segments of the outdoor traveller, some being naturalists, some resort lovers, etc.

Outdoor-Wilderness Segment: There are many different ways that markets can be segmented, and an equally diverse number of descriptors that could be attached to each segment. With respect to outdoor wilderness travellers, the Adventures of the Northern Wilderness Product Club identified three main sub sectors for wilderness travel to the Yukon5. Its research consisted of 800 telephone interviews and mail surveys to California, Vancouver, Calgary, Chicago, and Ontario. The identified segments were:

- Earthly Explorers: (24% *of respondents*) *like to keep it simple, lower budgets, into nature and roughing it, prefer to keep to one activity rather than trying them* all;

- Adventure Collectors: (*18% of respondents*) *like to sample lots of different* activities, looking for higher quality, with fun, shorter trips;
- Pampers Consumer Boomers: (*14% of respondents*) *Smaller segment but market expected to rise; looking for high quality, want to relax, but also* experience activities in a non-threatening way.

There was a fourth segment identified (*'No Thrills'*), but this sub-market prefer to stay closer to home for their wilderness trips and are not looking for any risk or adventure. Although this was noted as a weak market for the Yukon given distance and remoteness, it may hold some opportunities for the Kootenay region. In terms of product development and target marketing it would be beneficial for the Kootenay region to focus more on the Adventure Collectors and Pampered Consumer Boomers given their ability to pay, interest in winter, and the relatively more desirable (compared with the Yukon) climate offered in the local region, especially in the shoulder seasons.

Learning Traveller Segment: Learning travellers are often referred to as 'educated travellers' not because the trips they take have educational components but because they themselves have higher overall education levels than the population at large. *Elderhostel Canada* (since 2000 it has been re-named *Routes to Learning Canada – RTC*) has been the single largest provider of learning travel programs in Canada for 20 years. The North American Elderhosteller is on average 68 years old, and 90% have post secondary education (in a time when post secondary education was less accessible). Nearly 1 in 5 report having 7 or more years of post-secondary education. 7 The segments for learning travellers are:

Explorers are those looking for learning programs that offer opportunities to explore a new part of the world and learn about local area history, customs and cultures;

- *Activity-Oriented* are those seeking outdoor experiences and are interested in the natural environment;
- *Content-Committed are people who look for a specific subject of interest (e.g.* lepidoptery – the study of moths and butterflies);

- *Convenience-Oriented look for programs that are within a six-hour driving radius of* home.

Of the four segments, the last one is the one that would fit least well with the location and tourism product in the Kootenay Region. 'Activity-oriented' individuals and 'explorers', however, mesh perfectly with the strengths of the local tourism product, and the direction of the new product club.

Demand-Based Segmentation

Demographics

Understanding demographics is imperative to product development and segmentation, especially with regard to understanding trends in the market place. Demography (the study of age, sex, education, family status, life cycle etc.) is an excellent tool for product developers and marketers. According to the well respected demographer, David Foot, demographics accounts for "two-thirds of everything", (markets, social problems, demand for services etc.).

The subject therefore plays a key-role in decision-making regarding demand for tourism products.

Age in particular is an important example. The baby-boom generation is of prime importance due to its size (roughly 1/3 of the Canadian population – proportionally the largest of all the industrialized nations) and characteristics. It is well educated with above average income.

The front end is also approaching (within 10 years) retirement age and will therefore have the money and the time to travel. The 'echo' generation (children of the boomers) are also creating peak demands on certain products and services. Born between 1980 and 1995, the front end is into their twenties and taking part in independent, adventure travel. They are also much more technologically advanced and have been brought up in â generation with strong concerns for the environment Other sub sectors and age cohorts also need to be understood to more effectively communicate with them.

Lifecycle Segments: A recent and comprehensive travel motivations survey was undertaken for both Canadian and US travellers. The data was used to provide a series of reports and one 9 focused on demographic analysis of the various tourism market segments. The life cycle segments were as follows:

- Youth Market (18-35, no children under 20 living at home);
- Family Market (with children under 20 living at home);
- Mature Market (36-65 – no children); and
- Seniors Market (over 65, no children living at home).

Each one of these is broken down into sub categories, as shown in the pie chart below. The two largest segments are the Family Market and the Mature Market – accounting for over two thirds of the entire travel market. This, again, reflects the boomer bulge in the population. The single largest segment, at nearly one quarter of all travellers, is Mainstream Young Families (children under 12 living at home). A quick overview of the characteristics of the various segment follows:

Youth Market: (20% of the travel market): lower than average incomes, high energy approach to travel (extreme sports), high participation rate in activities, especially likely to seek out personal indulgence travel, use the internet as a research and booking tool.

Family Market: (33% of the travel market): above average education and income, most affluent of the four markets. Tends to be shorter-haul travellers (with children); important domestic market; greater focus on recuperative vacation experiences; less likely than average to take day and overnight tours; less than likely than typical American traveller to visit Canada.

Mature Market: (32% of the travel market): relatively well educated and affluent; slightly more than average likely to seek out exploratory vacation activities; more than likely to have gone on natural sightseeing vacations & visited cultural attractions; above average users of travel packages.

Seniors Market: Smallest of the four markets (15%): lower than average education and income levels; American seniors more likely than the average traveller to visit Canada, and most likely of all the markets to seek out exploratory vacation experiences, much less likely to view vacations as opportunities for relaxation. Above average participation in natural sightseeing (although generally less active in outdoor activities) and above average in cultural and heritage attractions; more likely than average to take guided tours; rely more on printed material and television for travel opportunities and information.

Although currently smallest, special attention should be paid to the seniors market, as its members look for exploratory experiences and prefer value-added components such as guided services. Although currently not a wealthy segment, the baby boomers are approaching retirement with higher income and education levels.

As can be seen, the largest sub-markets are mainstream young families, mainstream mature couples and mainstream youth. All the affluent segments are very important to the tourism sector as they tend to be better educated, well travelled, have the means to travel and are often looking for new experiences. The affluent sub-markets account for over one-quarter of all travellers.

Behavioural Segmentation

People's *'activities, interests* and *opinions* (AIO's) also play a key role in decision- making and travel habits. These behavioural characteristics (also known as psychographics), when used in conjunction with demographics, provide a much stronger marketing tool for tourism businesses and planners. By understanding people's AIO's and their subsequent motivations, certain sub-groups can be targeted more effectively, as well as reflected in new product lines.

Another TAMS report (Emergent Vacation Interests) 10 focussed on emergent themes in tourism and indicated which demographic sub market was likely to drive which emergent theme. A more detailed description of the report's findings (relevant to The Product Club) is outlined in the *Tourism Trends Discussion Paper.* Suffice to say the key emergent themes (in order of anticipated net change) were as follows:

- Intimacy & Romance
- Experiencing Different Cultures
- Natural Wonders
- Fine Cuisine and being pampered

- Escaping winter weather
- Adventure and Excitement
- Experiencing Unspoiled Nature
- Historic sites
- Hands on Learning
- Hobby or sport

Any product development should try and incorporate one or more of these themes if it is going to meet future markets. Selecting a couple that are most relevant to The Product Club-*experiencing unspoiled nature* and *adventure and excitement* -, the predominant sub-market driving both experiences is mainstream mature singles. Other important sub- markets that show great interest in these vacations are the young mainstream and mainstream young family markets.

The affluent family market is also a key driver. According to some travel writers 11, one of "the hottest trends in travel in 2002 was the family vacation", especially for affluent families. This may have arisen, in part, from the events of Sept, promoting a desire not to stray too far from loved-ones. With regard to transportation segmentation there is now even an airline designed exclusively for family travel: FamilyAir based in Los Angeles.

What the Sub-markets will be looking for

As noted, the largest sub-market is the mainstream young family market, accounting for 23% of North American Travellers. This group is looking for a number of outdoor activities, four out of the top five (in terms of anticipated net increases) of which are offered in the region. These are:

- horseback riding (12% expected increase);
- downhill skiing (11%);
- white-water rafting (10%); and
- kayaking or canoeing (10%).

The one not offered regionally (in the top five of emergent activities) is whale watching. Other notable outdoor experiences that are gaining in popularity within this single largest market segment are snowmobiling on organized trails (8%) and recreational biking (7%). Although smaller than mainstream markets the affluent segments require special attention due to their larger discretionary spending. In each sub-market the level of affluence varied. For example with affluent young couples, two-thirds of the market have household incomes between $40K and $80K with a third having $80K plus. With the affluent mature and senior couples 100% had income in excess of $80K. The table below lists the top three emergent vacation experiences in each of the affluent segments, followed by the emergent vacation experiences in the three largest segments.

There are a number of common threads. Intimacy and romance was top of the list of emergent themes in three of the five affluent markets and top of the list of two of the three largest markets. Natural wonders, different cultures, hands-on learning, being pampered and adventure vacations were all repetitive emergent themes.

The growing demand for exploratory and learning travel was highlighted with a recent travel write-up of a Scottish whiskey school (a 3-day learning experience). One individual was there after being involved in a climbing accident: "as he lay on his back looking at the stars [he] realized that he had always loved the night sky but knew nothing about it. He promised himself that, if he lived, he would never be so negligent with his passions." [Incidentally at least two of the individuals on the course (in their 30's) went because they had received it as a gift].

In the near future, increased numbers will have greater awareness of the fragility of life and there is likely to be an increased push in making memorable vacations. The Vancouver office of the Canadian Institute for the Blind, for example, has one new client walking through its doors every ten minutes. This is expected to double, to one person every five minutes, within the next fifteen years.

Activity-Related Accommodation

Nearly all (19 out of 20) activity-related accommodation types were more likely to be stayed in over the subsequent two years (at 2000) compared with the previous two years. Again this confirms the importance of experiential vacations.

Especially promising increases were expected in the bed and breakfast market. Less common activity-based accommodations (in other words niche markets, stayed-in by less than 10% of travellers) showed great potential relative to their market size. These included health spas, learning experiences, working farms, and wilderness lodges, which all suggest that more exotic forms of vacation are on the increase. Of particular note is the 'staying at a wilderness lodge that you can drive to by car', showing a two-fold (anticipated) increase. This study was conducted prior to September 11, and the increased fear of flying (and cost) may contribute to enlarging this segment still further. The increased interest in activity-related accommodation types amongst American and Canadian travellers.

Conclusions

A number of conclusions can be drawn from the data above, especially with respect to creating or enhancing product lines. These are:

- Market Segmentation is crucial. No business can be everything to everyone and those that can differentiate their markets will be in a much stronger position.
- Segmentation should not based purely on similar product attributes; a 'market pull' approach should be adopted where planners/operators first understand the needs/desires of individual market segments and then design packages/products to meet those needs.
- There is no right or wrong way to segment the products or market but segments, or niche markets, should be both focused and targetable.
- Developing and implementing new product lines is only half the battle; other real work comes in trying to reach the target market-identifying accessible (and focused) markets first and then designing packages and products that will draw tourists in.
- The Product Club should not expend significant effort and dollars on undertaking primary research into market segmentation. Significant analysis of the market place already exists.

- The Product Club should primarily focus on its strength: delivering a nature- based tourism product. Within this, there should be a mix of different activities and experiences offered, from themes promoting intimacy and romance to learning vacations.
- The Product Club should not solely focus on one lifestyle segment, e.g. the needs of current baby-boomers, because these will be replaced by a much smaller ("bust" population) in the years ahead. A mix is required and planning for future changes is important.
- The lines of segmentation are becoming more blurred as people mix activities.
- Special attention should be paid to emergent themes among segments. These include learning, intimacy and romance, heritage and historical trips, adventure and excitement, experiencing unspoiled nature, being pampered, health and spa retreats, bed and breakfasts related to activities, and lodges that can be driven to, among others.

The Application of Benefit Segmentation in Tourism Promotion

A basic starting point for tourism marketing efforts is a formal or informal marketing plan. In such a plan target market analysis or market segmentation is usually the first step and the most important part. An excellent market segmentation is half success of a marketing strategy. Promotion is particularly important in the tourism marketing strategy. A recurring problem in the tourism promotional area is "at whom should the promotional effort be aimed" and "what should be said to the prospective tourist". Market segmentation may give these questions good answers. Many people have proposed guidelines for dealing with the problem of identifying tourism target markets. They have attempted to position tourism products in the mind of the prospective tourists, or split up the market based on latent or overt psychological desires., price trip purpose, use type, or other characteristics of tourist in geography, socioeconomics and demography. However, some researchers have found with respect to the inability of demographics to explain important differences in travel and vacation behaviour. What is proposed here is a benefit segmentation approach which can combine many different ways of looking at the tourist and the travel market and actually simultaneously reduce marketing and promotional costs while increasing tourist demand. In other words, clever segmentation strategy can improve marketing and promotional efficiency for the tourism marketer. In addition, a tentative procedure will be rendered to help one to conduct a benefit segmentation research.

Tourism Marketing

In 1985 the American Marketing Association defines marketing as the performance of business activities that direct the flow of goods and services from the producer to the consumer or user. However, tourism industry is unlike many other industries in many ways: unseen before selling, intangibility, paying time and money before actually using, direct or indirect reservation in advance, far away from customers, combination of resources from a variety of businesses, cannot be stored, limited supply in the short term, instability of demand, and high elasticity of demand. The objective of marketing is to reflect the present marketing plan assessment, create the right image for the tourism product, and satisfy consumers. The most widely accepted method for this has been the development of marketing programs based on the 4 p's (product, place, price, and promotion). Within tourism generally price and place to visit is very difficult to be manipulated by tourist agencies in the short run. However, the product itself (various attractions in tourism industry) and promotion of that product (mass communications, direct mail, brochures, etc.), are much more controllable. The product itself can be improved to better match market desires but product calibration decisions involve long-term consequences since substantial developments require extensive time for planning and actual implementation.

The tourism industry can be differentiated from many tangible product businesses by the consumers' perception of risk when they buy intangible services. Promotion can reduce consumers' perception of risk. In addition, some features of tourism business, such as seasonal demand, price sensitive, selling without viewing the product, low brand loyalty, severe competition, and high substitution have made promotion play important role in tourism marketing. Promotion decisions involve the determination of copy appeals, media strategy, and production costs, and are easily controlled in the short run. Proper execution of the promotion task requires a thorough understanding of the levels and types of market heterogeneity faced by the tourism marketer. That is, a marketer needs to know his/her markets and their desires. Segmentation research can help with this task of identifying markets and can lead to more effective promotional strategies.

Market Segmentation on Benefits Sought

Generally speaking, market segmentation is based on four assumptions: (1) Tourists can be grouped into different but homogeneous market segments; (2) People in different market segment have different tourism needs and preferences; (3) A specific destination or tourist experience will appeal to some segments of the market more than others; (4) Tourism suppliers can improve their marketing efforts by market segments. Many ways exist to segment a market. The marketing literature is replete with examples of ways to group consumers based on geography, purchase behaviour, socioeconomic and demographic factors, use type, price, and various cognitive measures.

A method that has the highest usage in recreation or tourism is "benefit segmentation". It also uses a behavioral approach to segmentation but is the hardest to identify. This approach groups consumers according to benefits desired from a particular product category. It seeks to identify that part of the market that derives specific benefits from the product/service. The variables that a supplier has that are benefit based include recreational facilities and equipment, length of stay, transportation mode, experience preferences, and benefit expectations. With benefit-based segmentation, a supplier must determine what benefits potential customers are seeking from their tourist experiences. Groups are then formed of people who assign a similar amount of importance to the same product benefits. It is based primarily on cluster analytic method and has enjoyed widespread application. Once this is done, those benefits are presented to this market segment to encourage additional business.

The Procedure of Benefit Segmentation

The general approach of benefit segmentation consists of collecting data from various tourists by using survey instruments designed and applying appropriate statistical procedures to analyze these data. In brief, this approach includes two major phases: segment creation and segment testing.

Phase 1: Segment Creation

The first step is developing a set of attributes (benefits) which exhaustively describes the range of attributes available from and desired in the product. This list of attributes may include redundancies which are either real or perceived as real by the consumer. These benefits, for example, may be like scenery, cost of vacation, social activity, friendliness of people, cleanliness of environment, quality of shopping, quality of sporting opportunities, cultural opportunities, quality of accommodations, quality of entertainment, and so on. In practice it is usually developed from previous studies (content analysis of related literature), from judgment of a jury of experts, from perception testing of the relevant sample in the field (perhaps through focus groups), and pilot study of the instrument. This step is conducted to assure the list of attributes is clarity, concise, relevance, and validation, Engel, et. al.,., furnish a more thorough discussion of product attributes and their measurement.

The next step is eliciting subjects' assessments of the relative importance of each of the various attributes by Likert scale. For instances, "1" is very important and "5" is less important. In this way, an importance vector is created for each individual. Practically speaking, random sampling from a population of tourists is an impossible task. Generally, we can try to obtain a representative sample through randomizing time and location of questionnaire distribution. Cluster analysis.usually factor analysis of the importance vectors, is then employed in identifying groups of individuals in a benefit segment which is the package of benefits that they all are looking for when choosing a product or a service.

Phase II: Segment Testing

Segment testing directly describes the market structure. Each segment is described using several groups of variables such as principal benefits sought, general activities (lifestyle), interests, trip purpose, alternate destination favoured, different media habits and strengths, and opinions in travelling. These also include demographic and socioeconomic variables such as age, income, and size of family. Sometimes the discriminant analysis will be taken to test if demographic or psychographic variables are significant difference across each benefit segment. A summary of the overall profile of each benefit segment will be presented. Ultimately, promotional strategies are proposed for each of the segments which management wishes to reach.

Initially, each segment is described in terms of the unique, differential benefits sought by its members. This analysis is usually enhanced by a comparison of segments on their lifestyle and personality traits. Schewe and Calantone provide an example of this kind of comparison in a travel context. Also, demographic and socioeconomic statistics (SES) comparisons are made between groups to facilitate media purchases that efficiently reach target segments.

Next, purchase behaviour of each segment is evaluated. The assumption is that people tend to choose products which most closely fit their "ideal" in terms of benefits sought. Each group is identified by the benefits it seeks and the attractions (or brands) it prefers. From this point marketing strategy development draws on the manger's understanding of the situation. Key variables have been identified which make a segmentai.e. market position) unique.

Managerial Implications

Sometimes the benefits that customers seek determine their purchasing behaviour much more precisely than do geographical, demographic, or psychographic factors.. The tourism marketer can develop demographic profiles of those groups identified in the benefit segmentation in order to promote to those segments. This and other valuable information in such research have provided marketer for designing promotional appeals to its consumers and potential consumers, brochures, package tours, direct selling, point-of-purchase materials, or other media, to the product in the study, and training of branch office personnel. When introducing a new product/brand, the manager can develop copy appeals based on benefits of the new product/brand matching the desired benefits of an identified target segment. This can be especially effective where a new product or brand possesses more of a desired benefit, a differential advantage, than an existing product or brand. Alternatively an existing product/brand might be repositioned with new appeals to better appeal to a particular benefit segment. Each of these strategies, as well as others, depends on the strength each existing product has in its position and each segment's demand for the product's benefits.

Also important is the stability of the segments over time. People change, the environment changes, enough promotion to segments will in and of itself change the market. Just people's need for variety causes segmentation schemes to change over time. Thus, all segmentation schemes have time limits on their usefulness. In addition, this kind study provided the impetus for further marketing studies in the travel and tourism industry.

Conclusion

Benefit is one of key factors in tourist's decision process. People pay to buy a service or product because they can gain some kinds of benefits from this' service or product. Therefore, the tourism marketer should understand purchase behaviour based on the- benefits the consumers seek. Choosing target segments and promotional themes are crucial to marketing any product or service. Benefit segmentation provides an excellent technique for effective and efficient marketing. The wealth of information provided by the benefit segmentation technique can be directly translated into marketing and promotional strategy. No technique can eliminate the need for good managerial judgment and knowledgeability concerning products and markets. However, it is hoped that the above discussion of benefit segmentation with research recommendations, furnishes a convincing argument for its usefulness in tourism promotion.

The International, Local and Social Efforts Involved

India expects a tourist inflow of around 10 million in 2010. The country's tourism sector was growing steadily with 3.92 million tourist inflow in 2005 and 4.43 million in 2006, a confidence is being generated that the inflow would touch the eight million mark in 2009.

There is considerable government presence in the travel and tourism industry. Each state has a tourism corporation, which typically runs a chain of hotels /motels and operates package tours, while the central government runs the India Tourism Development Corporation. Divestment of these state-run tourism corporations have either already taken place or are in process.

Incoming foreign tourist arrivals have shown a 6% compounded annual growth rate over the last 10 years. The government has realised the potential and has advanced several incentives to promote infrastructure growth in the tourism sector. Current investments are likely to see hotel room capacity increase by 20% over the next three years, with several international hotel chains entering the hotel industry. With specialised types of tourism becoming a craze throughout the world, India is coming up with Dubai- type shopping tourism facilities at several places besides focusing on health tourism. At least four such destinations would come up soon and another is likely in West Bengal. Aurangabad near Ajanta-Ellora in Maharashtra is one of the leading shopping tourism destinations coming up amongst others like Noida in Uttar Pradesh with world class facilities, Shilpagram near Hyderabad, permanent art and crafts fair at Bhubaneswar.

Tourism in Aurangabad

The incredible India campaign has given a brand new dimension to the marketing of India as a country. Aurangabad and particularly Ajanta-Ellora have enjoyed a steady stream of local and international visitors from a long time, even before any specific promotion or campaign was done for it. The tourists are classified as " Budget Tourists" and " Star Tourists". They can choose the type of vacation they want to enjoy in this part of the country. It also enables the government and other bodies to subsequently divide their efforts on them The centre organizes exhibitions and trade shows especially in the Aurangabad region. These give an excellent platform for rural and ethnic culture of the region to be displayed before the international tourists. Various handicrafts, local crafts, food etc. are exhibited. Over the past 5 + years, Aurangabad has seen a regular flow of both national and international tourists. Acknowledged as one of the fastest growing tier-II city, Aurangabad offers a range of site seeing, shopping and experiencing opportunities. But amongst all, the most visited and most revered, still remain the beautiful Ajanta Ellora caves. In addition, the city has seen the development of relevant education providing institutes, courses – vocational, developmental etc. to provide world class atmosphere and service to the customers. The contributions of such entities were indeed exemplary.

Mentioning the infrastructure actors, the presence of three five star hotels in a tier–II city speaks a lot. Good quality roads, renovation of squares, bus stands, and railway stations, restoration works have been the focus to give a world class experience to the tourists. Promoting the place as a 'must see' on the list of the international Buddhist traveller has indeed been a national effort, but in line with that the contributions of local authorities can be seen in their adaptation of every heritage signage, symbol and story in their day to day activities.

The JBIC project

An entire project named 'Ajanta – Ellora Conservation and tourism development project' is dedicated to the conservation of Ajanta – Ellora site. MTDC (Maharashtra tourism Development Corporation) an undertaking of Maharashtra state conceived the Ajanta – Ellora Conservation and tourism development project and prepared in 1991 a master plan from Tata Consultancy Services, on the basis of which the Government of India requested the Government of Japan to consider grant of financial assistance for the project. The Government of Japan got the plan assessed from the Overseas Economic Cooperation Fund (OECF) now Japan Bank for International Co- operation (JBIC) and offered loan assistance for the implementation of the master plan as phase –I of the project. The government went into agreement for the loan in 1992. A Joint Venture of Pacific Consultants International (PCI) and Tata Consultancy Services (TCS) were appointed in November as consultants for planning and overseeing the implementation of the works under the loan. The objectives of the project are:

1. To conserve and preserve monuments and natural resources in the Ajanta-Ellora region.
2. To improve infrastructure in order to accommodate the increasing number of tourists to the region and enhance their experience by providing improved facilities and services.

The first phase consisted of building up essential infrastructure facilities. The consultants, then as was stipulated in Terms of Reference drafted a proposal for Phase –II. It was presented by the Ministry of Tourism for consideration of OECF in the Interministrial Meeting in 1998.

Phase –I and Extended Phase –I Expenditure

The project cost was estimated at Yen 4,406 million which is equal to Rs.817.1 million at the exchange of Rs. 1 = Yen 5.39. The support from JBIC was Yen 3,745 (Rs. 498.8 million) which was 85% of the total project cost.

Ajanta-Ellora Conservation and Tourism Development Project

Phase-II

The second phase of the Ajanta-Ellora Conservation and tourism development project with the Japanese Bank of International Cooperation (JBIC) sanctioning a soft loan of Rs. 300 crores became effective from July 31, 2003. the loan clearance was announces after JBIC held a series of talks with the central department of tourism and culture and MTDC in Delhi. The first phase of Ajanta– Ellora heritage circuit up gradation scheme won appreciation not only from Japanese government but also UNESCO. The second phase envisaged taking forward the conservation and a development scheme initiated in the first phase.

The second was targeted to be completed in 5 years time and was meant to generate additional employment in Ajanta-Ellora region. The plans envisaged restoration and repair of entire cave circuit of Maharashtra i.e between Mumbai and Aurangabad. The work carried out at these places includes structural reinforcement, chemical conservation of the paintings and artifacts, preservation of percolation within the caves, upgrading the environment, training conservation staff and improving visitor management system.

A Brief Account of the Work Being Done

Monument Conservation

It included the conservation and repair of he cave belt. Project packages of ASI (chemical branch) for chemical conservation of monuments., survey and maintenance/operation of equipments and purchase of equipments for conservation laboratory at Aurangabad and detailed documentation of heritage monuments.

The package included:

1. Protection of rock mass
2. Prevention of water seepage in the caves
3. Slope stability of caves and adjoining hills
4. conservation, preservation and protection of sensitive paintings
5. Surface water management
6. Landscaping the adjoining region
7. Visitor management
8. Restoration of essential / structural elements and investigate / exploration of surroundings

Aurangabad Airport (Executing Agency – Airport Authority of India)

The major work included to facilitate domestic and international flights to land in Aurangabad and the airport facilities to be upgraded. The development was aimed to significantly boost the international tourist traffic. The package included:

1. Construction of new passenger terminal building and ancillary support facilities
2. construction of new apron 500 x 400 and construction of taxi track

Afforestation (Executing Agency - Forest Department, Maharashtra) The central idea was to enhance the greenery adjoining the classic plains surrounding the caves. This was aimed to improve vegetation cover which will prevent soil erosion subsequently reduce pollution vicinity of the caves.

The package included:

1. Major afforestation activity in adjoining areas of the caves
2. Information and maintenance, erection of fire tower, fire line cutting every year, fire fighting equipments, display card on trees
3. Tourist facilities, camping and accommodation facilities, establishment of nature trails and watch towers.

Road (Executing Agency – Public Works Department, Maharashtra State)

A number of roads were selected for repair and up gradation. All the roads lead to tourist destinations and it was considered that these improvements will lead to reduction in time and commuting costs. Also the towns and villages in the vicinity of these roads will also benefit.

Water Supply (Executing Agency – Maharashtra Jeevan Pradhikaran)

Water supply and sanitation was the main focus. The aim was to provide essential facilities to tourists visiting the caves.

Tourism and Marketing and Visitor Management System (MTDC) Development of Ajanta Tourist Complex: which included construction of visitor information centre, arrival area, interpretation centre, site museum, virtual reality hall, cave replicas, restaurants, plazas and service areas.

Development of Ellora Tourist Complex: which included construction of visitor centre, arrival area, interpretation centre, site museum, virtual reality hall, restaurants, plazas, and service areas.

Public Awareness Activities

For promotion of Maharashtra and Buddhist circuits along with Ajanta-Ellora region using press, print, audio visual and electronic media.

Human Resource Development

Training of staff for maintenance and operation of tourism destinations, visitor management systems, and tourism planning and environment conservation was the main focus.

Computerization of tourist information:

A new system to be set up for computerization of tourist information.

Conservation of State Archeological Monuments

A number of sites, monuments and gates in the Aurangabad city and its vicinity were chosen for repair and conservation and also beatification so that it would act as an additional tourist attraction in line with the caves.

Development of Lonar crater: Lonar is the lake formed by an meteorite. Hence the focus was to promote it as a "must see" site. Roads, fencing, restoration, clearing of prosopsis plants, creation of visitor information centres etc. were undertaken. Additional sub projects at the vicinity of the caves: These included restoration and maintenance of various cave belts and regions. Development of access roads, signage, power and water infrastructure at these tourist places were on the list.

Micro Credit for Low Income Tourist Service Providers

This is the first of its kind in tourism sector in India and aimed at organizing and training service providers at tourist sites who are otherwise considered as nuisance by tourists and planners alike but are essential part of Indian tourism scenario. Along with the development of infrastructure in Aurangabad there is a need to cater to small necessities of tourists which are met by mushrooming hawkers whose service to tourists leave much to desire.

The micro financing sub projects aimed at organizing, training, and financing this low income segment. Women entrepreneurs will be given preference and suitable NGOs ha been identified to training, disburse and monitor the micro credit funding credit and recovery. The beneficiaries include of the scheme small restaurant owners, tea shops, kiosks, guides, photographers, hawkers, fruit vendors and taxi operators. This would make them more presentable as well as increase their entrepreneurial skills and abilities. The loan amount of the will be chanelised through rural banks.

Marketing the Shopping District

Aurangabad has an exclusive set up of mini markets and lanes dedicated to selling ancient craft. The areas near Panchakki, Ajanta – Ellora, Paithan, Daulatabad and the Aurangabad city have their own shops, which sell exclusive speciality items. Aurangabad has seen the thriving of many retail, government owned privately held outlets that offer a variety of regional handicrafts, clothes, jewelry, food etc.

This has immensely contributed to local employment generation. The marketing of Ajanta as a shopping destination is also a driving factor that made customers come to buy region specific products like Himroo shawls, jewelry etc. A best example is 'Paithani Saree' which is handmade and known to have originated at Paithan which is a 30 minutes drive from Aurangabad. On the way to Ajanta-Ellora there are number of government owned and also privately owned shops which sell Paithani sarees, Kurtas, Scarves handkerchiefs etc. All of these have a contributing effect on the marketing of India.

The shopping markets that have evolved in the form of mini shopping districts around the place/ site made the shopping experience more relevant to the heritage promotion of Ajanta and Ellora. Even the five star hotels that are running successfully here have exclusive galleries dedicated to the handicrafts made in this region. Here the international traveller gets a glance at the Indian culture. This is a good place for shopping for the tourist who does not want to be bothered by local vendors and sellers.

Rural Tourism- " Atithi Devo Bhava!"

This is the central idea behind all the tourism activities done by the government. The tourists are given the taste of the Indian hospitality and treated as 'God' just the way it is written is scriptures and taught to every Indian.

The authorities have very strategically promoted the theme of 'Rural Tourism'. The focus is on promoting rural culture and enabling employment generation. Tourism is considered to be the major revenue generator in these regions. Typically the allied and dependant areas like restaurants, tourist guides, handicraft shops have been considered to be the focus areas for revamping and enhancement. An active platform is given to boost the generation of income in rural households. Tourists can now stay at the very homes of rural citizens.

The government has started the ' Bed and Breakfast scheme' where they can stay at a local household and get an exclusive experience of the ethnic and rural flavour of India. The housewives get a chance to earn as they provide Indian food and shelter to these travellers. While staying with these local families these tourists get a chance to enjoy the day to day life of an Indian village. As this region is extensively dependant on tourism, here the government is also helping them out to get a more professional way to carry on their business.

Along with the handicrafts that are widely sold, special promotion is given to the Indian wear like sarees, kurtas etc. Also women are given a chance to set up their units where they can put mehndi on the hands of the tourists. An entire package of rural site seeing, staying with a local family and enjoying Indian flavours, traditions and handicrafts is being successfully sold to the tourists. India is internationally known to be a diverse yet very vibrant and colourful country. Marketing it as an 'rural experience' that is a must have for every tourist has many varied dimensions to it. The basic beneficiary is rural India and also the international tourist in many ways. On one hand it gives a good platform for rural India to showcase its culture and also earn from it. And for tourist, it is a very different and exclusive experience. The incredible India campaign has given a real boost to the inflow of international tourists. The global and local authorities are striving hard to maintain the eco friendly zone which they have recently declared around the caves.

Ajanta-Ellora Festival

A large crowd is pulled annually by the Ajanta Ellora festival, formerly known as Ellora festival, which sees a lot of national, state, local and international involvement. It is one of the best ways to study the marketing mix involved in promoting the site as a tourist attraction. Local students from institutes like hotel institutes, tourism courses etc. are invited to join the organizers and delegated various tasks to be a part of this mega event. It has been one of the drivers of tourism has been the Ajanta –Ellora festival that was started as a cultural event by the authorities. Many well known Indian artistes perform on this occasion. Of all the 4 P's the most used, necessary and exemplary were the heritage place itself, people involved, products/ services offered and the simplified processes in making Ajanta to top the traveller's list.

Shopping Tourism in South India

Tamil Nadu Shopping Travel Tours

Chennai

Chennai is well connected to little getaways from the city. These small towns, away from the rushing city life, give a closer insight into the Tamil and ancient Dravidian culture. Be it Mallapuram, Pulicat, Cholamandalam artists' village, Kovalam, or Kancheepuram, each has its own way of inviting people to Tamil culture Chennai Shopping Travel Tours. Chennai is known for its cotton & silk sarees, handloom works, Tamil handicrafts, gold jewelry, and other tradional Tamil stuff. It is home to some of the most swakiest retail outlets in the country. Poompohar emporium, Cottage emporium, Victoria Technical Institute market, T Nagar market, Nalli's Rasi and Kumaran Silks are some of the best places to shop from Chennai Shopping Travel Tours.

Chennai is a city where the traditional and the modern blend in life everywhere. From traditional vegetarian fair to fast foods, from nine-yard sarees to the latest in fashion, from ancient temple architecture to modern high-rise-with Indo-Saracenic and Victorian as stops along the way-from classical music and dance to discos throbbing to heady beats, Chennai has them all and many more vivid contrasts that are a pleasant surprise. And perhaps the most striking of them all is that here is a modern metropolis with beaches, parks and even sanctuaries in the heart of the City Chennai Shopping Travel Tours.

Chennai offers a wealth of nature and a rich historic past to visitors in the ambience of a city with every modern facility. Modern Chennai grew out of a small village when in 1639 a fishing hamlet called Madraspatnam was selected by early English merchants of the East India Company as a site for the settlement Chennai Shopping Markets India. There are a number of churches in Chennai that are connected with the life and times of St. Thomas Chennai Shopping Travel Tours. There are also several ancient temples around Chennai, and, within the city itself are two magnificent temples-a temple in Triplicane and another in Mylapore.

Shopping Attractions: Chennai offers a wide variety of traditional and trendy merchandise such as carvings on brass, stone, wood and ivory, leather bikinis, bags and shoes Chennai Shopping Markets India. Traditional items from all over Tamil Nadu can be bought from Chennai like Pattamara Mats and the leaf and palmyra-fiber handicrafts from Tirunellveli, Metal works from Tanjavur, bronze and brass castings and traditional jewellery from Kumbakonam, stone carvings from Mamallapuram and Silks from Kanchipuram. The most popular shopping centres are in Rannganatha Street in T. Nagar and Anna Salai Chennai Shopping Markets India.

Prime Attractions: Fort St. George: The British East India Company under the direct supervision of Francis Day and Andrew Cogon built Fort St. George in 1640 AD Chennai Shopping Markets India. The fort houses St. Mary's Church and fort museum. St. Mary's Church is the oldest Anglican Church in India built in 1680 and the tombstones in its courtyard are the oldest British tombstones in India. This ancient prayer house solemnized the marriages of Robert Clive and Governor Elinu-Yale, who later founded the Yale University in the States Chennai Shopping Markets India. Today the fort is used by the state legislative assembly and as the secretarial offices of the Tamil Nadu government Chennai Shopping Markets India.

The flagstaff at Fort St. George is still the tallest in India. South of the Fort is the War Memorial, a graceful monument built in 1939 in memory of the warriors who sacrificed their lives during the First World War. The Island Grounds, the biggest lung space in the city is situated on an island formed by the river Cooum. This ground is the eventful venue of Trade and the Tourist Fairs held periodically which are seasonal attractions. The High Court with the decorative domes and corridors reminiscent of Indo/Saracenic architecture and the adjacent Parry's corner are the important landmarks of Chennai.

Kapaleeshwara Temples, Chennai Holiday Tours

Fort Museum: This museum contains many relics pertaining to the tenure of the East India Company and British India. It has a collection of contemporary paintings as well as the rare exhibits of weapons, uniforms, coins, costumes, medals and some other artifacts dating back to the British period.

Kapaleeswarar Temple: The biggest temple in the city, it is dedicated to Lord Shiva. The temple contains inscriptions dating back to the 13th century AD, and is a fine specimen of the Dravidian style of architecture. The 37-metre gopuram is especially noteworthy for its intricate carvings that depict stories from Hindu mythology.

Sri Parthasarathi Temple: The temple built in the 8th century is dedicated to Lord Krishna. It was built under the patronage of the Pallavas. It houses the idols of the five avataras of Sri Vishnu and has a small temple shrine dedicated to Vishnu's consort, called as Vedavalli Ammai in the native language of the region.

Santhome Cathedral: San Thome at the southern end of Marina derives its name from St Thomas, the apostle of Christ who is believed to have come to Madras sometime during 52 AD. He was killed on St Thomas Mount just outside the city in 78 AD and was interned in San Thome beach where a church was later built.

Several years later, another church was built further inland and his mortal remains were transferred from the old church to the new one. In 1606 the church was rebuilt as a cathedral and in 1896 it was made a basilica. The beautiful stained glass window at the basilica portrays the story of St Thomas and the central hall has 14 wooden plaques depicting scenes from the last days of Christ. In the cathedral is a 3 ft high statue of Virgin Mary, which is believed to have been brought from Portugal in 1543.

Kanyakumari

The aura of the place is so mesmerizing that the tourists definitely like to take back little memoirs of Kanyakumari. Therefore, Shopping Tourism in Kanyakumari India is a very good place to look for handcrafted trinkets, palm leaf drawings, sea-shell crafts. Besides these, you can also shop for books of Swami Vivekananda and other mementos dedicated to this spiritual leader.

A religious destination of immense importance, Kanyakumari in Tamil Nadu is also frequented by hoards of tourists for the scenic beach and numerous tourist attractions that the land flaunts Shopping Tourism in Kanyakumari India. The southernmost tip of peninsular India, Kanyakumari must be visited on any tour to Tamil Nadu. Though not exactly known to be a shopper's paradise, Kanyakumari offers quite a few enchanting options to tourists for Shopping Tourism in Kanyakumari India Kanyakumari is an excellent shopping destination for buying various seashell items. Nothing better than to purchase beautiful seashell trinkets and souvenirs for your loved ones from this popular beach destination Shopping Tourism in Kanyakumari India ! While shopping in Kanyakumari, you can buy beautiful decorative items made of wood and bamboo. Palm-leaf utility articles are also good buys from Kanyakumari.

On the beachfront at Kanyakumari and within the temple premises there are several handicraft shops which sell many seashell products. The Tamil Nadu Co-optex Sales Emporium, Indco Products. Tamil Nadu Crafts and Poompuhar are some of the well known shopping centres where you can buy various handicraft items, textiles and other materials. Shopping in Kanyakumari must also include multi-colored sea sands and small curios made of numerous kinds of sea-shells. Traditional saris and other dress materials are also easily available in some of the shops at Kanyakumari Shopping Travel Tours What better gifts and souvenirs to carry home form this popular beach destination than beautiful trinkets made from seashells! While shopping in Kanyakumari, you will come across beautiful decorative items made of wood and bamboo.

Shopping Tourism in Tanjore India

The city of Tanjore in Tamil Nadu is a haven for craft lovers. The city draws much of its fame from the exquisite handicrafts and handlooms that its skilled artisans produce Shopping Tourism in Tanjore India. Weaving, painting, jewellery, woodworks are some of its renowned handicrafts which make for wonderful shopping in Tanjore Shopping Tourism in Tanjore India. Since long past Shopping Tourism in Tanjore India has been a princely state and under the patronage of the royals, tradition of art and craft attained a glorious height in Tanjore. Do remember to take back some artifacts while shopping in Tanjore.

Silk weaving is a major traditional craft in Tanjore. A lot of people are engaged in the profession Shopping Tourism in Tanjore India. They specialize in weaving silk saris with broad border and unique motifs laden all over with Zari work Shopping Tourism in Tanjore India. The saris are huge hit for weddings and religious occasions. Pick up graceful Tanjore silk saris while Tanjore Shopping Travel Tours Another must-buy in Tanjore is traditional paintings. Richly adorned paintings of mostly Hindu gods are quite popular with those who want to do Tanjore Shopping Travel Tours Check out Thalaiyatti Bommai (literally the head-nodding doll), which serve as great souvenirs of a Tanjore Shopping Travel Tours Thanjavur Plates (with sombu, coconut), brass and bronze idols, bowls and vessels are other items for shopping in Thanjavur. There are many shopping joints within the city. Several government run shops and private ones dot over the townscape, which you may explore for great variety and right price.

Visiting the craftsmen at work and buying directly from them is also a good option for Tanjore Shopping Travel Tours Shopping in Tanjore is an amazing experience. During your tour to Tanjore, you can go out shopping at the several markets in Tanjore. There are several shopping joints within Tanjore including government run emporia and private shops. You may also visit the craftsmen at work and buy directly from them. You can avail of a variety of authentic articles at good prices at all these places. Tanjore was formerly a princely state and under the patronage of the royals, tradition of art and craft reached a glorious height. Tanjore is renowned for its exquisite handicrafts and handlooms produced by its skilled artisans. Weaving, painting, jewellery, woodworks are some of its famous handicrafts which make for great Tanjore Shopping Travel Tours A prime traditional craft of Tanjore is silk weaving. While shopping in Tanjore, pick up some lovely Tanjore silk saris, weaved with broad border and unique motifs laden all over with Zari work. These saris are hugely popular for weddings and religious occasions.

Madurai Shopping Complexes

For a city sipped with history and tradition, it is not surprising to have an amazing corpus of traditional and ethnic. Products ranging from handicrafts to textiles and metallurgical artifacts. It is particularly known for the cottons and the batiks Madurai Shopping Complexes. If one is looking to explore all these products under one roof Madurai Shopping Complexes. Prithu Mandapam Market is the place to be Madurai Shopping Complexes. Madurai is also a nice place to shop for the traditional objects from greater Tamil Nadu as well. These are available in the West Tower Street, Handloom House, Khadi Crafts Madurai Shopping Complexes, etc. in addition to this, there are numerous flea markets and shops selling curios outside major tourist attractions.

While shopping in Madurai, you can buy locale manufactured cottons and batiks from Puthu Manadapam Market Madurai Shopping Guide. Just outside the eastern entrance of the Meenakshi Temple Madurai Shopping Guide. The interesting things about the rows of tailoring shops here is that they can stitch a dress for you in an hour or two. You can also pick up the famed Madurai silk and handloom sarees from big textile showrooms like the famous Hajeemoosa Textiles Madurai Shopping Guide. If you want to buy souvenirs in wood or brass, you should visit the Cottage industries emporium and other government emporiums nearby Madurai Shopping Guide. Madurai is also famous for its ethnically crafted jewellery if you want to indulge. In the pleasure of buying gold and silver ornaments. Madurai has also been a textile centre for long Madurai Shopping Guide. Here skilled tailors can reproduce your dress with cottons and printed fabrics at Puthu Mandapam. You can also visit the government Poompuhar Handicrafts shop Madurai Shopping Guide. The Cottage Arts Emporium and the Madurai Gallery for hand-woven silks and cottons.

Chidambaram City Travel Packages

Shopping in Chidambaram is restricted to local handloom and textile products. There are daily markets around commonly visited places like the Nataraja temple where tourists can buy souvenirs. They range from stone carved images of Shiva in the *Ananda Tandavam* posture, replicas of the temple, laminated or framed images of the gods and deities etc. apart from these, during the festivals there are large fairs throughout the city where villagers from the nearby areas set up their stalls.

One could buy trinkets of local jewellery, or refresh their taste buds with the local sweets and snacks. Beside these there are state handicrafts and khadi houses.

Chidambaram Tourism-Chidambaram is one of the most ancient and most celebrated of shrines in India. It is of great religious as well as historic and cultural significance. Tour to Chidambaram is the seat of the cosmic dancer Nataraja (Ananda Tandava pose; the Cosmic Dance of bliss). It is one of the Pancha (five) Bhutasthalas signifying the five elements of wind (Kalahasti), water (Tiruvanaikka), fire (Tiruvannamalai), earth (Kanchipuram) and space (Chidambaram). Tours to Chidambaram-There are several tourist attractions in Chidambaram. The Nataraja temple is located in the centre of the town and covers an area of 40 acres. The roof of the sanctum sanctorum is covered with gold plates. The presiding deity of the temple is represented by air, one of the five elements of the universe and is known as Akasa Lingam.

The Thillaikaliamman temple is on the northern end of the town. It was built by Kopperunjingan, who ruled between 1229 A.D. and 1278 A.D. Pichavaram is just 16 km from Chidambaram and ranks among the most exquisite scenic spots with abundant and varied tourism resources. Chidambaram Tours and the Annamalai University is a residential university founded by Raja Sir Annamalai Chettiar. It is on the eastern outskirts of the town and is a great centre of Tamil learning and Carnatic music, with facilities in various disciplines including Medicine, Engineering, etc. Chidambaram Tourist Attractions-The nearest airport to Chidambaram is Tiruchi which is 168 km. away. It is connected by rail with Tiruchi, Madurai and Chennai. It is also well connected by roadways with all major towns and cities.

Shopping in Rameshwaram City India

Rameshwaram Shopping is highlighted by the availability of wonderful handicraft items of the region. This is a haven for a variety of exquisite handicraft and decorative items. They can be bought from the many shops near the temples Shopping in Rameshwaram City India. These are made by the local craftsmen and are god souvenirs to take home. There are items made from palm leaf, beads and seashells. You can purchase exquisite handicraft items. The Rameswaram silk sarees are very popular among the ladies Shopping in Rameshwaram City India. There is a lot of variety and textures available at reasonable prices Shopping in Rameshwaram City India. Shopping in Rameshwaram City India markets in Rameshwaram are stuffed with these exotic decorative masterpieces. Which are very popular among the tourists, visiting this place throughout the year.

Shopping in Rameshwaram City India numerous shops near the temples of Rameshwaram sell exquisite showpieces made of seashells, beads, palm leafs, etc. The Rameshwaram shops are the ideal destinations for shopaholics and fashion freaks Rameshwaram Shopping Guide. The Khadi crafts available in the shops in the city attract them Rameshwaram Shopping Guide. The women swear by the famous Rameshwaram Silk Sarees and do not miss the opportunity to buy a few for their near and dear ones. Rameswaram is on an island in the Gulf of Mannar Rameshwaram Shopping Guide. Connected to the mainland at Mandapam by rail and by one of India's engineering wonders, the Indira Gandhi Bridge Rameshwaram Shopping Guide. The bridge took 14 years to build and was opened by Rajiv Gandhi late in 1988.

The town lies on the island's eastern side and used Rameshwaram Shopping Guide. To be the port from which the ferry to Talaimannar (Sri Lanka) departed before passenger services Were suspended more than a decade ago. as a result, there are now very few foreign visitors. The island is situated on the west of the Pamban bridge and is thronged by the marine biologists for research and observation. It is 20 km from Rameswaram via Mandapam Rameshwaram Shopping Guide. The island is famous for coral reefs and houses a wide variety of sea creatures in its reefs. This Lord Vishnu temple stands at the southern tip of Rameswaram in Dhanushkodi. It is the only temple structure that survived the 1964 cyclones Rameshwaram Shopping Guide.

Ooty Shopping Guide

It is an ideal place to shop. You can get Exclusive Nilgiri products including Nilgiri tea, fruits, natural oils like Eucalyptas. Toda embroideries and tropical plants are alsoeasy to get Ooty Shopping Guide. The co-operative Super Market and Municipal Market are the best places if you are looking for local fruit and general groceries. If looking for Indian handicraft and other material items then you need look no further than Kairali of Kerala Handicrafts and Poompuhar of Tamil Nadu Handicrafts Ooty Shopping Guide. On the slopes of the great Nilgiri range, the region grows some of the best qualities of coffee and tea in India. The sprawling plantations and the heady smell are feast to senses Ooty Shopping Guide You may choose to buy some coffee or tea while shopping in Ooty.

Handmade chocolates are also popular items for Ooty Shopping Guide. Also pick up aromatic oils and spices while Ooty Shopping Guide Besides, there is the wide variety of handicrafts of Tamil Nadu Ooty Shopping Guide. The ace craftsmen of Tamil Nadu are skilled in making fantastic Jewellery, painting, pottery, and stone crafts. Look for such artifacts as you go on shopping in Ooty. You may also come across some tribal crafts in the shops. The local bazaars are replete with private shops and Government run emporia, where you can shop till you drop Shopping Places in Ooty India. Many hotels have shopping arcades where of course the price would be a bit on higher side Shopping Places in Ooty India. The shopping malls of Ooty are flooded with natural products of forests Shopping Places in Ooty India. Ooty is a paradise for those who love shopping. Surrounded by tea gardens, the tourists can smell the enchanting scent of fresh tea leaves while taking a stroll in the long winding paths of Ooty. The fresh tea leaves are purchased by the tourists as a relic of the beautiful place of Ooty Shopping Places in Ooty India.

Another prominent itinerary in the list of items while shopping in Ooty is the pure and sweet honey which is available in all the stores and shopping centres of the place Shopping Places in Ooty India. The natural oil of Eucalyptus has a great demand among the shoppers because of its medicinal value. The markets of Ooty are full of fresh fruits that impart a colourful look to the place Shopping Places in Ooty India.

The exquisite piece of the embroidered items by the tribal community of Toda represents the rich traditional art and craft of South India. The delicately designed jewellery of Silver is another attraction for the tourists who purchase such items as souvenirs for their near and dear ones Shopping Places in Ooty India.

Shopping in Ooty offers the tourists to choose from a plethora of several eatable items and handicraft products that reflects the salubrious climate and the enriched regional culture of the place Shopping Places in Ooty India.

Mamallapuram Shopping Guide

Mahabalipuram is a favourite shopping haunt for South Indian artifacts, both wooden and granite based. The stone artifacts made by the locals are a collector's delight Mamallapuram Shopping Guide. They can be bought at the small side roads. They make excellent souvenirs and are reasonable and very attractive. They also reflect the creativity of the local craftsmen Mamallapuram Shopping Guide. Mamallapuram has revived the ancient crafts of the Pallava stonemasons and sculptures and the town wakes every day. To the sound of chisels chipping away at pieces of granite Mamallapuram Shopping Guide. Some excellent work is turned out.

The yards have controls to supply images of deities and restoration pieces. To many temples throughout India and Sri Lanka. Some even undertake contract work for the European market Shopping Places in Mamallapuram India. You can buy examples of this work from the Poompuhar Handicrafts Emporium or from the craft shops Shopping Places in Mamallapuram India. Which line the roads down to the shore temple and to the Five Rathas Shopping Places in Mamallapuram India. If you want a hammock, this is quite a good place to buy one Shopping Places in Mamallapuram India. For a book exchange service try Himalaya Handicraft on the main street. Exquisite soapstone images of Hindu gods, woodcarvings, jewellery and other similar products are also for sale. There are several Kashmiri shops too Shopping Places in Mamallapuram India. Mamallapuram is a place where one can shop for beautifully carved images of Hindu Gods in soft stone or wood. Decorative articles made from sea shells are widely available here Shopping Places in Mamallapuram India. There are some Kashmiri shops selling Hammocks here. There is even a Himalayan Handicraft emporium here which offers some good handicraft items from the Himalayan states.

Dharapuram Shopping Guide

This is definitely not a shopper's paradise. Only the local artifacts are available here. The local souvenirs are available at reasonable prices in the small shops and also by the road side. It also has a spillover from Erode and the neighboring cities of textiles and hosiery. This, however, is not a place on would recommend for shopping. It is basically a sleepy town with not much activity. The cities nearby are rich in exports, like Erode for Hosiery and Coimbatore for silks.

Erode also has a number of textile mills. When Tippu fell to the British, the East Indian Company took over the administration. Its famous for its aanjaneya temple Dharapuram Shopping Guide Tamilnadu. In ancient times Dharapuram was called as Viradapura which has significant links to Mahabharata Dharapuram Shopping Guide Tamilnadu. Dharapuram and Coimbatore got the status of Municipality on a same day.

Dharapuram Municipality is promoted 1st grade municipality on May 6, 1983. Dharapuram Town is situated along the bank of River Amaravathi with an extent of 7.02 Sq.km. The town has attained the status of a Municipality in the year 1916 and functioning as the First Grade Municipality from

09.05.1983. The town developments completely depend on the agricultural activities and Commerce and Trades Dharapuram Shopping Guide Tamilnadu. Once upon a time Dharapuram was a Capital for South NOYYAL Dt, and Bhavani was a North Noyyal Dt. That time Erode was a village Dharapuram City Tour Guide.. It is a sleepy village at the foot of the Nilgiris Mountains Dharapuram City Tour Guide.

It is about 90 Kms from Coimbatore, in the district of Erode. It is situated on the banks of the river Amaravathi. This is a tributary of Cauvery. One side of it is fairly garlanded by Kodaikkanal Mountain Ranges Tamilnadu Travel Tourism India. Dharapuram City Tour Guide town is residing on the banks of the holy river Amaravathi, a tribute to Cauveri.It has a rich history with the famous Hindu dynasties being a part of it.Tamilnadu Travel Tourism India.

Kerala Shopping Guide

Shopping in Kerala is as exciting as touring the mystical place. Kerala is famous for its local crafts and you will find a traditional touch in each and every craft item in Kerala. Apart from the usual knick-knacks, there are many eatables that you can buy in Kerala Shopping Guide. The famed banana chips are available in each and every shop in Kerala. While in Kerala Shopping Guide, shopping can be done in major cities like Kochi Kerala Shopping Guide.

Trivandrum, etc. In all major cities, you will find not only the flea markets but also glittering malls and showrooms. Kerala is famous for gold and every road in Kerala's major cities will have a huge jewellery shop. You will be amazed to see the amount of gold that is bought by people Kerala Shopping Guide. Indian gold is pricey so check the on going rates before you buy anything Kerala Shopping Guide. Apart from jewellery, Kerala is well-known for its ivory carvings, pottery, brocade fabrics and earthenware products. It is an unforgettable experience to shop for those small traditional items in Shopping Places in Kerala India

Also famous are the Indian spices that are available in Shopping Places in Kerala India You can choose from turmeric, pepper, ginger powder and other exotic spices that are available only in Kerala. The most famous shopping centres in Kerala are in Trivandrum on the M.G. Road. You can buy the famous wooden "Kathakali" face as a remembrance of this beautiful place. You can also buy the traditional Indian attire known as "Sari".

Kerala is famous for its variety in saris and you can find some really good colours and designs here. Do not hesitate to bargain a bit on the prices Shopping Places in Kerala India. Owing to the abundance of forests and coconut groves in Kerala, wood, coir and coconut shells traditionally remain the base of such handicrafts. A whole range of souvenirs and trinkets are made from these Shopping Places in Kerala India. Artifacts made of teak, deep-wine rosewood and fragrant sandalwood may arrest your eyes while shopping in Kerala. Buffalo horn is also popular with Kerala artisans as a raw material for the handicrafts Shopping Places in Kerala India. But the sea-fringed state of Kerala is also the land of spices. Since long past Kerala has carved a niche of its own in the global spice market for its rich flavored spices. Spices are used in medicines, preservatives, perfumes and above all in cooking.

Cochin

Cochin is a haven for shoppers from all parts of the world. You can buy here some authentic metal-ware, camel-bone carvings and also wood-made structures. Unsurprisingly, there are also articles that are made of coconut and bamboo cane Cochin Shopping Travel Tours. If you are looking for handicrafts then there are many options like jewellery stores and garments and handmade fabrics. The major hubs for shopping are MG Road, which is located at the centre of the city Cochin Shopping Travel Tours.

There is also Marine Drive for shopping lovers (do not confuse it with the one in Mumbai). Weekdays are the best days to shop, as most of the shops are closed on Sundays Cochin Shopping Travel Tours. As travellers loiter around the old city, the cosmopolitan character clearly comes to the forefront that are well reflected in the Mansions and structures built in the place Cochin Shopping Travel Tours. Discovered by the Portuguese, the island city with the lagoons and canals with the fishing hamlets is today one of the busiest port of India Cochin Shopping Guide. Cochin lies on the direct route to the countries of east Europe and Australia and is proud to possess all the three forms of transport in one particular region Cochin Shopping Guide. Fort Cochin: Called the Old Fort, the Fort Cochin is the first and the foremost fort built by the Europeans in India and is among the most important travel attractions of the city. Initiated by the Dutch, the Fort was also developed by the Britishers Cochin Shopping Guide.

The Fort as a whole consists of many amazing structures Cochin Shopping Guide. The Fort houses the memory of Vasco Da Gama, the first European to land on the coast of India in the year 1498. The old fort comprises a huge Portuguese style mansion, the St. Francis church and the basilica of Santa Cruz Cochin Shopping Guide.

Chinese Fishing Nets: The huge Chinese cantilevered fishing nets were brought by the Indian traders from the royal court of Kubla khan, the famous Mongol Emperor and founder of the Yuan Dynasty of China Cochin Shopping Guide. These nets were erected by the traders in around 1350 to 1450 AD and are set up on the teak wood and bamboo poles. The nets offer an interesting sights when they are lowered in to the sea to catch the big cats underwater Cochin Shopping Guide.

Mattancherry Palace: Constructed in the year 1557, the magnificent Palace was presented to Raja Veera Kerala Varma of Cochin as a gift by the Portuguese Traders. Complete with extraordinary murals and scenes from the epics of Ramayana and Mahabharata, the palace also displays the Dutch maps of Old Cochin. The royal coronation and the palanquins are splendidly presented. Renovated in 1663 by the Dutch, the palace show case the wonderful attires of the Maharajas who ruled the place from earlier times.

St. Francis Church: The St, Francis Church has the reputation of being the first church built by the Dutch in the year 1503 AD. It is also the burial place of Vasco De Gama, the portuguese trader and sailor, the first European to discover India. The great traveller was buried here in 1524 before his remains were taken to Lisbon, Portugal in about 1538.

Bolghatty Island: The narrow and elongated island widely known for the famous Bolghatty Palace was constructed by the Dutch in 1744. The island hold the only picturesque golf course of Cochin among its prime attractions.

Calicut Shopping Guide

Shopping in Calicut is a pleasure for people from all across the world. Its most popular joint for shopping is Sweet Meat Street – yes, it is a street which goes back to the ear when there used to be streets lined with stalls of sweetmeat. Here, you can get fancy clothes at reasonable rates and prices Calicut Shopping Guide. Also, Mavoor Road is one such place where you can get fancy and good clothes. Big Bazaar Road is your cup of tea if you are looking at wholesale spice market Calicut Shopping Guide. Then there is Comturst Store near town hall that sells handloom fabrics. These are manufactured locally in the factories Calicut Shopping Guide.

Climate: Due to its nearness to sea, the place has a hot and humid climate. Summer starts from March and continues until May. Maximum temperature recorded in the month of May is 36°C and minimum temperature recorded in the month of December is 14°C. Southwest monsoon arrives in the first week of June and average annual rainfall is 254 cm Calicut Shopping Guide.

Past: There is not much known of the early history of Calicut except for some prehistoric rock-cut caves that have been found at many places of the district Calicut Shopping Guide. During the Sangam age, the district was under the Chera administration until AD 1122. This was the time when this region was a major centre of trade between Kerala and the outside world Shopping Places in Calicut India. The city of Calicut came into existence in the 13th century when Udaiyavar, the king of Ernad, conquered the area around Ponniankar and built a fort at a place called Velapuram, now known as Calicut. Interestingly, the name Calicut is derived from 'calico,' the fine variety of hand-woven cotton cloth said to have originated from this place Shopping Places in Calicut India.

Shopping Places in Calicut India outer world came to know about India in 1498 when Vasco da Gama came to Calicut and obtained permission to carry out trade from here. Quickly in succession came the English and Dutch. Disputes over the control of Calicut continued for a long time until 1792, when the East India Company went into an agreement with the local Zamori rulers to directly administer this area. Kerala was declared a state in 1956, and Calicut today is one of the most important centres of trade and business in this progressive state Shopping Places in Calicut India.

Sites To Visit: Kappad is the place where Vasco da Gama set foot for the first time when he came to India on May 27, 1498. There is a small stone monument at the beach to commemorate that event Shopping Places in Calicut India.

Pazhassirajah Museum is located on the East Hill. It is run by the State Archeological Department. Ancient mural paintings, antique bronzes, old coins, models of temples, and megalithic structures are on display here Shopping Places in Calicut India. Situated next to Pazhassirajah Museum is an art gallery displaying paintings of Raja Ravi Varma. Dolphin's Point is a good place to watch dolphins playing in the sea early in the morning. On this beach are also situated Calicut Town Centre, Lions Club, and a lighthouse. Two crumbling piers, more than hundred years old, stand out into sea at Kozhikode beach. The beach is easily accessible from the city and provides a good view of the setting sun. The place also has a Marine Life Aquarium open whole day.

The Science Planetarium at Jaffarkhan Colony is the best place to unravel the mysteries of universe and enlightens about the planets and stars. The Science Centre has an interesting array of games, puzzles, and scientific gadgetry, which can keep a person busy for the whole day. The planetarium and Science Centre are in the same complex. Mananchira, which was the palace tank of King Mana Vikrama, has been now turned into a traditional architectural splendor with carpeted green grass and surrounded by ethnic buildings. The place also has a musical fountain.

Sites Nearby: Beypore (11 km) is a small coastal town known for its shipbuilding industry for centuries. It is still a favourite destination to buy large boats. Vadakara (48 km) is a commercial centre of martial arts and the birthplace of Tacholi Othenan, a legendry hero of North Malabar. Ninety-eight kilometres away from Calicut is Tellicherry and Sultan Battery famous for their breathtaking scenery. Thusharagiri is famous for its waterfalls and lush green forests. It is at a distance of 11 km from Kodenchery, a place abounding in rubber plantations, coconut, pepper, ginger, and spices of all sorts. There is a dam at Kakkayam, located around 45 km from Calicut. The place offers challenging trekking and rock-climbing through river path and numerous waterfalls.

Shopping Tourism in Alleppey India

Alleppey is a haven for shoppers. It has all the ingredients to make it a shopping paradise. Here, you can shop for some very authentic coir products and carpets. You can also see how coir are manufactured here. The city has many shops that sell coir matting and carpets. You can get it all at very reasonable prices here. However, being tourists you may have to bargain it with the local shopkeepers.

However, the quality of coir products is so good that most of you may not paying a tad higher price for it. Alleppey is also a magnificent destination if you are looking to purchase pepper, coconut oil or cardamom. Indian Holiday offers an excellent range of Alleppey tour packages to make your India trip a bit more special. The architectural splendor and the modern outlook of this capital city make Alleppey the dream destination for tourists.

Alleppey the backwater destination of Kerala is famous for its beautiful backwaters houseboat cruises and seafood. If you are looking for an idyllic retreat amidst the emerald green waters, palm fringed shores and lush acres of greenery then Kerala Backwaters is the ideal destination for you. Alleppey is widely known for its good quality coir products and carpets, and shopping in Alleppey for these products will be a fascinating experience. You can get glimpses of the coir manufacturing process at Alleppey-right from the coconut husk to the final rope/coir yarn stage. The numerous shops that sell coir matting and carpets are frequented by a regular number of tourists and the fine quality, variety and reasonable prices make these a much sought after product while shopping in Alleppey. Alleppey is also famous for the pepper, coconut oil, areca nut, cardamom, and sugar available here. In the markets in Alleppey you will also find hoards of fresh fruit and vegetables, which you will be more than delighted to buy.

Tourist attractions: The central area of Alleppey town is called Mullakkal, where you will come across a number of gold and silver shops. Renowned for gold and silver ornaments, these shops are places worth visit on your shopping spree.

Kumarakom Shopping Travel Tours

Shopping in Kumarakom is a damn good experience for people from all parts of the world. You can go shopping to Kottayam, which is 15 km from the city or can shop in the interiors of the city Kumarakom Shopping Travel Tours. There are many craftsmen in Kerala, so you will find a lot of handcrafted items in this culturally rich state. There are camel bone carvings that are reasonable and also look very striking Kumarakom Shopping Travel Tours You can also purchase many reasonable and high-quality handcrafted items of wood, coconut shell, cane and bamboo and more Kumarakom Shopping Guide

There are also many other items like jewellery and garments that are worth having a look at Kumarakom Shopping Travel Tours. Although not one of the hottest shopping destinations in Kerala, Kumarakom is a pleasant place to indulge in some leisurely shopping when you are free and not wandering into the depths of the wildlife sanctuary or cruising down the charming backwaters Kumarakom Shopping Travel Tours Kumarakom Shopping Guide. Shopping in Kumarakom can be a nice experience because the various items available here are generally of good quality and would tempt you to pick souvenirs from the shops scattered in the town Kumarakom Shopping Travel Tours Kumarakom Shopping Guide.

Some of the best buys while shopping in Kumarakom include metal-ware, camel-bone carvings, wood carvings Kumarakom Shopping Guide. Articles made of coconut shell, bamboo and cane, embroidered screw-pine (pandanas palm) mats, grass mats, and various other types of handicrafts items Kumarakom Shopping Guide. The people of Kerala are wonderful artisans and all these finely crafted items are much sought after by tourists visiting Kumarakom Shopping Guide. Shopping in Kumarakom can also include various antique items, jewelr. Readymade garments, and ethnic hand-woven textiles, which are also easily available in the local markets. You will also find various gift items typical of the state of Kerala during Kumarakom Shopping Guide These can range from products as diverse as lampshades and fashion accessories like earrings, to brass lamps, 'kathakali' masks and so on Kumarakom Shopping Guide.

Other decent buys at Kumarakom include fresh and aromatic spices which are quite abundant here. But if you want to indulge in an extensive shopping spree, then Cochin-at about 70 km from Kumarakom, will be the perfect shopping haunt for you.

Munnar Shopping Guide

Not a surprise, the best thing you can buy here is tea. Tea is brought to shops here direct from estates. Besides being reasonable and high on quality Munnar Shopping Guide. Iit is easily available and you can smell it and tell that there cannot more fresh aroma anywhere in the world. Like many other parts of Kerala, you can also find here a lot of handcrafted items Munnar Shopping Guide

At a reasonable rates and of high-quality Munnar Shopping Guide. Besides, tea you can also shop for spices here as there is rich spice plantation also here Munnar Shopping Guide. If you are a real tea lover, you can even visit factories and carry a few leaves as samples, and can also taste various flavors. Shopping in Munnar is not-so-promising Munnar Shopping Guide.

The markets are minus glitz and glam of a showroom—a local bazaar set up. Besides the local veggies, woollens, tea, coffee, spices, spices, seasonal fruits etc. are seen arranged not-so-aesthetically in the narrow lanes of the this bazaar Munnar Shopping Guide. The majority of bazaars are owned by the private owners but the presence of Government Shops can also be felt in the market. Munnar's best buys are all its local products Shopping Places in Munnar India.

Munnar is all meant to buy tea and better quality tea, which cannot be procured anywhere else in the country. Tea and history is 25 years old in Shopping Places in Munnar India Several tea kiosks and shops are full-fledged engaged into tea selling. Shopping Places in Munnar India a s many the smaller and larger tea shop are owned by local people. Lay your hand on the best quality tea such as colonial tea (lowest Rs 140 for half kg), Lemon Tea, Green Tea, etc. Unlike tea, strawberries are seasonal pick ups. Fresh and best in quality, strawberries are sold at chosen outlets.

Spices are available in abundance in Munnar. Every shop and other nook and corners are engaged in selling tea and spice such as cardamom, cinnamon, nutmeg, clove, etc. So be it spice shopping or tea shopping in Munnar it will always be an interesting experience for the tourists. Top Tea Station in Munnar has a collection of rare fruits like the passion fruits and tree tomato.

Shopping Tourism in Trivandrum

Trivandrum being the most important city of Kerala, economically and culturally. Certainly has a shopping experience to offer to people of all tastes. You can shop here for valued handcrafted items such as jewellery, garments and household items. Things may be little expensive here as they are being sold in commercial markets. However, you can choose from a wide range of fabrics and materials like wood, ivory, coconut. Chalai is the local market here. You may have bargain a little bit here to get reasonable prices.

But all in all you will get good and long-lasting stuff. A Trivandrum tour is left incomplete if you return without shopping in Trivandrum. More often than not shopping is an integral part of a tour. Everyone wants to take back some artifacts, utilities or souvenirs after touring a region. The rich tradition of art and crafts make for a great shopping in Trivandrum. Metal work is an ancient art in this part of Kerala. The ace craftsmen of Trivandrum make exquisite items out of bell metal. Pick up some kitchenware, brass lamps and many other objects d'art while shopping in Trivandrum.

Coir products are also a wonderful speciality of Kerala. Floor coverings, doormats, floor Matting and rugs come in a range of colours and designs, which are made of coir or coconut fibers. These along with coconut shell crafts are huge favorites with those who want to do some shopping in Trivandrum. Wood carving and horn carving is also interesting art forms in Kerala. You may be on the look out look for beautiful artifacts carved out from animal horns as you go on shopping in Trivandrum. Don't forget to pick up miniature snake boats and kathakali masks while shopping in Trivandrum that make for fantastic souvenirs of a Trivandrum tour. You would find many shopping joints in Trivandrum. Some are run by the state government while others are private ones. Drop in at M.G. Road in the city to where you may come across large variety of local handicrafts for shopping.

Thrissur Shopping Guide

As Thrissur is well known as the cultural centre of Kerala, this city abounds in religious and cultural items all around. The rich cultural and traditional activity here makes it well organized in the production of artistic and craft products, which also forms major shopping articles available here for tourists Thrissur Shopping Guide. These handicrafts are mainly based in producing wonderful woven silk cloths and jewellery Thrissur Shopping Guide. Coir handicrafts, crafts of coconut shells, carvings of horns, carvings of woods, works of brass, carpet making and other household articles comprises the major portion of handicraft products in Thrissur Shopping Guide The Kathakali Mask is the best bought souvenir of visiting Thrissur Shopping Guide

Thrissur in Kerala is renowned for its mesmerizing variety of silks. Bell metal curios, brass work, textiles and gold jewellery are typical buys, the shopaholic would find hard to resist when in Thrissur Shopping Guide If you are making a choice for a true memorabilia of the place from a wide array of display Shopping Places in Thrissur India. Thrissur's very own culture to take home the true flavour of the region Shopping Places in Thrissur India. The silk produced in Thrissur are possibly the best buys while in the city. A variety of materials in myriad hues are sure to attract the tourists and visitors Shopping Places in Thrissur India. Artifacts made of brass are also popular for their intricacy and use in common everyday life. Exquisitely crafted ornaments and embellishments in gold with in distinctly South Indian designs and alignments are also preferred by many Shopping Places in Thrissur India.

The shops of Thrissur are welcoming with well behaved sales person who are always ready Shopping Places in Thrissur India With a smile to help you decide what is best for you if you find yourself lost in the huge variety available. The best part is, you can shop at your own pace for delightful souvenirs to take back home. Surabhi, Kairali or other government emporiums are good places to shop for things that are related to the culture and tradition of Kerala in general and Thrissur in particular Shopping Places in Thrissur India.

Periyar Shopping Guide

There are not much of shopping centres in Periyar. This place is mainly dedicated to the wildlife sanctuary and its staunch visitors Periyar Shopping Guide. People visiting this place rarely ask for shopping centres too Periyar Shopping Guide. In fact, there is no particular product of Periyar sold or available in the city Periyar Shopping Guide.

Sprawled over an area of about 780 sq. km. in the Idukki District of Kerala, Periyar is one of the major tiger reserves in India. Renowned worldwide as being home to a large number of wild elephants and tigers, and a host of other animals and birds Periyar Shopping Guide.

Although not one of the hottest shopping destinations in Kerala Periyar Shopping Guide. Periyar offers some pleasant options for tourists to indulge in some leisurely Shopping in Periyar. In fact, an avid shopper will find it impossible to return from a trip to the Sanctuary without shopping in Periyar Periyar Shopping Guide. But, if anyone is bound to shop in Periyar, he can shop for spices, which is the best thing available in this city. Periyar is a place with variety of spices. It is also exported to other places of the nation Shopping Places in Periyar India. Cardamom, Cinnamon, Pepper, Ginger, Anise, Mace and Nutmeg are some important spices a visitor can shop for. Shopping Places in Periyar India being a land of spices, the most sought after items for tourists visiting the sanctuary is a wide variety of exotic spices. The slopes of the Western Ghats at Periyar grow a number of spices like pepper, cardamom, cinnamon, ginger, nutmeg, mace and anise. Spice trading having been a mainstay of the local economy of the region,Shopping Places in Periyar India spice-scented air at Periyar welcomes tourists and tempts them to shop for some excellent quality fresh spices that are grown in abundance here.

While shopping in Periyar, you can also buy T-shirts with exclusive Periyar Wildlife Sanctuary motifs of tigers and elephants. These can serve as excellent souvenirs for your loved ones back home Shopping Places in Periyar India. But if you want to go on a shopping spree in Periyar, you can head for Kochi, located about 190 Km from the sanctuary. At Kochi you can find numerous shops and a large variety of items to buy including souvenirs and local handicrafts. Kumily, located nearby, is a famous shopping centre and spice trade centre Shopping Places in Periyar India. A wide variety of spices and handicrafts are also available at the shops in Kumily.

Kollam Shopping

One can find many places like markets and malls in Kollam for shopping. Some of the most popular items for shopping in this city are jewellery, products of handloom and handicrafts and the textiles.

The most common shopping centres in Kollam are Rani Fancy, Rani Gold Covering and Fancy Centre. Chungath Prince Jewellery, Sky Jewellery, Sunny Jacob Jewellery. Dazzles, Lifestyles, Supreme Textiles and Sudarshana. Kollam is also a place of Ayurvedic centre as it has a good collection of medicinal herbs grown in the forests of this place.

Thevalli Palace: This is a beautiful and historically renowned palace situated on the banks of Ashtamudi Kayal (backwater) Sasthamkotta 26 Km. northeast of Kollam city. Sasthamkotta is situated on the bank of Kallada river. There is a temple dedicated to Lord Sastha. Sasthamkotta lake The place in known for the Sasthamkotta fresh water lake. The natural gift is set amidst scenic surroundings covered by hills on the three sides.

Thenmala: 70 km from Kollam, Thenamal is a small hill town amidst thick forest. Thenmala is an interesting picnic spot to enjoy natural scenery. The main attraction is trekking. Boating facility also available. Best Season-September to January

Thenmala Deer Park: The another attraction of Thenmala is the Deer Park. Thenmala Rock are about 5000 year old, which are worth seeing.

Kottarakkara Kathakali Museum: Kottarakkara Thamburan Kathakali Museum, is the memorial of Kottarakkara Thamburan (King) the father of the Kathakali. Exhibited here are various models of Kathakali, Kathakali classes and ornaments. Mahatma Gandhi beach & park at Kochupilamoodu, Thirumullavaram beach and Ashramam picnic Village, are some of the important spots of local sight seeing. Mahatma Gandhi beach lies just 2 Kms. from the town. It is fascinating place for an evening. Thirumullawaram Beach is 5 kms. from the town.

Palakkad Shopping

The city of Palakkad is not much popular or characterized with market infrastructures. The city doesn't have any particular distinct product of its own Palakkad Shopping Info. This city is not commercially built up to the level. It is an agro-based civilization. Generally goods like textiles, handicrafts, handloom products and agricultural products take the main share of Palakkad markets Palakkad Shopping Info. As for the history of Palakkad goes, very little is known about it. Evidence in form of relics suggest that Palakkad existed during the Paleolithic age Palakkad Shopping Info. First millennium AD saw the Perumal rulers exercising their control over the land Palakkad Shopping Info. This control was later disintegrated into smaller divisions by the Perumal governors Palakkad Shopping Guide.

Accounts of William Logan, the Scottish author of the Malabar Manual also mentions Palakkad as one of the Malabar region that was captured by the Pallavas of Kanchi Palakkad Shopping Guide. Another record describes a war that was fought by the king of Palakkad in 988 AD to stop the invading army of King of Kongunadu at Chittur. The victory of Palakkad in that war is still celebrated in the form of a festival. Palakkad Shopping Guide 1757, yet another invasion by the Zamorins made the then Raja seek the help of Mysore ruler, Hyder Ali.

Hyder Ali obliged and eventually secured Palakkad for himself and later his son, Tipu Sultan. However, with the defeat of Tipu in the third Anglo Mysore war of 1792. Palakkad Shopping

Guide along with other Malabar territories (belonging to Tipu) passed of to the British. The British made Palakkad a part of the Malabar District of Madras Presidency which post independence became a part of the Madras state. In 1956, when Kerala came into existence, Palakkad became a part of it.

Shopping: Palakkad has a quiet a good number of options for shoppers Palakkad Shopping Guide. There is a big bazaar (Valiya Angadi) where shops sell items like traditional bell, peacock villakus, thooku or hanging villakus, nilavillakus and utensils Palakkad Shopping Guide. Tranvancore sarees, Kerala souvenirs and jewelleries are other options for shoppers.

Shopping Places in Wayanad India

Despite the beautiful natural delights of Wayanad, this city also has beautiful shopping centres in and around the city. The major count of the products sold here are the spices of Kerala.Shopping Places in Wayanad India The handicraft and handloom products of this city are a good bought that one can get as a memorandum for visiting the city.

The crafts here are mainly done with coconut shells, ivory, canes, wood and metalsShopping Places in Wayanad India. Other items like garments, textiles and furniture are also available in excellent quality and at suitable costs. One can also get fresh nutritious vegetables, fruits, fish and chicken etc. Shopping Places in Wayanad India.

One should not forget to get the mask of Kathakali to commemorate your visit to this city Shopping Places in Wayanad India Evidence in form of relics and edicts indicate inhabitation of the area as early as in the New Stone Age. However, recorded history is available only from the time of the 18th century Shopping Places in Wayanad India.

In earlier times the land was ruled over by the Veda rajas and later it came under the Pazhassi Raja of the Padinjare Kovilakom of the Kottayam family. During the reigns of Hyder Ali of Mysore, Wayanad was came under his rule, however with the defeat of his son, Tipu Sultan, at the hands of British, the entire Malabar region went to the British. This was followed by an intense revolution led by the Pazhassi Raja. The revolution ended only after the death of the raja himself.

The British reign ushered in an era of tea and other cash crop cultivation. Roads were laid down in the precarious areas of the regions thereby opening up newer land for cultivation. With the increase in the British power, organized cultivation came into limelight.. The very nature destinations that soothed your soul a little Wayanad Shopping Places Information Guide While ago now transform themselves and present opportunities to become adventurous. So, undertake a trekking expedition to the peaks, boating rounds in the lakes Wayanad Shopping Places Information Guide Game viewing in the sanctuaries and have a close look at the carvings of the caves Wayanad Shopping Places Information Guide. When you are free from all this, visit the revered temples of the region that each have their own story

Thiruvananthapuram Shopping Guide

This city of Thiruvananthapuram is an excellent place for shoppers Shopping Places Information Guide. One can find almost all sorts of articles relating luxury, household, garments, jewellery, gifts, foods and many more Shopping Places Information Guide. The SMSM Government Emporium is the right place for shopping souvenirs and handicraft items Shopping Places Information Guide. Varieties of handicraft and handloom wonders are available in various range of quality and cost.

Rosewood sculptures or sandalwood sculpture, carved items, bronze creations, fabrics and the Kathakali mask are the best buys of the city Shopping Places Information Guide. Chalai is a market where local people come for marketing. All type of items for regular utility is available in this market. Kerala depicts the rich heritage and culture of South India Shopping Places Information Guide. From its remarkable temple architecture to the beautifully sculpted idols, it displays the excellence of the artisans of Kerala. Metal Work is an ancient art of the city of Kerala, which has been carried on for generations Thiruvananthapuram Shopping Guide. If you are interested to go for some Thiruvananthapuram Shopping Guide Then you can pick up some of these kitchenware, decorative items and brass lamps from Kerala. The coir products of Kerala are equally famous. From floor coverings Thiruvananthapuram Shopping Guide. Doormats, rugs or mats, the coir products are found in almost all the shops of Kerala. They are made of coir or coconut shell fibers. Along with this beautiful coconut shell crafts are also available. Shopping in Thiruvananthapuram or a tour to Thiruvananthapuram remains incomplete If you do not buy the miniature elephants or the snake boats which are the typical symbols of Kerala. The miniature Kathakali masks are also beautiful souvenirs Thiruvananthapuram Shopping Guide.

Andhra Pradesh

Shopping Places in Hyderabad India

The City of Nizams has many shopping centres. It has historically been a rich trading and commerce centre. Hyderabad is a haven for those who love to buy handicrafts Hyderabad Shopping Guide. It also sells many kinds of perfumes which have been famous since the times of Nizams. You can go shopping in Charminar Area, where you will find ethnic garments, jewellery and handcrafted items. Hyderabad Shopping Guide Some of the shops here remain close on Fridays. There are also many street-side bazaars, where you will also find many locals shopping. Book lovers will find the Abids Bazaar a nice place to Hyderabad Shopping Guide You many find here old books which have become a rarity.

Shopping in Hyderabad city is one remarkable experience one wishes to have too often Shopping Places in Hyderabad India. The markets in the city are provided with all that makes the heart pound and the purse to lose control. Shopping Places in Hyderabad India continues to be one of the best to provide precious stones and antiquities in the sub continent and at large. The best buys in the city include jewellery, pearls, handicrafts, apparels, leather goods and traditional crafts. Abids, Basheer Bagh, Nampally, Begum Bazar, Laad Bazar and MG Road are main shopping areas in Hyderabad city. These places feature some of the best stores and showrooms in Shopping Places in Hyderabad India

The pearls and jewellery for which the place has been notorious over years can be purchased from Laad Bazar. At Laad Bazar are present a lot of shops that sell the mentioned products and more including semi precious stones, glass beads and colourful bangles Shopping Places in Hyderabad India.

Shilparamam, an arts and craft village presents exquisite pieces and objects. The traditional handlooms, textiles, carpets can be had from this place and that too for genuine prices. Some other related items merchandised in the city include brass ware, Nirmal paintings, Kondapalli toys and Bidri ware. Bidri is an ancient art and in modern times can be found in forms like vases, ashtrays, ornaments, nameplates etc. The souvenir and handicrafts centre opened by Andhra Pradesh Tourism at Ravindra Bharati and Mahtaab Restaurant are great places to shop. Some other popular places to look for the things include Handloom House-Nampally, Kalanjali-Nampally, Lepakshi-Tank Bund, Central Cottage Industries Emporium-S.D.Road Secunderabad.

Vijayawada City Travel Packages

The malls and the markets of Vijayawada are almost busy for the whole weeks but still busier are the Sundays. The street is overcrowded with shoppers in the city. The people moves all around the city to find their shopping items. All items of need are available in the city Vijayawada City Travel Packages. Generally the most displayed items of the city include the electronic goods and garments for all. The most interest inculcating part in the city to shop is the heavy discounts and free gifts on purchases. The most rushing day of shopping is on the day before Makar Sankranti. Shopping in Vijaywada is truly a memorable experience Vijayawada City Travel Packages. One can shop for anything ranging from handloom products, handicrafts, furniture to pearl jewellery, silver jewellery and textiles in Vijayawada City Travel Packages. Apart from these, there are also things like exquisite antiques, leather goods, pearls as well as semi precious stones. Vijaywada is also well known for beautiful toys that are made in the nearby villages of Kondapalli and Machlipatnam. Vijaywada is the Kalamkari paintings and kalamkari works. Some of the most popular markets for shopping in Vijaywada are around MG Road. Eluru Road, Besant Road and Governorpet. Other than these popular places Vijayawada Shopping Guide. There are a number of shopping malls and market places in Vijaywada where you can shop to your hearts content.

Ranging from handloom products to handicrafts, furniture to textiles, pearl jewellery to silver jewellery, you can set off with anything and everything in Vijayawada. Besides these knick-knacks, the city has wonderful antiques, leather goods, pearls as well as semi precious stones to offer. Kalamkari paintings and handiworks are things not to be missed on your visit to Vijaywada, the third largest city of Andhra Pradesh Vijayawada Shopping Guide.

Regarding shopping places, MG Road, Eluru Road, Besant Road and Governorpet are some of the popular markets in Vijaywada. There are many shopping malls that dole out maximum number of things under one roof. In the nearby areas, Kondapalli is a nice place to get colourful toys, made from light-weight wood. You can also browse the local markets, where you can find most of the items at reasonable price Vijayawada Shopping Guide.

Shopping Tourism in Warangal India

Warangal is an excellent place for shopping, and its handicraft are world famous. It is famous for Metal crafts, Banjara Fabrics, Warangal Rumals, and Nakashow Paintings. Visitors would surely like the Warangal Carpets, which have huge demand in India. People of Warangal are associated with wooden industry, therefore its wooden handicrafts move very fast. Apart from wooden craft, Pembarthi Metal crafts attract tourists. Cloth symbolizes the culture of country and everyone would wish to get involve in it. Warangal "Banjara Fabric" is capable to entice visitors. Embroidery is done to make it look nice. Banjara Fabric is available in variety of colours. Another exquisite item to buy from Warangal is its Warangal Rulams. For those who love shopping, the Warangal city of Andhra Pradesh has some good deals to bargain for. Since the region is famous for handicrafts like brass ware, carpets, scroll paintings etc., your question regarding 'what to buy' would never arise. Infact, it would be unfair not to have a glimpse of such amazing artifacts. Once seen, it is sure that you would not be able to resist buying those amazing knick-knacks.

Another fact about these handicrafts is that they are made by observing traditional techniques and methods. Till day, artisans in local villages practice the time-honored art. The exclusive carpets from the region are popular amongst the national as well as the international markets. Regarding the shopping places in Warangal, you can browse the local markets. Though they have limited range of products, it is exceptionally good and you will get not go home empty-handed. For special and selected items, you must explore the shopping places that are known for particular products. Like Khadi Gramodyog Bhandar at Subedari and Hanamkonda is the best place to get premium Khadi items that offers authentic items at reasonable rates. Podduturi Complex, near Warangal, is a nice place to shop for Lepakshi handicrafts. To get the best brassware and gift items, Hanamkonda is the right place to opt for.

Vishakhapatnam Shopping Travel Tours

The main shopping centres of Vishakhapatnam are located on the main road stretch of Jagadamba Junction to Old Post Office, Kurupam Market, Dwarka Nagar, Daba Gardens and One-Town Area."

The best deals in the famous Narayanpet, Kalamkari, and Pochampali, printed fabrics and wall hangings can be found in Khadi Grammena Udyog. Lepakshi, Girijan Co-Operative Society and Eastern art Museum are other such places. Where you can get exclusive handicrafts of Vishakhapatnam. Wooden toys called Etikopaka are also famous of this region. You can find a great variety for young and old alike at Kondapalli. Vermillion boxes and bangles are also found here. Perhaps industrial centre is the exact term for Visakhapatnam.

However, with its sun-kissed beaches and beautiful landscape, the city is also a big hit in the tourism market of Andhra Pradesh. Though Vizag is not a shopper's paradise, it has some quality things to set you on a shopping spree. Indeed you must be pondering over the question of 'what of buy', so here comes the answer. From this port city, you can purchase jewellery, handicrafts, clothes and traditional South Indian metal utensils. Apart from curios and artifacts, sandalwood products-varying from wood carvings to sculptures-are really nice antiques to splurge. Other famous things of the region are spices, pickles, spices, soaps, perfumes, musical instruments, handmade paper and Indian tea. While shopping from the local market places, keep in mind that you are required to indulge in some bargaining. Before purchasing anything, it is better to confirm rates at other shops too.

To get handicrafts, Lepakshi Emporium Eastern, Art Museum and Girijan Co-operative Society are good places that offer most of the famous state works. Dabagardens is a great place to buy sports gears, ranging from cricket sets to skates. If you want to buy jewellery, then Kurupam Market is the popular gold and silver souk. Owing to the proximity of many shops in markets, you can get great bargains. Markets at Waltair, RTC Complex, TSR complex, Jagadamda Junction, Kurupam and Dwaraka Nagar are quite popular amongst the people.

Karnataka

Karnataka Shopping Guide: Shopping Guide in Karnataka is an adventure and involves a lot of fun. Karnataka is regarded as a shopper's paradise from all parts of the world. Shopping is almost regarded as exciting experience Karnataka Shopping Guide. Lively, busy and active, Mysore's street markets are an essential part of Karnataka life Karnataka Shopping Guide. They are grand for bargain hunting and all sorts of goods are on sale, from clothes to antiques. The state boasts amazing handicraft by the rural artisans, old antiques and the fantastic silk and cotton weaves and much more Karnataka Shopping Guide.

Shopping Malls in Karnataka is world famous for sandal woodworks Karnataka Shopping Guide. Exquisite sandal wood carvings can be found in this state. Other than this you can shop for metals, stone and wood stuffs. The artisans of Karnataka are traditionally skilled in making striking objects. The woven silk fabric of Mysore is also worth a buy as you shop in Karnataka. Besides these Mysore Paintings and Bidriware are also a must buy while shopping in Karnataka. Shopping Guide in Karnataka- Several Government Emporia and exclusive private shops mark all over the state of Shopping Places in Karnataka India. Shopping in Karnataka and Shopping Malls in Karnataka takes a delightful turn as you travel to lovely Udupi that is admired for its mythological figures cast in metal, shop for crafts cast in bell metal in Mangalore, buy metal crafts in Bidar, Sravanbelgola and Nagamangala that is renowned for its bronze objects Shopping Places in Karnataka India

Shopping tours in Gulegudda in Karnataka open up a lavish land of Ilkal saris, Lambani jewellery and Kinnala paintings Shopping Places in Karnataka India. You can also shop for the famous Mysore paintings with their subtle patterns in a riot of vegetable dyes and gold leaf work.

Shopping for pendants, delicate baskets, and wooden caskets with inlay work, sandalwood pens and exotic bookmarks is a delightful adventure in Shopping Places in Karnataka India.

Sandalwood: Sandalwood of Karnataka is renowned for the exquisite carvings on wood. The sandalwood products range from idols of deities and finely wrought chariots to decorative pieces such as paper cutters, boxes, name cases, trays, photo frames, and combs Shopping Places in Karnataka India.

Mysore Silks: Mysore is famous for its luxuriant silk sarees. These sarees enchant one and all with a riot of colours and traditional patterns woven in real gold threads and brocade. They are a must have on everyone's shopping list.

Metalware: Metalware craft has taken distinctive forms in different regions of Karnataka.

Bangalore Shopping Guide

Bangalore is also well abound in places of Shopping. There is a beautiful hill called Nandi Hill at a distance of about sixty kilometres from Bangalore. Nandi Hill is popularly known for it's being health care resort. The lakes and the valleys viewed from this hill resort are awesome Bangalore Shopping Guide. It is tourist's delight to visit this resort during summers. Moving for about 28 km from the city is the big Banyan tree. It is also the major amazing factor to the visitors Bangalore Shopping Guide. This big Banyan at Romahalli is spreading over and area of three acres to surprise. There are lot many more places for Shopping in Bangalore.

Commercial Street: Commercial Street is one of Bangalore's busiest shopping areas Bangalore Shopping Guide. While garment, hosiery and textile stores are in a majority here, you can also find shops selling shoes. Art supplies, stationery, novelties, jewellery, travel kits, sports and general goods. The side streets are also worth exploring. You never know what you might find there Bangalore Shopping Guide. Things may be inexpensive, especially if they are unbranded Bangalore Shopping Guide. The clothes may not be of very good quality but you can bargain on some great deals here.

Brigade Road: Brigade Road is a favourite hangout for youngsters as they have a variety of shopping options available accompanied by entertainment Bangalore Shopping Guide. One can get just anything here: Electronic equipments, kitchen appliances toys, music, garments and shoes. There are malls like Fifth Avenue and Mota Royal Arcade, which are worth exploring Bangalore Shopping Guide. You'll get a variety of products that range from cheaply priced to very expensive.

M.g. Road: It's a very popular commercial area and has many sari stores. The Raymonds and Cotton World showrooms are also located here. Jamal is the place to go for buying Bone China and cutlery. Gangaram and Higgin Botham are very popular bookstores, also located at M.G.Road Shopping Places in Bangalore India Shopping Centres to look out for on M. G. Road are Shrungar Shopping Complex, Barton Court, Public Utility Building, Spencer's Super Market, the Coir Board showroom, Natesan's Antiquarts, Kids Kemp, Saree Kemp, Cauvery Arts and Crafts emporium and others Shopping Places in Bangalore India.

Residency Road: If you are looking for steal furniture or handicrafts, Residency Road is the place to go to Shopping Places in Bangalore India. Some of the state emporiums are located on this road: Gangotri, the Uttar Pradesh Government Handicrafts showroom, offering brassware, wooden furniture, jewellery, etc. Mriganayani, the M. P. Government Emporium, Utkalika, the Orissa Government Handicrafts Emporium and Gurjari, the Gujarat State Handicrafts Emporium Shopping Places in Mangalore India. There are other markets that specialize in the products they sell; Richard Square is famous for cutlery and crockery, Avenue Road is known for its stationery, stainless steel ware and silver jewellery, Chickpet is famous for its silk sarees, silver and gold jewellery and textiles Shopping Places in Mangalore India.

Bibliography

Burkart, A and Medlik, S: *Management of Tourism*, The, London, Heinemann, 1975.

Clark, Mona: *Interpersonal Skills for Hospitality Managers*, London, Chapman Hill, 1995.

David L: *International Tourism Policy, New York*, Van Nostrand and Reinhold, 1990.

Donald E. : *Public Personnel Management: Contexts and Strategies*, Upper Saddle River, NJ: Prentice Hall, 1998.

Donald M.: *Customer Service in the Hospitality and Tourism Industry*, Englewood Cliffs, Prentice Hall, 1994.

Douglas C: *Practical Tourism Forecasting*, Oxford, Butterworth Heinemann, 1996.

Eberts, Marjorie: *Careers in Travel, Tourism, and Hospitality*, Lincolnwood, VGM Career Horizons, 1997.

Elliott, James: *Tourism: Politics and Public Sector Management*, London, Retailed, 1997.

Fowler, Peter: *Heritage and Tourism: In the Global Village*, London, Retailed, 1993.

Hinkin, Timothy R.: *Cases in Hospitality Management: A Critical Incident Approach*, New York, Wiley, 1995.

Hoffman, Edward: *Project Management Success Stories: Lessons of Project Leaders*, New York, John Wiley & Son, 2000.

Hubert, B.: *A Host of Opportunities: An Introduction to Hospitality Management*, Chicago, Irwin, 1996.

Ireland, Lewis: *Quality Management for Projects and Programs*, Upper Darby, PMI, 1991.

Judi Radice: *Restaurant & Food Graphics*, Glen Cove, PBC International, 1994.

Larkham, P J: *Building a New Heritage: Tourism, Culture & Identity in the New Europe*, London, Routledge,1994.

Leivadi, S: *Sociology of Tourism, The: Theoretical And Empirical Investigations*, London, Retailed, 1996.

Nijkamp, Peter: *Sustainable Tourism Development*, Aldershot, Avebury, 1995.

Norman G.: *Hotel, Restaurant, and Travel Law: A Preventive Approach*, Albany, Delmar Publishers, 1993.

Peters, M: *International Tourism*, London, Hutchinson, 1969.

Prentice, R: *Conceptualising The Experiences of Heritage Tourists*, 1997.

Robert C.: *Cases in Hospitality Marketing and Management*, New York, John Wiley, 1997.

Rosemary E.: *Managing Employee Relations in the Hotel and Catering Industry*, London, Cassell, 1995.

Rosenzweig, J. E.: *Organisation and Management*, New York, McGraw Hill International, 1963.

Sherman, Barry: *Telecommunications Management*, New York, McGraw Hill, 1995.

Slinn, Judy A: *Tourism: Management of Facilities*, London, Pitman: M & E, 1993.

Stallworthy, E.: *Waste Management Towards a Sustainable Society*, Auburn House, New York, 1990.

Swarbrooke, J.: *Marketing Tourism, Hospitality and Leisure in Europe*, London, International Thomson Business Press, 1996.

Thomas, F.: *Introduction to Management in the Hospitality Industry*, New York, Wiley, 1995.

Timothy R.: *Cases in Hospitality Management: A Critical Incident Approach*, New York, Wiley, 1995.

Tribe, John *Corporate Strategy for Tourism, London*, International Thomson Business Press, 1997.

Var, Turgut: *Tourism Planning*, London, Retailed, 2002.

Weiler, B: *Ethnic Tourism*, Belhaven/Wiley, 1992.

Index

I

M

N

R

S

T

U

❑❑❑